Finding Wisdom

Finding Wisdom

Learning From Those Who Are Wise

To Debbie —
The purpose of life is to
discover your gifts
The word of life is to develop them —
The meaning of life is to give them
away. (anon.)

Thanks for all you do for me!
Merriam

Merriam Fields Bleyl, PhD

To order additional copies of this book, contact:
Xlibris Corporation
1-888-795-4274
www.Xlibris.com
Orders@Xlibris.com
68202

Contents

To those who made it possible:

Philmer Bluehouse
White Elk*
Odd Mathis Hætta
Misae Itani
Ibrahim Muthoka Kang'eri
Bethwell Kiplagat
Helaman Krause
Walter Krause
Kristian Kristensen
Wangari Maathai
Ole Henrik Magga
Mburu James Gakunji
James Mbatia
Nizhoni*
Fleur Ng'weno
William Olotch
Shandiin*
Yuichi Takenaka
Hiroshi Shimoguchi

and to Robert for his loving support

[*Not an authentic name. These individuals prefer to remain anonymous.]

But where shall wisdom be found?
And where is the place of understanding?

—Job 28:12

Acknowledgments

*We are like dwarfs sitting on the shoulders of giants. We see more, and
things that are more distant, than they did, not because our sight is
superior or because we are taller than they, but because they raise us
up, and by their great stature add to ours.*
—*John of Salisbury,* Metalogicon *(1159)*

While conducting research in Africa, I became intrigued by the sculptures
of people huddled together, human pyramids, reaching high by standing
on one another's shoulders. The sculptures reminded me of quotations like
the one above, acknowledging the fact that we truly accomplish little on
our own in this life. That certainly is true of this book.

A generous group of individuals assisted me in my search to find the
wise. These individuals were key to this project. Dr. Richard Hansen put me
in touch with Dr. Betty Migongo-Bake at the United Nations Environment
Programme, Nairobi, Kenya. Dr. Migongo-Bake, in turn, introduced me
by e-mail to Jagi Gakunju, CEO of AAR (Africa Air Rescue Plans), located
in Nairobi. Margie Anderson put me in contact with Alberta Burroughs,
who helped me locate Western participants for this study. My friends, Al
and Andrea Yazzie, called Sunlatsa "Sunshine" Jim-Martin to ask if she
could help me locate wise individuals on the Navajo Nation. Sunshine, who
is much like her name, helped immensely. Kunio and Fumiko Hatanaka
assisted in finding wise individuals in Wakayama Prefecture of Japan. Finally,
Sveinung Elkeland, the director of the Norwegian Institute for Urban and
Regional Research (NIBR) in Alta, Norway, volunteered Sigrid Skålnes and
Stig Karlsted to locate Saami participants who met the wisdom criteria. It is
obvious that this book could not have been written without the help of those
generous and unselfish individuals who were willing to assist me, giving so
bountifully to the project of a friend or a literal stranger.

This book is dedicated to the nineteen individuals who eventually agreed to be interviewed and to share their life stories with me. These incredible individuals have enriched my life with their friendship, with their willingness to relate their life stories and ideas, and their patience in putting up with the many delays of this project. I am more than indebted to them.

Another group of individuals without whom this book could never have been written is those who served as translators for Norwegian/Saami, Japanese, Kikuyu and Swahili, and German languages. These individuals spent hours interpreting during interviews, and in addition, some of them listened to tapes for additional hours to determine if I had rendered the translations correctly. I thank Robert Burke, Mr. Ditley, Jagi Gakunju, Michael Hansen, Elizabeth N. Kang'eri, Edith Krause, Linnea Kristensen, Kirstin Lyng, David Mutinda, Karin Olson, Ann Om'mani, and Steven Bleyl for their translation skills.

These acknowledgments would not be complete without mentioning the support and encouragement given by my husband, Robert, and our four children. *Finding Wisdom* had its beginning as I spent the month of January 2001 in my son Erik's family beach house on the Outer Banks of North Carolina. The solitude and beauty of the beach that winter inspired the framework for this book.

Well over one hundred individuals have been intertwined in the finalization of this book. I marvel at and appreciate their selfless donations of time and energy. I am overwhelmed and humbled by their contributions and their support.

Preface

Wisdom is not a product of schooling,
but of the lifelong attempt to acquire it.
—*Albert Einstein*

Wisdom is probably the most written-about human quality or attribute in the traditional literature of the world. The idea of wisdom is timeless—it has not changed much in the five thousand years of recorded history. The peoples of every culture have been fascinated by it. Everyone benefits from the companionship of those who generate wise thoughts and actions. Yet knowing and defining wisdom has proven difficult. Especially frustrating is the fact that even those who study the characteristics of human beings don't actually know what wisdom is or how a person acquires it. All agree, however, that wisdom is rare.

In spite of that rarity, I have sought over the past ten years to discover the role wisdom plays in contemporary human life. I chose to explore wisdom by finding and interviewing known wise individuals—people from differing cultures. Looking for the ultimate contrast in cultures and also considering the feasibility of travel to various countries, I chose to interview wise men and women from the Japanese, Kenyan, Navajo, Saami/Norwegian, and Western European cultures.

Narrowing each of these broad cultures to include specific geographical locales, I searched for and eventually found five willing individuals to act as cultural liaisons, so to speak. These men and women asked numerous people who lived in each chosen area to select and nominate individuals (excluding their relatives) whom they *believed* to be wise. If a person received at least three nominations, I arranged an interview with him or her. I was unsuccessful in interviewing several nominated wise individuals because of scheduling difficulties, but most of the nominees went out of their way to meet with me.

I began my quest wondering what these wise individuals would be like. Would the life stories of these "wise ones" give any clues as to what made them wise? Would their personalities be the same? Would they be wise in similar ways?

In the pages that follow, you will learn about nineteen noble, wise, and humble individuals—a few of the wise ones I met on my quest. These real men and women are quoted extensively throughout this book. All were magnificent and patient teachers. They often spoke metaphorically—through stories, poetry, art, and song—giving me new perspectives from which to view my own life. My experiences with these individuals were transformational, and I found myself in complete agreement with Ellen Langer, a distinguished Harvard University professor of psychology, who noted,

> Hearing or reading about another person's life dilemmas or circumstances that differ from our own challenges our tendency to "mindlessly" accept our preconditioned thoughts and responses—those we have accepted at face value without context and/or emotion.[1]

As I traveled the world and met many wise, extraordinary men and women, my preconceived ideas and assumptions about people were challenged and changed.

Finding Wisdom also explores whether or not wisdom is something that contemporary men and women—we "regular folks"—can attain. In presenting the characteristics of those known to be wise, I attempt to make a case for wisdom being the pinnacle of human development, suggesting that the outward manifestation of wisdom transcends culture. The wise have much in common.

The life stories reiterated here contain clues about wisdom. Each of the men and women about whom I have written is a wonderful example of the *consummate* person described hundreds of years ago by the Spanish philosopher and Jesuit scholar Baltasar Gracián.

> Words and deeds make the consummate man. It is to voice what is good and to do what is honorable; the first evidences a good head, the second a good heart, and together they give birth to a great soul.[2]

Each wise person—each *great soul*—I interviewed helped me to better understand the intrinsic value of wisdom. Wisdom can increase our mindfulness in our dealings with one another. Hopefully, understanding wisdom's essential and vital role in guiding humanity mindfully and sanely into the future will become apparent. I believe that we can all agree with Robert Sternberg, the renowned Yale psychologist and researcher of wisdom, who said, "If there is anything the world needs, it is wisdom."[3]

Endnotes

[1]   Ellen J. Langer, *Mindfulness* (Reading, MA: Addison-Wesley Publishing Co., 1987), 4.

[2]   Baltasar Gracián, *The Art of Worldly Wisdom*, trans. Martin Fisher (New York: Barnes and Noble, 1993), 118. This is Gracian's most famous book outside of Spain. It was translated by Joseph Jacobs in 1892 from *Ordculo manual y arte de prudential* (1657). Baltasar Gracián y Morales lived from 1601 to 1658. His works influenced Voltaire, Nietzsche, and Schopenhauer.

[3]   Robert J. Sternberg, *Wisdom, Intelligence, and Creativity Synthesized* (New York: Cambridge University Press, 2003), xviii.

Chapter One

Why Wisdom?

Ugi ukirite hinya.
"Wisdom outweighs strength."
—*Kikuyu Proverb*

"Jambo!" said Muthoka. A wide grin brightened his handsome age-lined face, putting me immediately at ease.

"Jambo!" I replied, using the only Kiswahili word of greeting I knew.

I first met Muthoka in September 1999 at Wajee Nature Park, a wildlife refuge located 160 kilometers north of Kenya's capital city, Nairobi. Muthoka, a highly respected Kikuyu[1] medicine man, was well-known in the Mukurwe-ini area of Kenya. I would soon discover why.

Months before, I had set out from my home in New Mexico to learn more about people living in various places around the globe—people who were reported by their kinsmen, community, or tribe to possess the quality of wisdom. Jagi Gakunju, a Nairobi insurance executive, was instrumental in helping me find wise individuals in Kenya. He arranged for me to meet with Muthoka. My husband Robert accompanied me to Kenya and helped with the audio and video equipment utilized in every interview.

Muthoka
(Line drawing by Cris Fewox, Rio Rancho, New Mexico.)

The two-and-one-half-hour drive from Nairobi to Wajee Nature Park[2] on that bright September Saturday morning, with Jagi at the wheel, took us through the cultivated lands and the spectacular scenery of the Aberdare foothills. The Aberdare Range, also known by the Kikuyu name *Nyandarua*, is a volcanic mountain range running directly north of Nairobi for nearly one hundred miles (160 kilometers). As we traveled north, I observed that the lower slopes of the Aberdares, well-known for their rich soil, were farmed extensively. In addition to coffee and tea, greenhouses filled with flowers for export lined the roadway.

We stopped in a small town for lunch at an Indian restaurant. I ordered sambosas—deep-fried triangular-shaped curry puffs filled with ground lamb, potatoes, and vegetables—and they were delicious. Continuing on our journey, Jagi drove to a scenic point where a river flowing out of the Aberdares suddenly cascaded as a beautiful waterfall one hundred meters to the floor of a canyon. Four such rivers flow out of the Aberdares, supplying water and hydropower to millions of Kenyans, including those countless farmers who live in small towns and, most critically, the three million residents of Nairobi.

We continued our road trip, but before we reached the higher areas of the Aberdares, Jagi steered the car off the tarmac, and we slowly completed the remaining trip toward Mukurwe-ini on unpaved and rutted roads. Along the way, we passed throngs of people walking along the sides of the dusty roads—mainly women and children. Many women bore large bundles on their heads, while others bore large bundles on their backs. Mothers with babies carried them on their backs, securely cradled in brightly colored woven cloths.

Wajee Nature Park is south of the town of Nyeri, the capital of Kikuyuland.[3] The main industry of the area is farming—coffee and tea, as well as maize. It is a beautiful part of the country. Lord Robert Baden-Powell, founder of the Scouting movement and a hero of the Boer War, and his wife are buried in the Nyeri town cemetery. Baden-Powell once wrote, "The nearer to Nyeri, the nearer to bliss."

When we reached the humble small town of Mukurwe-ini, Jagi stopped the car in front of a small building. It was a small grocery store. A group of eight men was gathered outside. As Jagi climbed out of the car, he greeted the men, who, peering in through the car's open windows, looked a bit startled to see Robert and me sitting in the car. We smiled. They smiled back. Feeling inadequate, I wished then that I could speak Kiswahili.[4] When Jagi came out of the store, he was carrying a large cloth sack. He explained that he had picked up a "gift" for Muthoka—ten kilos (twenty-two pounds) of sugar.

Continuing on, we then drove down a dirt road for a short distance. There on the side of the road we found the sign marking the entrance to Wajee Nature Park. As we entered the driveway and drove into the park, a tranquil scene awaited us. The equatorial sunlight filtered through the leaves of the indigenous trees, painting the dusty Kenyan ground a dappled reddish brown. Melodic songs rang out from the branches of the numerous trees, chorused by the various exotic birds that found refuge in Wajee Park. Though I wasn't in Kenya to observe the local birds, I could not help but hear and enjoy the abundant colorful avian singers who flitted about in the greenery. The task at hand, however, was to interview Muthoka.

Muthoka sat on a bench in front of the house that served as the headquarters at Wajee Nature Park, waiting for us to arrive. He was chatting and having tea with several men whom I learned later worked at the park. Wearing a stylishly braided black yarn wig that served to protect his balding head, Muthoka was dressed in a Western-style camel-colored sports coat, shirt, and long pants. Well-worn brown leather sandals covered his calloused and dusty bare feet. His dark eyes twinkled as he talked and joked with his companions. I learned from Jagi that Muthoka only spoke Kikuyu peppered with a few words of Kiswahili and that he was around one hundred years old. Jagi, in addition to being the Kenyan cultural liaison, chauffeur, guide, and facilitator of the interview, also served as a capable and invaluable interpreter of language and culture.

As we climbed out of the car, Muthoka and the other men stood to greet us. Jagi handled the introductions. As Muthoka walked toward us, he relied on two walking sticks to steady his gait, but otherwise, he moved with the agility of a much younger person. I could not help but notice the respect and deference that the Wajee Park staff members paid to him. In the Kikuyu culture, older individuals are held in high esteem, especially those well advanced in years and those who possess special skills, as Muthoka did.

The scheduled interview with Muthoka took place outside, on a shaded veranda, one hundred yards south of the park's headquarters. As we walked toward the veranda, Muthoka conversed with Jagi in Kikuyu. I assumed he was asking for details about what was going to happen that afternoon. Muthoka was not accustomed to meeting, let alone talking to, foreigners—especially American white women.

Before the interview began, Robert began to assemble the audio and video recording equipment. Muthoka watched this process with great interest—his curious and agile mind took in all of this new-to-him technology. As Robert unfolded the tripod and placed the camera on it, Muthoka ambled close to the camera to study it. Jagi was setting up his own video camera, and Muthoka asked him questions about what the cameras would do. Robert pointed his camera at Muthoka and recorded him for a few minutes. He then rewound the tape and showed Muthoka that the camera had captured not only his image but also what he had been saying during the taping. Muthoka actively questioned Jagi about how it all worked. His quick wit, humor, and intelligence were immediately evident. He was delighted when Robert informed him (through Jagi) that he would receive a copy of the tape that he could play on the VCR at the park headquarters whenever he wanted to see it.

Once the equipment was in place, Muthoka and Jagi sat down on camp chairs in the shade of the veranda. Muthoka removed his wig, revealing his bald head. I sat down in a chair facing them. It was warm, even though we were sitting in the shade.

Once we were all seated, Robert attached a microphone and cable to Muthoka's jacket. (Not only was the interview videotaped but also audiotaped.) Looking down at the audio cable, Muthoka took hold of it with his right hand, pulling it out from his chest. Looking quizzically at Jagi, he asked, "Why do I have this string attached to me?" Jagi briefly explained the function of the tape recorder, and the interview commenced.

Muthoka answered my questions about the major events of his life and about some of his experiences as an elder in his community. I hoped that the life story of this wise man would reveal something about the wise in particular and wisdom in general. I was not disappointed.

Born in the fertile highlands of Kenya, Muthoka didn't know the date of his birth. He said, "I don't know the exact year or day that I was born. I remember many events from my youth, but no one in my generation knows exactly when they were born." Muthoka shook his head from side to side, explaining, "No one kept records then."

Not having knowledge of a birth date was not unusual for older African men and women. Before acquiring a written language, tribal societies, such as the Kikuyu, had no way to record the exact dates of certain life events like birth, death, or marriage. Thus, the year of Muthoka's birth was approximated from his stage of life when certain events with known dates took place. In Muthoka's case, the significant event from which he calculated his age was the confrontation between the English and the Germans in Tanzania during World War I.

Muthoka said, "I'm close to one hundred years old. I don't really know my age for sure. British soldiers came to our village when I was a young boy. They told my friends and me that we had to help them because they were fighting the Germans far to the south. We were asked to carry luggage on our backs a long distance."

The conflict to which Muthoka connected his age erupted in August of 1914, when Britain declared war on Germany. Britain, Kenya's colonizer, began compulsory participation of African natives, under the Native Followers Recruitment Ordinance, soon after—in 1915. On a massive scale, twelve- to sixteen-year-old Kikuyu boys were conscripted into the "much hated and ill-fated Carrier Corps, a military labour unit in which Africans were used as little more than forced labour."[5] These young boys ported British supplies and luggage on their backs from the foothills of the Aberdares in Kenya toward the German-occupied Tanganyika (now the United Republic of Tanzania). It is estimated that at least three carriers were recruited for every soldier in the field.[6] Muthoka was one of those young boys. Thus, he was born between 1898 and 1901, making him between 98 to 102 years of age at the time of our interview.

Muthoka told me that his birth family consisted of two older sisters, and because his father was polygamous (a common practice among the Kikuyu),[7] he had stepbrothers as well. Both of Muthoka's parents died when he was very young. His father died when he was about five or six; his mother died not long after. Muthoka's maternal grandparents, Munuhe and Warûgûrû, died before he was born.

Even though his mother died when he was a young child, it was evident early in the interview that Muthoka felt a strong, secure attachment to her. He brought a well-worn unpainted wooden stool to the interview. As he began to talk about his mother, he reached down to the side of his chair, picked up the stool, and placed it on his lap.

"This was my mother's stool," he told me quietly. "It is one of my most prized possessions."

Stools play a significant social role in many African tribes. Men carried their own stools to community and other meetings. This action stemmed from age-old beliefs. In many communities, the stool was a ritual symbol of power and divinity—with a leader's stool being elaborately and ornately carved, and a woman's stool simply constructed.

Traditionally, stools had either three or four legs, with three-legged stools being the norm. Today stools stand also as reminders of memories past and present—sculptures that remind one of stories and of ancestors that may guide one's affairs.[8] Each person's stool is still a treasured item among the Kikuyu people.

As Muthoka tenderly held the well-worn wooden stool in his dark, calloused, and wrinkled hands, he explained, "The stool is part of Kikuyu culture. This particular stool was actually used by my mother. Stools were always used in storytelling. Instead of having three legs, this stool has four legs—because four legs make things firm [stable]. Because this belonged to my mother, I keep it as a memory of some of the stories that were told around this stool. When Kikuyu children are young, normally they sit with their mother to hear stories every night around the fire pit in the center of the hut. And most of the stories come from your mother, rather than your father, around the fireplace."

Thus, Muthoka retained a vivid memory of his mother sitting on her stool each night, teaching the important stories, legends, and traditions of the Kikuyu to her small children.

I asked Muthoka, "What kinds of stories did your mother tell you?"

He laughed, and then replied, "Most of the stories told to the children were more like riddles, but riddles that would teach. For example, one of them says, 'Go around from me, and I'll go around the other side. Then we'll meet.' Then the child is asked, 'What does that mean?'"

Muthoka looked at me for my answer to the riddle. I shrugged my shoulders, having no idea what it meant.

Muthoka smiled, saying, "It is the description of a house—since the house is round. Another similar riddle is, 'You go this way, and I'll go this way, and we'll go and tie a dress around your mother.'"

Again, Muthoka looked at me, waiting for my answer. Once again, I had no answer.

"That is a riddle that means 'a round house.' You see, the old houses had sticks that were flexible to tie [they could be woven]—so you go around the house. I go this way and that way—weaving the sticks [the dress] around the house [your mother]."

I conceded that I was not good at solving riddles. However, since this experience with Muthoka, I've often thought that riddles are a wonderful tool for teaching people to think "outside the box," as we in the West like to say.

Until recently, the tradition of telling stories, riddles, and proverbs to the younger generation every night around the fireside existed everywhere in Africa. In this manner, everyone learned cultural beliefs, expectations, traditions, and customs; they were passed on orally,[9] generation after generation. As Muthoka noted, each tribe's beliefs and customs were most often related in the form of stories and riddles that young people were asked to solve.

Euphemisms and proverbs are ubiquitous in the language of the Kikuyu. Many of them have counterparts in all cultures. For instance, the Kikuyu proverb "*Ndukanine nduma mbira,*" literally translated as "Do not make home affairs known," is often heard in its Western form as "Don't wash [or air] your dirty linen in public." The proverb "*Gatinyinyiraga gatari gakunye*" translates to "Nobody cries that has not been pinched" or the more familiar "Where there's smoke, there's fire." Other Kikuyu sayings relate specifically to Kikuyu culture—such as "*Alea eri ni nyungu igiri ein ningi,*" which translates to "Two wives are like two pots of poison."[10]

With the death of his parents, five-year-old Muthoka, in keeping with Kikuyu tradition, was raised by his uncles—his father's older brothers. From his uncles he learned the role of a Kikuyu man, including how to slaughter cattle, sheep, and preferably goats for special religious sacrifices, rites of purification, and celebrations within the tribe.[11] During such times, the tribal elders passed on long-held Kikuyu customs to the younger men. Women weren't allowed to be near the group of men at these times.

Although his uncles taught him the ceremonial ways of the Kikuyu, at some point Muthoka came into contact with Scottish missionaries. The first Christian missionaries, the Holy Ghost Fathers, arrived in Kenya in 1889. Fifteen years later, Scottish missionaries came to Muthoka's village and sought to Christianize the local population. They established a hospital in the area. In addition, the Bible, a book that the villagers had never heard of before, was introduced.

These well-meaning men convinced the people of Mukurwe-ini that their tribal religions weren't good enough. They offered a new religion—calling it "a better way" to worship. Consequently, they persuaded most Kikuyu tribal members to become Christians—in this case, Protestants. The missionaries convinced Muthoka that, as one of God's children, his Kikuyu name alone was not sufficient. He must have a Christian name because African names were not considered "holy." Thus, at his baptism, Muthoka became Ibrahim Muthoka Kang'eri. He adopted his father's name, Kang'eri, as his surname.

The priests brought literacy to the people as well. They established a school where male children were taught to read and write English. Muthoka attended the Scottish mission school briefly—only long enough to learn to write his name. Even so, he remembered being in a classroom as being a joyful experience.[12]

He explained, "When I went to the school—the formal school—that was my happiest moment. I had no responsibilities, I had company around me, and I didn't have to think anything about tomorrow."

Muthoka spoke of his teachers in that school with fondness. More than ninety years later, his eyes twinkled as he smilingly said, "I still remember Ibrahim Karoe, Jonathan Kibutu, and Simeon Karecho. They taught me many things, including how to write my name—Muthoka!"

During this same time, Watiri, an influential Kikuyu elder in Mukurwe-ini, also stressed the importance of becoming literate. Muthoka agreed with him. He said, "Education changed the thinking of the people. It opened a lot of people's eyes."

For Muthoka, learning to write his name was the extent of his "formal education." Since he and his friends were conscripted into the British Carrier Corps, Muthoka spent little time in the classroom. From that point on, he experienced an education of a different sort.

The Kikuyu celebrate the entrance of both men and women to adulthood with a ceremony that includes circumcision.[13] When Muthoka was nearly twenty years old (in 1920), he was initiated and accepted as a Kikuyu man. Initiation was performed in groups of young men (age fourteen to nineteen) at a specific period every year or two. Muthoka's initiation group was named Romemo Riko. These men became a close group for the rest of their lives. They took responsibility for one another as they progressed through the various stages of life together.

Following initiation, individuals were encouraged to marry. Muthoka did in fact marry his sweetheart that same year (1920). Muthoka and his wife subsequently raised a family of two boys and four girls, and at the time of our conversation, they had been married eighty years and had grandchildren, great-grandchildren, and great-great-grandchildren. All of them addressed Muthoka as "my father."

Throughout his life, Muthoka gained knowledge and skills in the traditional Kikuyu manner. He sought out and learned from people who were experts in a specific skill or understanding. Through quiet observation, by watching what they did, he learned. Early in life, he began to acquire a vast knowledge of the medicinal properties of the indigenous plants of Kenya as well as other traditional skills.

This is not to say that Muthoka's life was smooth and easy following his forced service in the British Carrier Corps. I asked him, "How did you earn a living for your family before you were an elder?"

He replied, "I was a mason. I built houses for people. When I was a young man, I worked in a quarry and also built houses. I was even in Nairobi as a mason on building construction sites."

Nairobi, the large capital city of Kenya, attracts many people in search of jobs and financial gain. However, Muthoka made it clear that he had no desire to go back to Nairobi. He tapped his hand repeatedly on the arm of his chair as he emphatically and decisively stated, "The *quality* of life is here [in Mukurwe-ini]. The cities do not have the good quality of life that is here. My family is here, my friends are here, my wife is here, my land is here—what should I go for and do in the city?"

According to Kikuyu tradition, once a man becomes a grandparent, he is eligible to become an elder. Several factors are necessary in order for one to become an elder: age (the older one is, the more respect he or she receives), being married and having grandchildren, experience (as in his accomplishments), and a special knowledge. As noted, Muthoka was a well-respected elder. He possessed many skills, especially knowledge of the medicinal properties of plants.

Throughout his life, Muthoka remained a follower of the traditional Kikuyu religion. Muthoka acquired his knowledge of herbal medicine by self-training. Among the Kikuyu, herbal medicine is considered a sacred practice, and that may explain why Muthoka did not explicitly tell me how he acquired it. He merely said, "It was by observation—not by sitting down and being trained. I looked for and followed the people who *were there*."

I asked Muthoka, "What do you do when people come to you for help?"

He quickly answered, following Jagi's translation of my question, "I listen to them. But I can help people because I have learned many things in my life. For instance, if your body is feeling like it is being cut to pieces, I know the herbs that treat this particular illness. If someone cannot eat meat and has no appetite, I know the herbs that can restore the appetite. If someone has a problem with their stomach [worms], I know the herbs that will help."

Muthoka further explained that he knew the treatment for aching bones, impotence, and venereal diseases. He knew which plants, herbs, and procedures could heal illnesses, including mental illness. He also practiced veterinary skills. Not only was he well-known in Mukerwi-ini and the surrounding environs as a man to whom one could go for medicines for various ailments, but also as one who could provide helpful counsel as well. Individuals in his community often went to him for his commonsense advice. Thus, Muthoka was known to be, and was revered as, a wise man.

I also inquired about the process whereby Muthoka gained his reputation as a wise person in his community. He looked down at the ground briefly, as if embarrassed at being called wise.

Then, lifting his head and looking at Jagi, sitting next to him, Muthoka said, "When I started being appreciated as an elder within the community, it built much more confidence in me. Before that, I would give advice, but I didn't have much confidence in myself. Many in this community went to certain people for advice, but they soon found that their counsel didn't work. So they would go to someone else, but eventually they lost hope in finding someone who could help them. The building of my own confidence started when I was entered into the class of the elder. Eventually, people felt that if they came to me, they could be helped. So they would come to me. I would advise them. They were satisfied with what I told them, and they didn't have to go to anybody else. But I can't remember the year itself. It was before the year that is called 'The Emergency' here. This area was under The Emergency—during the Mau Mau insurrection."

Before the turbulent period in Kenya known as The Emergency, many Kenyans, especially those of the Kikuyu tribe, pushed for independence from Britain.[14] They had lost their lands to white settlers, and they were being heavily taxed by the British. By that time, Muthoka was well established as an elder. By the 1950s, the Kikuyu tribe organized a nationalist movement that proposed independence from Britain. This movement developed into the Mau Mau Resistance Movement, a long war of resistance that helped to bring independence to most of Africa by the early 1960s.

The British came down hard on the Kikuyu during this time, many of whom sympathized with the Mau Mau and longed for freedom and land reforms. Jagi clarified the situation, explaining, "The Nyeri area was the epicenter of the Mau Mau activity. The general of the Mau Mau army, Gen. Dedan Kimathi, was from Nyeri and had the best operation in the forests for the guerrillas. Mount Kenya and the Aberdare Range were the hiding places of the fighters. They were heavily bombed by the British, especially between 1953 and 1956."[15]

Life was most difficult for Muthoka during this time. In all, more than a hundred fifty thousand Kikuyu people, including Muthoka, were held in detention "villages"[16] that were more like concentration camps. Muthoka was incarcerated in Mihuti village, one of the barbed wire-enclosed "villages" where interrogation or "reeducation" took place. No proof of wrongdoing was necessary in order for the British to incarcerate a person. All that was needed was an allegation that the man, woman, or child had connections to the Mau Mau. Brutal treatment awaited those forced into the villages. Government officials even threatened Kikuyu people who had no Mau Mau connections unless they gave bribes to them. It was a treacherous time for the Kikuyu. Yet Muthoka survived. His life as a respected elder continued in Mukurwe-ini. He helped others whenever he could.

When it came to giving people advice, Muthoka noted that he didn't go about telling people what they ought to be doing with their lives or what they should be eating or drinking unless it was specifically asked of him. If they asked him, Muthoka would try to help.

"Most of the things I tell them," he said, "are actually stories [euphemisms or proverbs]. I don't normally say things bluntly. So for instance, if someone is suffering from impotence and is sent to me, I would tell him a story about the particular way he needs to proceed—he will remember a story better than my advice. I suggest that he should go and find a certain type of banana—*mutore*. He eats. And in the story, I may suggest certain herbs. Then he will come back to see me. If he does that, he will come back with a baby to say 'thank you.' So solutions to problems are given through stories and sayings."

I asked Muthoka, "How do you know what stories or things to tell people?"

He answered that it was only when an individual came to him to ask for his opinion that he seemed to intuitively know what to say or do. People's questions energized him.

Tapping his left hand on the arm of the chair, Muthoka smiled and said, "Nothing pleases me more than helping others—whether it be people with worms in their stomachs, infertility problems, family relationship troubles, various diseases, or problems with their livestock."

Jagi then asked Muthoka, "How do you get this feeling?"

Muthoka replied, "One of the moments when I feel good is when I am treating people. When that feeling [knowledge or wisdom] entered me, it got into me and never left me. And when I transfer it to people, they come back with a very good smile, showing that they have been healed. There are people who come with worms in their stomach, and then in the end, I tell them the herbs to use. Later on, they say they have no stomachache, and they feel better as well. There are some people who can be helped, even in these days when venereal diseases have become so common. There are herbs that can be used to treat those particular illnesses."

After these comments, Muthoka whistled and then laughed. His whistle conveyed to those in his culture that he is *good* at his work—he's on the "cutting edge."

Muthoka then talked about the extent of his knowledge. "My knowledge goes more with this local area—from Nairobi to the Kambali area. People from other parts of the world come here, but I don't know much about the world at large. Even the local people who listen to the radio don't tell me what's going on in other parts of the world." He then chuckled and said, "They don't know what's going on either!" Muthoka then added, somewhat apologetically, "I don't know about the current affairs of the country."

As to material possessions, Muthoka had few. He mentioned his friends although he lamented that most of his friends had died long ago. His family was the most valued thing in his life, but he acknowledged that livestock signified wealth in Kikuyu society.

"To have *property*, to me, is important," Muthoka clarified. "In the traditional ways, to have livestock and to have children—these are most important. However, you should not have children before you have the property." (To the Kikuyu, property is the equivalent of wealth: cattle, goats, and then children.)

Asked what possessions he'd like to have, Muthoka smiled, saying, "In these days, I'd like a stone house, and if I was younger, I'd like a car! Those things are valuable."

Jagi asked, "Would you like an airplane?"

Muthoka laughingly replied, "I haven't yet reached that stage of life!"

Muthoka then explained, "I wish that I was younger, and I would show you how I was as a younger man. When I was younger, I was very virile. As a young man, I was 'walking on water.' You could look at me and see how agile I was because I was burning like electricity. I was very strong when I was younger."

Jagi leaned out of his chair toward Muthoka and murmured something. Both he and Muthoka immediately began to laugh. Jagi did not translate their exchange. I later asked another Kikuyu translator, Ann Om'mani, who listened to the tape, what was so funny. It seems that Jagi told Muthoka that he could eat the bananas he was referring to earlier—the ones that assist people to conceive children. Muthoka laughed at the idea that he could give himself a prescription (an aphrodisiac) to become young again.

I, clueless about what had just transpired, asked Muthoka about his health. He said, "I had a very meat-based menu, and I kept myself very healthy. So I feel that the agility, the sexual appetite I had, and the ability to stay alive was mainly from my eating habits—a meat diet. Meat, for me, is what builds the body. Therefore, eating meat has always been an integral part of my diet." (I later learned that most Kikuyu's don't eat much meat—they do eat a variety of vegetables.)

Muthoka continued, "You should know that in terms of age, I am still agile and virile—meat is good for the body and brain. My habits have not changed over time." He then spoke passionately of his wife, comparing her to the "fire" that kept his life in balance. "Up till now, I sleep with my wife in the same bed. She is like fire. We keep each other warm. I get warmth from her, and she gets warmth from herself. When we are together, sitting alone in the house, we are like logs of wood in fire. We are like two young people."

I asked Muthoka if he ever gave marital advice to others.

He nodded his head in the affirmative, saying, "Traditionally, first of all, people don't divorce. That is because the wife belongs to the community. So when you marry, it's like the community gets married—it is not just a man and a wife. So the question of not doing what you are not supposed to in a marriage does not even occur. There are many homes where that togetherness is there because you get pleasures and good blessings from the community."

I followed up by asking, "What kind of problems, if any, do you see in Kikuyu marriages?"

"Among the older generation," Muthoka mused, "a wife hitting her husband has never been heard of. It would never occur. However, the newer generation has a big problem with striking one another. Respect for one another has gone, and some of them have come to me and asked me for advice. I always tell them stories and examples of the way we used to live—including the things they shouldn't do."

Muthoka continued, saying, "One of the things that has changed in marriages is that girls are not respected today before they get married like they used to be. Now girls are getting pregnant before they marry, and the men do not take the responsibility. They just go and impregnate another, and then they just leave. Those things are bad! There is no respect for women."

I commented, "Perhaps the women do not respect themselves."

Muthoka added, "Many women have loose morals—they engage in premarital sex too easily. They have no respect for themselves. They should not make it so easy for the men." He nodded his head, saying emphatically, "That's what I believe!"

We talked about the trees and animals that lived in Kenya's forests, and Muthoka expressed concern about the planting of foreign trees. He told me, "I'd like the indigenous forest to come back because that is where the wisdom and the medicine is."

We were at the end of the interview, and Muthoka's next statement surprised me. "If you want to take a challenge," he said, "I'd like to take you tomorrow morning and show you some of the trees and plants of the forest. You can take herbs with you that you can use for a long, long time. There are roots that can help you. I'll give you the prescription of what they do."

He wanted to introduce me to the indigenous plants that were so useful to him in helping others. I told Muthoka, "Of course! I'd be honored to do so."

Muthoka then smiled at me, his dark eyes twinkling, and rose from his chair to depart. He put his hat/wig back onto his bald head. Looking over at my husband and the cameras, he removed the microphone cord from his jacket and placed it on the chair. Then he said, "Robert! Sawa sawa (*Sawa sawa* is a Swahili saying that means OK.)

Muthoka then exclaimed to Jagi, "My spirits are full of charge. I am very happy when I get people to talk to. I get moments like this, and I feel wonderful."

Jagi, walking to his car, retrieved the previously purchased sack of sugar from the trunk and presented it to Muthoka, who seemed pleased with the gift. A Wajee Camp staff member then escorted Muthoka to a small sedan that was parked in front of the main house, helped him into the front passenger seat of the vehicle, loaded the sack of sugar into the backseat, and drove Muthoka to his homestead.

Jagi Gakunju arranged for my husband and me to spend the night at Wajee Nature Park where we had the once-in-a lifetime experience of staying in a typical Kikuyu dwelling.[17] Men skilled in traditional construction built the mud hut then painted it white. Located on the park ground, the hut was a round structure called a *rondavel*. In the customary manner, its door faced east, there were two small windows, and the roof was comprised of long grasses and twigs.[18] Our rondavel was equipped with modern conveniences—two cots, sleeping bags, and a small nightstand. The bathroom facilities were available, after a walk across the grounds, in a *choh* (pronounced *choo*)—or outhouse.

That evening the camp staff prepared a delicious dinner, including several authentic Kikuyu dishes—including *kinyegenya* and *irio,* with *ucuru,* a traditional millet beverage, to drink—and, of course, many kinds of bananas. Irio is a dish made of boiled peas, potatoes, corn, spinachlike greens, and often lima beans, all mashed together. *Ugali* is made from white cornmeal and is somewhat like stiff grits. We ate outdoors, around a warm and inviting campfire, learning more about the Wajee Nature Park and its history from Jagi and others at the park.

A rich variety of birds, over 108 species, found sanctuary at Wajee Park, including the *ndutumba* (tambourine dove) and Hinde's Pied-babbler. As night approached, the calls and songs of the birds quieted. Robert and I headed to our rondavel; the faint sound of drums and singing could be heard in the distance and continued into the night. This pleasant and soothing music, emanating from the homes of people living near the park, lulled us quickly to sleep.

The next day dawned bright and sunny. We woke at 6:30 a.m., just as the equatorial sun began to stream through the door of the hut. Robert and I hiked to a spot at the northern boundary of Wajee Park, from which we could see Mount Kenya. No clouds hid the top of the mountain—a somewhat unusual occurrence—leaving this magnificent mountain clearly visible, its jagged summit reaching more than seventeen thousand feet toward the heavens. The old religion considered *Kirinyaga* (Mount Kenya's Kikuyu name) a sacred and holy place. It was considered the birthplace of the Kikuyu tribe.

Soon after breakfast, Muthoka arrived at the main headquarters of the park in a sedan driven by a Wajee Park staff member. He stopped to have tea with the staff at the house. As he was finishing his tea, Robert and I walked over to the porch of the house where Muthoka was sitting on a bench. Muthoka greeted us, "Jambo!" Robert and I replied in unison, "Jambo."

David Mutinda, the manager of Wajee Park, approached the three of us. He had agreed at dinner the evening before to be the interpreter and Muthoka's helper. Muthoka, full of energy, suggested that we begin our walk. I also brought a notebook and pencil to take notes at Muthoka's insistence. Robert carried and operated the video camera. We entered the forest, loudly announced by the chirping birds. The terrain was steep in places, and large roots occasionally snaked across the surface of the path that Muthoka chose to take.

The experience of walking through the forest with Muthoka was surreal and has become, for me, an unforgettable and treasured memory. Within view of the Kikuyu's sacred mountain—Mount Kenya—I found myself hiking the hillsides of an indigenous African forest, guided by a wise one-hundred-year-old Kikuyu elder who knew the qualities and uses of every plant in sight.

Within seconds of entering into the trees, Muthoka plucked a leaf off a vine that was climbing up and around a tall tree trunk. He said the tree was a *murembu* tree. The vine was called *muhukura,* and its leaves would make a person "healthy and strong." He then asked David Mutinda to dig into the reddish clay around the base of the murembu to obtain a piece of root. Using his bare hands, David cleared a bit of earth to expose the tree roots. He had a bit of trouble breaking off a piece of root, even though he utilized a long knife, but was eventually successful. He handed the root to Muthoka.

As Muthoka held the white root in his hand, he explained, "This root is prepared by crushing it and then boiling it in water. This results in a tea. Drinking one cup of that tea in the morning and one in the evening will relieve the pain of arthritis."

Muthoka handed the root to me. I had to ask David how murembu was spelled so I could record it in my notebook.

Muthoka moved on. He seemed to gain even more energy as he walked, supported by his two canes, in amongst the bushes and trees. He stopped every few minutes and pointed out many of the sacred plants of the area. Trying to impart some of his vast knowledge to me, he explained their qualities for healing and other uses. He told me that this information could be useful to me. He insisted that I take samples and label them in my notebook—which I did.

We walked deeper into the forest. The birds seemed to sing and chirp even louder from the branches of the trees over our heads. Muthoka pointed out a *mukindi* tree, whose bark, when boiled in water and sieved, made a flavoring for soup that would reduce body fat. The bark of another tree, the *miriri,* or red stinkwood (*Prunus africana*), also made a tea that would strengthen a person's immune system; it was also useful in treating prostrate problems.

We climbed up a small hill, stopping at a muituya, a wild fruit tree that produced edible fruit. Another stop was in front of a *mutundu* tree. I was told that mutundu leaves were well-known for the antiseptic properties of their sap. Another tree, the *muringa,* was a refuge for bees; and honey could be gathered from the hives in its trunk.

Muthoka searched awhile for a *ndegenya* plant that he wanted me to see. After one was located, he explained, "When the roots of the ndegenya are boiled in water, they make a tea that eliminates worms. It is also given to cows with digestive problems or difficulties with their udders."

Another bush, *muu* (*Markamia lutea*), helped with prostrate problems. With a smile, Muthoka cautioned me, "You need to be careful as you gather the foliage of the muu. This shrub is known to be a favorite hiding place for leopards." Throughout our expedition, we saw many *luthiri*, a member of the fern family, and *mutuma*, a broad-leaved plant, both used for thatching the roofs of huts.

Muthoka led this extensive tour not at all with an attitude of boasting or of self-importance but simply as a humble man who wanted to help a fellow human being to appreciate and understand the beauty and resources of an unfamiliar land, culture, and belief system. He was successful! I returned to America with an immense appreciation for the depth of human capabilities and a profound sense of awe for this compassionate, gentle man whom many in the West might condescendingly label "illiterate" but whom I then knew to be incredibly knowledgeable and wise. Fortunately, Muthoka's own people recognized him as both and showed him great respect.

Muthoka was the sixteenth wise person I met in my quest to learn more about wisdom. I was genuinely saddened in 2002 when I learned that he passed away. He had lived a long, productive, and meaningful life. Except in the area of Mukurwe-ini, Kenya, where Muthoka was well-known, his death went unnoticed by the world. With his death, Muthoka's knowledge, experience, wisdom, and sense of humor are lost to all of us.

Many people lament that wisdom seems to be a vanishing human quality.[19] It does seem that people, especially those living in Western cultures, often refuse to listen to or believe in certain sure words of wisdom. Why should this be the case? Why don't people always recognize the wise path? Why can't we always act wisely?

One reason given by wisdom researchers is that the world has changed drastically in the past few centuries. Some believe that humans have outgrown their need for the wise man or woman in their midst. Humanity's knowledge of physical processes and social phenomena has exploded exponentially. We now live in a time of unparalleled information and knowledge. Far more information presently exists in the world than any one person can

assimilate in a lifetime or even several lifetimes. Yet success in life depends
on our mastery of such. In addition, we need to know the answers to the
pressing questions of "Which knowledge is indispensable for living a good
and productive life?" and "How do we learn to make wise choices?" We still
need wisdom.

Since about the time of the French philosopher René Descartes
(1596-1650), Western cultures have relied on science and technology to
build a marvelous and technically tuned world. Miraculous discoveries
and unparalleled progress in many fields of knowledge presently bless
our lives. Some believe, however, that there may be a downside to all our
technical expertise; namely, that in this mushrooming growth of science
and technology, the concept of wisdom appears to have been abandoned.
Since science and technology exemplify a type of knowledge quite different
from that of wisdom, perhaps this is only to be expected. Heinz Pagels, an
American physicist and critic of science, wrote,

> It is a sign of the times that many people cannot tell the difference
> between information and knowledge, not to mention wisdom,
> which even knowledge tends to drive out . . . . Science shows what
> exists but not what to do about it.[20]

The major differences between science and wisdom lie in their basic
epistemology. Science utilizes method, techniques, and technology as its
means of operating. Efficiency, productivity, power, and effectiveness are
its values. Knowledge from this perspective combines what the British
philosopher Gilbert Ryle[21] called the "knowledge of that" and the "knowledge
of how."

People of every culture have spent a lot of time and energy cultivating the
"knowledge of that" and the "knowledge of how." These forms of knowledge
are crucial to our present existence, and they have brought about the high
standard of living and the scientific prowess enjoyed by many of us. This is
knowledge gained by attending traditional educational institutions, through
specialized training, or through the written word. It appears that science has
become the ubiquitous religion of the Western world and an ever-advancing
technology the determiner of lifestyle choices.

Wisdom, on the other hand, is difficult to describe. That knowledge that
the communication professor emeritus Walter Fisher[22] called the "knowledge
of whether"—whether or not some things are desirable to do beyond
what is instrumentally feasible, technologically possible, and monetarily

profitable—is not so easily learned or taught. This form of knowledge appears to be lacking in Western cultures. But in people's interactions with each other and the earth itself, the "knowledge of whether" ought to be paramount. Dee Hock, the financial wizard who essentially invented the present credit card economy, aptly described our present situation as being "fat on data and information and starved for wisdom."[23]

Wise individuals like Muthoka, although usually possessing a heightened "knowledge of that" and "knowledge of how," seem *to act* from their "knowledge of whether." Individuals who are deemed by their neighbors and friends to be wise often seem to "know" when asked which problems are important and which are trivial. They often intuitively understand the "knowledge of whether." They seem able to answer the many "why" questions as well. Their peers, especially in non-Western societies, often seek their guidance. Where does this "knowledge of whether"—this wisdom—come from? The life stories of wise individuals may yet reveal the answer.

These individuals, whom I call the wise ones, are rare—yet they are more numerous than we might think. They might be our next-door neighbors, our parents or grandparents, our siblings, our own children, or our friends. How are we to recognize them? How are they treated in our wisdom-deprived modern technological era? Do the wise have a place in our contemporary chaotic world of cell phones, computers, the Internet, the electronic chip, and space travel? It seems that human beings desperately need wisdom, but as our lives are filled with the products and the "knowledge of that" and the "knowledge of how," we are in danger of losing the "knowledge of whether," or the wisdom we may already possess.

To my knowledge, no one keeps statistics on how many wise men and women are living in the world at present. There is no "society of wise people." Today in Western cultures, for the most part, wise women and men are not acknowledged as such, even if their accomplishments are notable. Perhaps they should be. The wise ones like Muthoka provide humanity with a solid base—they bring their experiences, insights, compassion, and vision to their own communities. As Mihalyi Csikszentmihalyi, an eminent wisdom researcher, has noted, the wise offer all of us "hope, identity, and purpose in our lives."[24] We have much to learn from them.

Endnotes

1   http://www.mnsu.edu/emuseum/cultural/oldworld/africa/kikuyu.html (10 May 2007). There are forty-six different tribes in Kenya. The Kikuyu (Gîkûyû) represent the most populous ethnic group. They total 7.4 million, equal to about 22 percent of Kenya's total population. They are the most economically active ethnic group in Kenya.

2   Wajee Nature Park, a ten-hectare (twenty-five-acre) park had been Jagi Gakunju's childhood home. His father, Reverend Wajii, dedicated the homestead for the conservation of indigenous plants and animals of the area. Mr. Gakunju inherited the land following his parents' deaths and established Wajee Nature Park. More information can be found on the park's Web site: www.wajeenaturepark.com (20 July 2007).

3   The Africa Guide, http://www.africaguide.com/culture/tribes/kikuyu.htm (10 May 2007). Although members of the Kikuyu tribe are found in other parts of Africa and the world as well as Kenya, historically, they have been extremely successful in what is now called the Central Province of Kenya, in the Nyeri and the Mukurwe-ini areas, the area of the Aberdare south of Mt. Kenya. It is the home of elephants, antelopes, leopards, buffalo, the rare black rhinoceros, plentiful birds (270 species), and colobus monkeys. The Kikuyu have occupied this part of Africa—with its fertile soils and, at one time, plentiful rains—for at least four hundred years. They expanded into the area through purchasing land, blood brotherhood, and intermarriage with those who already lived in the area—that is, until the British colonized Kenya in 1898. An agricultural people, the Kikuyu grew sugarcane, yams, maize, beans, and other vegetables. They also raised cattle and, for religious purposes, sheep and goats. Trade with other groups flourished in Kikuyu societies. Thus, members of the tribe have accrued a reputation of being good businesspeople.

4   World Information Zone, http://www.worldinfozone.com (23 May 2007). Kiswahili (or Swahili) is the African language spoken in eastern and central Africa. "The language that grew out of the mix of Arabs and Bantu is one of the most common and widespread of the *lingua franca* (a *lingua franca* is a secondary language that is a combination of two or more languages): Swahili or Kiswahili, from the Arabic word *sawahil*, which means 'coast.' Swahili is primarily a Bantu language with some Arabic elements; it is written in the Arabic alphabet. Like the language, the Swahili culture was a mixture of the two cultures, Bantu and Arabic. Kiswahili is a national language in Kenya, Tanzania, and Uganda."

5   Tim Parson, "Wakamba Warriors Are Soldiers of the Queen: The Evolution of the Kamba as a Martial Race, 1890-1970," *The American Society for Ethnohistory* 46 (1999).

6   John Reader, *Africa: A Biography of the Continent* (New York: Alfred A. Knopf, 1998). Although World War I is often thought of as primarily a European war, the contribution of Africans was certainly significant. "By the time of the armistice [World War I] in November 1918, more than two million Africans had contributed directly to the European war effort, either as soldiers or as porters and labourers; more than 200,000 gave their lives . . . . Over one million African troops were recruited during the war." (Reader, 605-606).

7   *Emergency in Kenya*, updated April 27, 2005. www.globalsecurity.org (15 June 2007). It was common among the Kikuyu, especially in previous times, to be polygamous. The husband provided each of his wives her own home.

8   African Art treatise. Home Gallery: African Tribal Arts and Ethnic Textiles Web site. 15 June 2006. www.african-tribal-arts.com/stools.htm. Also, Mosha describes the functions of the stool in African societies in his text. R. Sambuli Mosha, *The Heartbeat of Indigenous Africa: A Study of Chagga Educational System* (New York: Garland Publishing Co. 2000.)

9   Clemente K. Abrokwaa, "Indigenous Music Education in Africa," In Ladislaus M. Semali and Joe L. Kincheloe, eds. *What is Indigenous Knowledge? Voices from the Academy.* New York: Farmer Press (1999). "All African cultures have relied on oral tradition teaching methods since time immemorial. Pre-colonial African societies preserved their history, cultural traditions, values, and climatic and environmental knowledge through oral tradition. The elders of the various communities are able to recall past events and history with astonishing accuracy. The oral system of learning and record keeping was, and is, passed on to the younger generation. Consequently, Africans tend to rely on their memory, and are able to listen and then store detailed and complex information for very long periods of time. Even today the majority of the African population, including well-educated individuals, continue to use oral tradition in their efforts to preserve ethnic information, and to employ memory in business agreements rather than use written records." (Abrokwaa, 204-205.)

10   Mister Seed Web site. 2005. www.misterseed.com/link%20pages/PROVERBS2.htm (15 April 2007).

11   Personal communication with Ann Om'mani, March 16, 2000.

12   Jomo Kenyatta (1898-1978), the first prime minister of a self-governed Kenya, also received his preliminary and elementary education at the Scottish mission

center at Thogoto. He was baptized a Christian and given the name John Peter. He then changed the name to Johnstone before adopting the name Jomo in 1938. These mission schools brought literacy to many individuals.

[13] *Historian* (Winter, 1998). At the present time, governmental, religious, and secular groups are actively discouraging female circumcision, *clitoridectomy,* a painful and risky procedure. Theodore Natsoulas, "The Kenyan Government and the Kikuyu Independent Schools; From Attempted Control to Suppression, 1920-1952,"

[14] Personal communication from James Mbatia, Nairobi, Kenya, September 1999.

[15] Personal communication from Jagi Gakunju, May 16, 2007.

[16] David Anderson, *Histories of the Hanged: The Dirty War in Kenya and the End of Empire* (New York: W. W. Norton & Co., 2005), 5.

[17] W. Scoresby Routledge and Katherine Routledge, *With a Prehistoric People* (London: E. Arnold Publishers, 1905). The specifications for building such a hut are quite specific. The hut is built from twenty poles with a fork at the top of each one. The poles are placed in a four- to five-meter-diameter circle and "then withies are woven around the tops of the uprights to form a wall plate which carries the thrust of the roof; a centre pole is erected and poles are lashed into the woven withies and pass across the diameter of the circle being tied to the centre pole each time as well as joining the wall on the other side of the circle. The wall uprights with the forked tops are then used to carry the roof poles. Throughout the whole Kikuyu building process no timbers are greater than 6 cm in diameter."

[18] In traditional Kikuyu families, each married woman had her own *rondavel,* where she and her daughters slept. Cooking was done over a central fireplace. The father and older sons slept in an adjacent smaller hut—one that also harbored the goats and other livestock, keeping them safe throughout the night.

[19] Aleida Assmann, "Wholesome Knowledge: Concepts of Wisdom in a Historical and Cross-Cultural Perspective," In *Life-span Development and Behavior,* edited by D. L. Featherman, R. M. Lerner, and M. Perlmutter (Hillsdale, NJ: Lawrence Erlbaum Associates, Inc., 1994), 12; Mihalyi Csikszentmihalyi, "Toward an Evolutionary Hermeneutics: The Case of Wisdom," In *Rethinking Knowledge: Reflections Across the Disciplines,* edited by R. F. Goodman, and W. R. Fisher (Albany, NY. 1995: State University of New York Press); D. N. Robinson, "Wisdom Through the Ages," In *Wisdom: Its Nature, Origins, and Development,* edited by R. J. Sternberg (New York: Cambridge University Press, 1990c) and others.

[20] Heinz Pagels, *The Dreams of Reason: The Computer and the Rise of the Age of Complexity* (New York: Simon and Schuster, 1988), 149.

[21] Gilbert Ryle, *The Concept of Mind* (Chicago: Univ. of Chicago Press, 1949).

[22] Walter Fisher, "Narration, Knowledge, and the Possibility of Wisdom," In *Rethinking Knowledge: Reflections Across the Disciplines*, edited by R. F. Goodman and W. R. Fisher (Albany, NY: State University of New York Press, 1995).

[23] Dee Hock, *Birth of the Chaordic Age* (San Francisco: Berrett-Koehler Publishers, Inc., 1999), 229.

[24] Mihalyi Csikszentmihalyi, *The Evolving Self* (New York: HarperCollins, 1993), 286.

Chapter Two

What of Wisdom?

Learning is not wisdom—
You can learn to pick a lock or steal a neighbor's car,
But it would be wiser to do neither.

—*Wise Saying*[1]

What is it that makes a person wise? Some say that wisdom comes with age. Some say it comes from the difficult and painful experiences of life. Some say it comes from trials and tribulations that have no connection to one's own choices. Some say it is indicative of an expertise in the practicalities of life. Some say wisdom is a gift from God. People have many opinions. Yet however wisdom is attained, it seems to be a uniquely human attribute—one that, though rare, is "no respecter of persons or cultures." Wise individuals live in all societies throughout the world. I believe they have much in common.

On the southwestern end of Honshu Island, the mainland of Japan, lays Tanabe (田辺市), a city of approximately eighty-six thousand in the Wakayama Prefecture. Situated on the coast of the Kii Peninsula, surrounded by rugged mountains and dark green forests, Tanabe is a fishing port where the processing of marine products is an important commercial industry. Citrus orchards dot the hillsides. Rocky outcrops jut out into the Pacific Ocean, separating the shoreline into numerous small bays and beaches. The area is not only beautiful but also revered by the Japanese people—it is said to be the place where gods descend and reside. It is also the home of Misae Itani (hereafter called Itani-san, reflecting her proper Japanese name and title [Japanese individuals customarily address each other by their surnames, followed by an honorary title, with *san* being the most common title]).

Fumiko Hatanaka, one of the people who nominated Itani-san as a wise one, made arrangements for me to meet with her. Hatanaka-san accompanied my son Steven and me to picturesque Tanabe on the morning of July 20, 1999. Steven, who is fluent in Japanese and English, served as our interpreter. Tanabe was not bombed during World War II, and its confusing maze of streets remain much as they had been in medieval times—a labyrinth of narrow pathways. Finding parking for the car was a challenge, but not impossible, and the three of us were soon walking down the narrow street where Itani-san lives.

Itani-san's home, the same house where she was born, was a typical old-style Japanese home, resembling a townhome or row home. All the homes in her neighborhood were similar. They were one-story structures built entirely of wood. Streetside, the fronts of the homes were narrow,[2] but each dwelling extended a long way back into the city block. Called a *machiya*, each town house had a unique architecture, consisting of rooms off a long hallway (*tori-niwa*) that led from the front of the home to the rear. There were subtle variations in the architectural features of the front of each townhouse, making each home slightly unique.

As we approached Itani-san's home, I noted a line of individuals stretching from her door and down the street. Hatanaka-san explained that Itani-san was very popular with her neighbors and those who knew of her in the Wakayama Prefecture. Throughout each day, many people sought her out to ask for her help.

Because we had an appointment, we went to the front of the line and were met by Itani-san's friend, a lovely middle-aged woman who ushered us through the front door into the *tori-niwa*, a long hall. All the *washitsu*, shoji-screened rooms, in the *machiya* were on the left side. Passing by one screened washitsu, Itani-san's friend led us to the second room back from the door where the open screens revealed a reception room. The tatami-matted room was elevated nearly thirty inches above the corridor—a large step-up for a Westerner like myself. A low table covered by a lovely lace cloth sat in the center of the room. The family shrine was prominent on the right-side wall of the room. Itani-san stood by the table in the room. As the three of us approached down the tori-niwa, she bowed to us in the Japanese traditional greeting. I bowed formally[3] as well upon seeing Itani-san.

After leaving our shoes in the tori-niwa and undergoing appropriate verbal introductions, Itani-san expressed some concerns. In her humble way, Itani-san was not convinced that she was an appropriate person to interview for a study on wisdom. After much discussion with her friend, Hatanaka-san, and Steven, Itani-san agreed to talk with me.

An agile diminutive Japanese woman, with dark hair and expressive dark eyes, Itani-san, then seventy-eight years old, graciously invited me to sit across from her at the low table on a *zabuton*, a low chair or cushion. She offered us tea or a soda. Steven assembled the recording equipment then sat down at the end of the table with us. Hatanaka-san and Itani-san's friend knelt on the tatami mat next to the family shrine.

Itani-san's expressive hands were strong; her voice was melodic. She was apologetic, explaining that she had difficulty seeing things well. When she was ten years old, she lost her eyesight—completely in one eye and partially in the other. Because of her condition, she had difficulty learning to read and write the difficult Japanese language, but she persevered and learned to do so. Thick glasses helped her limited eyesight.

After the video camera and audio recorders were turned on, Itani-san told me her life story.

Misae Itani was born to a family with seven children. She clarified this number by telling me, "but many of them died young." Her father, she reported, did not talk a lot; but he worked hard, as did her mother. Tragically, her mother died at age thirty when Itani-san was ten years old.

Itani-san explained, "My mother was delivering drinking water to all the houses in the town day and night—she worked herself to death!"

Itani-san's father died prematurely as well. A maternal aunt, her mother's oldest sister, took over the care for her and her siblings. This aunt also died not long after she assumed responsibility for Itani-san and her siblings. Following her death, the second oldest maternal aunt looked after the children of the family.

Besides a strong work ethic, Itani-san's mother was remembered for her high priority in giving service to other people. She did so without seeking any compensation. Itani-san chose to do the same thing. She was not attached to the material things of the world and, apparently, never had been. Itani-san's friend related that when Itani-san was young, the family planted fields of vegetables to supply them with food. They became frustrated because Itani-san constantly gave away all of their vegetables to other people in their neighborhood—to the extent that the family found itself in a precarious position. The family even contemplated giving Itani-san away to another family because she was "starving" everyone at home.

After her friend related this story to me, Itani-san shyly smiled and exclaimed, "I like to give things to people!"

At nineteen, Itani-san married. "My first husband," she said, "was a wonderful person, and he was very nice to me. I was very happy. We eventually had a beautiful baby, but tragically, he passed away when he was a toddler. Then shortly after our son's death, my husband died unexpectedly of a stroke. He was only thirty-six years old!"

The deaths of her son and husband devastated Itani-san. She somberly explained, "Everyone died here in this house. And I was lonely. Everyone died!"

When she was twenty-eight years old, Itani-san remarried, but she and her second husband had no children. At the time of my visit to Japan in June 1999, her husband of fifty years was hospitalized with heart problems. (He passed away later that year.) When I asked Itani-san about him, her eyes filled with tears; and she choked back her sadness and fear, unable to speak.

Itani-san's strength and determination enabled her to turn her thoughts and energies toward helping her neighbors and friends. She preferred to focus and talk of positive things. Therefore, she didn't talk much about the difficult times in her life although they were numerous. She did remark, however, "I have learned much from the various events of the twentieth century—the depression, the wars, and such. I admire people who have the heart to find and express their will [spirit] and are able to work hard despite hard times."

Itani-san worked hard all her life and planned to continue to do so even as she approached her eighties. She was extremely skilled at her occupation. She used massage and herbal medicine to help those who come to her for relief from their physical ailments. With great effort because of her disability, Itani-san earned the appropriate certificates to practice her occupation, as required by the government of Japan.

Itani-san, a generous and kind woman, used the Japanese word *suku* whenever she referred to her occupation of helping people. In Japanese, the word *suku* is typically used to refer to the concept of saving people, including their souls. Moreover, Itani-san also healed injured psyches, and people regularly consulted her for wise advice.

To this day (August 2009), Itani-san, now eighty-seven years old, continues to help people from her humble Tanabe home. She treats people sent to her by medical doctors in the area and also individuals for whom there is little hope of recovery from disease or illness.

When I asked about her ability to help so many people, she simply explained, "You can't help people without love."

Being a loving individual, Itani-san focused on the good things and the good times of her life, and she tried hard to "not have bad feelings toward anyone." She also told me, "My ability to serve others and help them is something God has given me, but I also need to do my part."

A faith healer, Itani-san suggested that everyone would function better by doing "as God has said, that is, to hold our hearts"—a Japanese phrase with Buddhist overtones. It refers to thinking and disciplining one's mind in such a way that one can turn disadvantages into advantages.

Itani-san explained this phrase by relating the following analogy on life: "Some flowers bloom in spring, some in summer, some in the fall, and some in the winter. Therefore, one can always look forward to the next season. Although each flower will not be blooming at the same time, there is always another flower that will bloom in the next season. Always anticipate or expect the next flower blooming. Don't let yourself become depressed. Proceed forward with each step. If you do so, your life will open up."

Itani-san has "held her heart" throughout her lifetime. In spite of her blindness, she has been able to find a purpose to her life through serving and helping others. She explained, "I am very proud of my work. I believe people must be proud of what they do. My main purpose is to help people through the power of words, love, and beauty."

At one point in our conversation, I asked Itani-san, "What is wisdom?"

Once she heard my question, reiterated in Japanese by Steven, her response was calm, confident, and immediate. She answered, "The knowledge that is called wisdom is something that is given by God, but action on a person's part is also necessary."

As Itani-san and I talked, my eyes were drawn to the family shrine in the corner of the room next to the tori-niwa (hallway). It was covered with photographs, mementos, and small strips of paper called *omikugi*. The omikugi are associated with Buddhist temples and worship. They are received at the many temples throughout Japan and contain words, poems, phrases, and messages that bring blessings to one's self, family, and others. Interestingly, there were actually two shrines in the corner. A Shinto shrine was placed directly above the Buddhist shrine.

Itani-san blessed individuals regularly not only with her services but also with her love and her prayers and chants. Before I left her home after our second interview, Itani-san gave me a special Buddhist blessing—pronouncing a prayer over my head, at the same time shaking a long prayer stick with tambours that produced a shower of sound that descended over me. Although

I did not understand the words she chanted, I felt her goodwill toward me and I had a sense of her wisdom.

As I was about to leave, Itani-san said to me, "I had some concerns when I learned that you wanted to meet with me. But after I have had this chance to meet with you, I realize that you are a good person, and I am thankful that we have met."

After uttering this gracious statement, Itani-san handed me a white envelope, stating that she had not had time to go shopping because her husband was in the hospital. However, she wanted to give me a gift "to show my feelings toward you." She added, "I believe in God, and I like to give the offerings on the altar here [in her home] to people—no matter what God they worship."

Steven and Hatanaka-san motioned to me that I was *not* to open the envelope. I learned later that opening the envelope in her presence would have been considered extremely rude.

Itani-san continued, "If all the different countries would 'hold their hearts' in a way that they helped the people in distress, then the world would become a peaceful place. I am not educated, but I feel I have a simple, pure heart. I am happy because I have good relationships with the people around me, and they take good care of me."

Itani-san and I again formally bowed to each other in farewell; and Hatanaka-san, Steven, and I returned to the car. As we drove away from the old part of Tanabe where Itani-san lived and the brown-wood row houses with their black-tile roofs faded from sight, I asked if I could finally open the envelope Itani-san had given me. Hatanaka-san, with Steven serving as interpreter, said that it would be appropriate to do so then.

I opened the white envelope's flap. There inside, Itani-san's gift to me, wrapped in white rice paper, was a crisp ten thousand yen bill, at that time approximately ninety U.S. dollars.

Overwhelmed, I remembered Itani-san's words. "I like to give things to people." I was reluctant to take such a large amount of money from Itani-san, but Hatanaka-san and Steven informed me that returning the "gift" to her would be viewed as an extremely rude gesture on my part.

I had given Itani-san a small piece of San Felipe Pueblo pottery; but when I finally returned to New Mexico, I sent her luxurious thick white towels to use in her work, wrapping them in the best paper and ribbons I could obtain. A few months later, Hatanaka-san informed me, through Steven, that Itani-san had placed the attractive blue ribbon that had been wrapped around the box of towels in a prominent place on the family altar. I assume the towels were given to others who were in need.

Itani-san's "gifts" to me and to others were not only of physical objects but included spiritual blessings as well. She viewed wisdom as "a gift from God." She was the first, but not the only, person that I interviewed who expressed this belief.

In Kenya, following my meeting with Muthoka, I met with a wise man who defined wisdom in the same way—Mburu James Gakunju. Mburu turned out to be the older brother of Jagi Gakunju but was nominated as a wise man by several other Kenyans.

A dignified, humble, and thoughtful man in his early sixties, Mburu certainly did not claim to be a wise man. My interview with him took place at Wajee Nature Park as the golden Kenyan sun was beginning to set and darken the bright blue sky on September 11, 1999. He replied to my questions with confidence and conviction in his voice.

I asked Mburu the usual question. "What is wisdom?"

He, like Itani-san, was confident in his answer to my question. Hardly had the question left my lips when he quickly answered in his perfect Kenyan English, "Wisdom is a gift from God!" He did not hesitate with his answer.

Like Muthoka, Mburu lived north of Nairobi in Mukurwe-ini, near Nyeri, Kenya. Kind, fit, gracious, and extremely humble, Mburu was most cordial and polite during the interview. He was impeccably dressed in a suit, white shirt, and tie. As he told his story, it became clear that he was a compassionate man who was also deeply religious. Wisdom, to him, was simply a gift of God; and it differed significantly from intelligence.

The fifth of ten children, Mburu was born and raised in the Nyeri area of Kenya. During our conversation, he spoke frequently of his father, whom he admired and still tried to emulate. His father, the Reverend Wajii, now deceased, had worked for the Presbyterian Church and counseled many people.

Mburu said, "My father was that kind of a person—a wise person . . . . He was consulted [by other people] in many things. He was a teacher first of all, and he then became a church leader. Leading in a church means you are a counselor—because you have to counsel many, many people. By so doing, you learn a lot of things."

Mburu was close to his father. He told me that his father regarded him as a friend, not just as his son. Mburu felt close to his mother as well. "My mother is not alive, but I cannot live a month without remembering what my mother told me."

He mentioned that one of the "greatest" things his mother told him was to treat his female children differently than his male children. He said, "In our culture, girls are more *dangerous* than boys."

When I asked him to explain "dangerous," he replied, "Girls are more *dangerous* because my daughter can have children out of wedlock, and if she has children, she will bring those children to me as her parent. They will be added to my own children—whether I like it or not. So the burden will be too big for me as a parent. Thus, my mother told me, 'Take care of your boys differently than your girls.'"

When Mburu's parents became older, they put him "in charge of their gate" (their temporal affairs and care). Mburu would go every morning to light fires for them, to check their house, and to keep them company. He would do the same every evening. He viewed this responsibility as a privilege rather than a duty.

Educated in church schools, Mburu finished his formal schooling and then received special training as a public health worker. That field exposed him to the problems of people and gave him some insight and knowledge as to why they have had them. He continued his learning after school by attending workshops and seminars.

Mburu's life was not always calm and pleasant. The Mau Mau movement caught him in its tentacles when he was only a teenager. He became a Mau Mau warrior during The Emergency, joining with two of his brothers.

Mburu explained, "My father and mother were not members of the Mau Mau movement, and they were not harmed by the Mau Mau or the British. This was because my father, a reverend and a leader of the Presbyterian Church, never publicly condemned Mau Mau. He was known to have prayed to God to arbitrate the dispute between the two functions—even though his two high-quality bulls were stolen by the Mau Mau."

Mburu and his brothers were captured, arrested, and detained by the British. He reported, "I was held for six months in a detention camp and released after the tribunal found me innocent. I was nineteen years old."

Mburu was fortunate. During the Emergency, the fate of convicted Mau Mau fighters was not pleasant. They were denied the right of appeal and hanged immediately after their convictions. David Anderson, a lecturer in African studies at Oxford University, wrote,

> State execution is a mighty weapon, and in the colonial context it has generally been used sparingly. Not so in the Mau Mau emergency. Kenya's hanging judges were kept busy. Between April 1953 and December 1956, the Special Emergency Assize Courts tried a total of 2,609 Kikuyu on capital charges relating to Mau Mau offences in 1,211 trials. Around 40 per cent of those accused were acquitted, but

1,574 were convicted and sentenced to hang over this period . . . .
In total, approximately 3000 Kikuyu stood trial between 1952 and
1958 on capital charges relating to the Mau Mau movement."[4]

When Mburu was twenty-four years old, he married. He and his wife
have five children, all of whom were adults at the time of our conversation.
Asked about his hobbies, he replied that he enjoyed agriculture—planting a
garden and growing his own vegetables. He said his father had encouraged
him to plant indigenous trees and to care for them, telling him that if he
did so, he would never want for anything. He believed his father gave him
wise advice.

Mburu's adopted a motto, which was "Be principled," by which he meant
to say that he valued honesty and self-mastery. He took excellent care of his
own health, watching what he ate and exercising regularly. He understood
the value of balance in his life.

When we talked about the problems life could present, Mburu said,
"Life, of course, is like that . . . Sometimes things may be very good;
sometimes things may be very bad. There is no life that is straightforward—it
has the ups and downs. It was ups and downs for me. In some things, you
feel stressed because of a certain situation. You are not in charge. Nobody
is fully in charge of his life. And you cannot be happy all the time, nor can
you be sorrowful all the time. There is—what do they call it?—balance."

Mburu's life story illustrated his great faith and his service to others. At
the time of the interview, he was a retired social worker but spent his free
time, without remuneration, serving disabled individuals in the Nyeri area.
Kenya has more than its share of disabled, ill, and poverty-stricken citizens.
AIDS has taken a terrible toll on the population, and thousands of children
have been orphaned as their parents have been taken by the disease. Mburu,
a devout Christian, enjoyed serving others and, like Itani-san, recommended
such service to everyone.

It was dark when our conversation ended. Mburu's calm and humble
manner and his deep understanding of human nature set me at ease in this
country that at first seemed so different from my own. We talked of many
issues. He brought up the problems inherent in raising teenagers. I sensed
from him that raising children in rural Kenya is fraught with problems for
parents and for children, the same as it is in New Mexico or London or
Oslo—everywhere. No matter what their culture, most parents care for and
worry about their children. They seek wisdom—that *gift* "far more precious
than rubies."[5]

Mburu and I continue to communicate through mail and e-mail. He has continued learning and studying as well as helping those in need. Through a distance-learning program, in 2005, he earned a degree in theology. The last time I spoke with him, he was finishing another degree—one in counseling.

He wrote to me, "Counseling knowledge is in high demand in this country, as the world has become a global village. Our people, especially the youth, are susceptible to adopting foreign cultures which would be detrimental to their future lives."[6]

Mburu plans to do everything he can in his wisdom to help make his tiny corner of the planet a safe, healthy, and beautiful place to live for everyone.

As I began to meet some of the wise people of the world, the reality of the relatedness and the inherent similarities of all human beings became indisputable. As I looked at wisdom and its importance to contemporary life, I still didn't have a satisfactory idea of what wisdom was? Although Mburu and Itani-san easily defined it from their point of view, social scientists and philosophers—those who formally study wisdom—are hard-pressed to comprehend it.

Even though wisdom has been a subject of research in the social sciences since the early 1970s, academic researchers still have difficulty agreeing on its definition. Robert Sternberg, the well-known psychologist who has conducted extensive research into intelligence, creativity, and wisdom,[7] lamented that wisdom is an "elusive psychological concept."[8] Most of the definitions that have been suggested have been dependent upon the point of view or the emphasis of the researchers' particular domain of inquiry or field of study.

Because wise people are found in all nations and cultures, wisdom must be a universal quality or trait of humankind. Therefore, a definition of what wisdom is and how it manifests should be apparent to all. But such does not appear to be the case.

Webster's New World College Dictionary defines wisdom as "the power of judging rightly and following the soundest course of action based on knowledge, experience, understanding, etc."[9] Of course, the problem with this definition is that the phrase *judging rightly* is subjective and vague; thereby it is prone to various interpretations. After all, with the West's predilection for moral relativism, who is to say what is right? Another dictionary, *The Oxford English Dictionary*, not only defines *wisdom* as (a) "the ability to judge rightly in matters relating to life and conduct" but also as (b) "knowledge, learning, or erudition, especially in relation to philosophy or science" and (c) "wise discourse or sayings."

The Dictionary of Etymology[10] reports that *wise* means (a) "knowing or learned" and (b) "prudent." The word *wise* stems from the Indo-European word *wede*—meaning "to see" or "to know." S. G. Holiday and M. J. Chandler, psychologists who researched wisdom extensively beginning in the 1980s, wrote, "The meaning of the word *wisdom* has seemingly remained constant across centuries and over . . . languages. . . . *[T]he term is still used in a manner consistent with the ancient meanings of seeing and knowing*"[11] (emphasis added).

Synonyms for *wisdom* include *discernment, discrimination, judgment, prudence, sagacity,* and *sense. Use the Right Word: A Guide to Synonyms* gives the following description of wisdom:

> Wisdom is a broad term, embracing the meanings of all its synonyms in addition to outranking them all in suggesting a rare combination of discretion, maturity, keenness of intellect, broad experience, extensive learning, profound thought, and compassionate understanding. In its full application, wisdom implies the highest and noblest exercise of all the faculties of the moral nature as well as of the intellect.[12]

It appears that wisdom is much like the Heisenberg uncertainty principle.[13] In quantum physics, while conducting research into the nature of the electron, when researchers expect to see the electron as a particle, they find a particle; when they expect to see the electron as a wave, they find a wave. Thus, it seems to be with wisdom. Depending on whether wisdom is viewed developmentally, psychologically, philosophically, spiritually, biologically, or anthropologically, it is seen and understood somewhat differently; and thus, its definition varies.

Perhaps defining wisdom is difficult because wisdom is like other common human qualities, such as courage, love, or compassion—it is dependent upon the *context* in which it is expressed, and it cannot be easily parsed or divided into definitive pieces or conditions as modern scientific investigations are prone to do. Obviously, a more specific definition of wisdom is required and preferably one that could include all contextual and even cultural viewpoints. Such a definition does not exist.

William Damon, a Stanford University professor of education, discerns wisdom to be comprised of "many diverse components of human judgment, cognitive appraisals, learned behavioral 'scripts,' emotional (or 'gut') feelings, moral awareness, and spiritual consciousness (the latter being the least understood by psychological science)."[14]

The renowned contemporary philosopher Robert Nozick succinctly described wisdom as being conducive to the "best" life as well as "an understanding of what is important," but then added,

> Wisdom's understanding is a special one, special in three ways: in the topics it concerns—the issues of life; in its special value for living; and in its not being universally shared. Something that everyone knew might be important but would not count as wisdom. [15]

The academic definition of wisdom that I have most appreciated and use when speaking on the topic is actually a definition of what wisdom is not.

> The essence of wisdom . . . lies not in what is known but rather in the manner in which that knowledge is held and in how that knowledge is put to use. To be wise is not to know particular facts but to know without excessive confidence or excessive cautiousness. Wisdom is thus not a belief, a value, a set of facts, a corpus of knowledge or information in some specialized area, or a set of special abilities or skills. Wisdom is an attitude taken by persons toward the beliefs, values, knowledge, information, abilities, and skills that are held, a tendency to doubt that these are necessarily true or valid and to doubt that they are an exhaustive set of those things that could be known. [16]

Understanding how the people of another culture see wisdom may help those of us in the West to understand and define it. Few social scientists have written about wisdom from the point of view of a non-Western culture. However, anthropologist Keith Basso's book, *Wisdom Sits in Places*,[17] discusses aspects of Western Apache life in Arizona, including their concept of wisdom. Basso's translation of an important definition of wisdom given to him by his wise Western Apache tutor, Dudley, reveals how Apache conceptions of wisdom seem to use words that differ markedly from those of familiar Western thought about wisdom—and yet they also illuminate the underlying similarities of wisdom in all cultures.

Dudley told Dr. Basso that to be wise, one must have a smooth, resilient, and steady mind. One had to seek "the trail of wisdom," and it would be best to start young. A smooth mind is alert and able to see danger on the trail. A resilient mind is not easily frightened and is able to think clearly. A steady mind is not angry, arrogant, or proud. Apache individuals are told that to achieve a steady mind, "You must learn to forget about yourself!"

As quoted in Basso's text, Dudley explains,

> How will you walk along this trail of wisdom? Well, you will go to many places. You must look at them closely. You must remember all of them. Your relatives will talk to you about them. You must remember everything they tell you. You must think about it, and keep on thinking about it, and keep on thinking about it. You must do this because no one can help you but yourself. If you do this, your mind will become smooth. It will become steady and resilient. You will stay away from trouble . . . . Wisdom sits in places. It's like water that never dries up . . . . You also need to drink from places. You must remember everything about them. You must learn their names. You must remember what happened at them long ago. You must think about it and keep on thinking about it. Then your mind will become smoother and smoother. Then you will see danger before it happens. You will walk a long way and live a long time. You will be wise. People will respect you.[18]

Basso wrote that every Apache person can aspire to wisdom; however, it is a long and troublesome process, private and public, involving much introspection and many disheartening setbacks. Few attempt it. Apache individuals who have successfully pursued the trail of wisdom become mentors for others.

The idea of wisdom is consistent, no matter where one looks. Like the Cibeque Apache, people of every culture seem to know how wisdom manifests among its peoples. They also recognize wisdom's opposite—foolishness. It appears that wisdom always refers to those acts of exemplary human behavior that are admired, condoned, and encouraged by every society and that leads to positive human advancement. Misae Itani, Mburu James Gakunju, and Ibrahim Muthoka Kang'eri represent two different cultures, yet their ideas on wisdom and their wise actions are similar. Like wise Cibeque Apache individuals, they were able to forget about themselves.

Endnotes

1   David Baird, *A Thousand Paths to Wisdom* (Naperville, IL: Sourcebooks, Inc. 2000), 31.

2   www.kansai.gr.jp/culture_e/build/living/machiya1.htm (23 May 2007). During the Edo period (1600-1867) in Japan, taxes were levied based on the width of the property at the street. Thus, narrow widths of buildings meant lower taxes. Kansai Window, Kyoto Life Arts Center, Japanese architecture,

3   A formal bow is seen as Japanese people meet one another for the first time. It is a deep and long bow given before they introduce themselves. The Japanese custom of bowing (*ojigi*) is an important nonverbal form of communication—one that shows respect for others.

4   David Anderson, *Histories of the Hanged: The Dirty War in Kenya and The End of Empire* (New York: W. W. Norton & Company), 6.

5   *Holy Bible, King James Version*, Old Testament, Proverbs 8:11.

6   Personal communication, June 28, 2007.

7   Robert J. Sternberg's extensive research into creativity, intelligence, and wisdom notes that the three are different human attributes, but that of the three, wisdom is the least related to creativity and intelligence. Robert J. Sternberg, "Understanding Wisdom," In *Wisdom: Its Nature, Origins, and Development*, edited by R. J. Sternberg (Cambridge, England: Cambridge University Press. 1990a); and Robert J. Sternberg, "Intelligence and Wisdom." In *Handbook of Intelligence*, edited by R. J. Sternberg (New York: Cambridge University Press, 2000b), 631-649.

8   Robert J. Sternberg, "Understanding Wisdom," In *Wisdom: Its Nature, Origins, and Development*, edited by R. J. Sternberg (Cambridge, England: Cambridge University Press. 1990a), ix. In fact, a reporter for *Psychology Today* once asked Sternberg what he looked forward to working on in the future. His reply was that he would really like to "crack" the problem of wisdom. Robert J. Sternberg, "Sternberg: A Wayward Path to Wisdom" *Psychology Today, 31* (1998), 88; Robert J. Sternberg, "Implicit Theories of Intelligence, Creativity and Wisdom," *Journal of Personality and Social Psychology, 49*, (1985), 607-627. He has been working on it.

9   Webster's New Collegiate Dictionary, p. 1533.

10 Robert K. Barnhart, *The Barnhart Concise Dictionary of Etymology: The Origins of American English Words* (New York: Harper Collins, 1995), 884.

11 Stephen G. Holliday and Michael J. Chandler, "Wisdom: Explorations in Adult Competence" In *Contributions to Human Development, 17*, edited by J. A. Meacham, (New York: Karger, 1986) 10.

12 S. I. Hayakawa, *Use the Right Word: A Modern Guide to Synonyms and Related Words* (New York: Funk and Wagnalls, 1968), 690.

13   Isaac Asimov, *Atom: Journey Across the Subatomic Cosmos* (New York: Truman Talley Books Plume, 1992). Physicists early in the twentieth century decided to accept the idea of a nuclear atom—a positively charged nucleus with negatively charged electrons around it. What kept the electrons in place? Niels Henrik David Bohr (1885-1962), a Danish physicist, won the Nobel Prize in 1922 for showing that classical physics did not apply to determining the structure of the atom; quantum theory was needed.

The electron was visualized as spinning around the nucleus in an orbit—much like a miniature solar system. However, it did not take long for physicists to find that it wasn't quite that simple. The German physicist Werner Karl Heisenberg (1901-1976) thought that the solar system image of the atom was not realistic, and he felt that physicists would need to describe nuclear behavior numerically—not in terms of orbits of electrons. In 1925, Heisenberg devised *matrix mechanics*—using a mathematical device (a matrix). Also in 1925, Davisson proved the existence of electron waves, and Erwin Schrödinger (1887-1961) felt that the electron waves could explain the electron orbits—and he invented wave mechanics to mathematically explain it.

As it turned out, wave mechanics and matrix mechanics are equivalents. The term quantum mechanics describes both systems. In 1927, Heisenberg demonstrated that if you tried to measure the exact position of an electron and its exact momentum (which is its mass multiplied by its velocity), the device that one used to conduct the measurement would affect the position and the momentum of the electron. The best you could do would be to get a combined position and velocity, plus a little fuzziness—an unavoidable inaccuracy. "The uncertainty of the position multiplied by the uncertainty of the momentum, if both are taken at the absolute minimum that can be obtained, comes to an amount closely related to a fundamental constant of quantum theory." (Asimov, 120.)

14   William Damon, "Setting The Stage For The Development of Wisdom," In *Understanding Wisdom: Sources, Science and Society*, edited by Warren S. Brown (Philadelphia, PA: Templeton Foundation Press, 2000), 339.

15   Robert Nozick. *The Examined Life: Philosophical Meditations* (New York: Simon and Schuster, 1989), 267.

16   John A. Meacham, "The Loss of Wisdom." In *Wisdom: Its Nature, Origins, and Development*, edited by R. J. Sternberg (New York: Cambridge University Press, 1990), 187.

17   Keith Basso, *Wisdom Sits in Places: Landscape and Language Among the Western Apache* (Albuquerque, NM: University of New Mexico Press, 1996).

18   Ibid., 126-127.

Chapter Three

Who Are The Wise?

Nothing doth more hurt in a state
than that cunning men pass for wise.
—*Sir Francis Bacon*

Describing the qualities and attributes of those who are actually known to be wise seems even more difficult than describing wisdom itself. The wisdom researcher Robert Sternberg has given a description of the wise individual based on his research into wisdom (conducted primarily in Western cultures) that fits with my own ideas about wise persons.

1. The wise individual has a certain "sagacity"[1] that differs from mere intelligence.
2. The wise individual is one who listens to others, knows how to weigh advice, and can deal with a variety of different kinds of people. In seeking as much information as possible for decision making, the wise individual reads between the lines as well as makes use of the obviously available information.
3. The wise individual is especially able to make clear, sensible, and fair judgments and, in doing so, takes a long-term as well as a short-term view of the consequences of the judgments made.
4. The wise person is perceived to profit from the experience of others and to learn from others' mistakes as well as from his or her own. This individual is not afraid to change his or her mind as experience dictates.

5. The wise person tends to offer the right solutions to complex problems.[2]

These characteristics are relevant to a description of wise Westerners, but what about non-Western wise persons? Do differences in cultures and even in epochs lead to differences in the characteristics of the wise? For instance, if there are wise individuals in France and in Samoa, are they similar in any way? Can a person from America recognize the wisdom of a person who is considered wise in Borneo? Was a wise person of ancient Athens anything like the wise person living today in New York? Or Berlin? Or London?

Wise individuals have not been compared across cultures. In fact, with the exception of a few biographies, wise people in non-Western cultures have been overlooked or not considered at all. If wisdom is the epitome of human development and is therefore *universal in nature*, a wise person in one culture should have similar characteristics to a wise person in any other culture—or even from another epoch. To my knowledge, no one has investigated to see if such similarities do actually exist.

Long before I began to look for wise individuals to interview, I considered the characteristics and traits of those deemed to be wise—as reported in Western research and in the writings from other cultures that I have read. Subsequently, I made a list of the qualities of the wise gleaned from these sources.

- Wise individuals are highly respected by others.
- Wise individuals are often sought out by others.
- Wise individuals live long, productive lives.
- Wise individuals continue to grow as persons throughout their lives.
- Wise individuals have the ability to make sound moral judgments.
- Wise individuals exhibit many dimensions and abilities.
- Wise individuals possess knowledge, but aren't necessarily "educated."
- Wise individuals possess the ability to locate and solve problems.
- Wise individuals are humble.
- Wise individuals express gratitude.
- Wise individuals are understanding
- Wise individuals can discern what is "good" for individuals and society.

When I began my search for wise ones, I found that people in *non-Western* cultures could easily identify those among their contemporaries whom they considered to be wise men and women. Such is not the case among those living in Western cultures, however. When I pressed an American or a Western European to name a wise person, many, especially those of Judeo-Christian background (if they answered at all) claimed that King Solomon of the Old Testament was a wise man. Others with Buddhist, secular, or New Age leanings answered that His Holiness the Dalai Lama of Tibet is wise. I reasoned that if wisdom is a universal human trait, King Solomon and the Dalai Lama would have common attributes. Here are two wise men, separated by three thousand years in time and representing vastly different cultures. Examining what we know of both men's lives might help us learn more about the wise among us.

KING SOLOMON

> And God gave Solomon wisdom and understanding exceeding much, and largeness of heart, even as the sand that is on the seashore. And Solomon's wisdom excelled the wisdom of all the children of the east country, and all the wisdom of Egypt.[3]

The story of Solomon, the ancient king of Israel, recorded in 1 Kings and in Chronicles (Old Testament) is familiar to all readers of the Torah or the Old Testament and to most Westerners. A brief reiteration of the story follows.

Solomon was famous for his wisdom, his wealth, and his efforts in building the Israelite temple in Jerusalem. He was the tenth son of polygamous King David; he was the second son born to David's wife Bathsheba (their first son was Adonijah). The name *Solomon* is probably derived from the Hebrew word meaning "peaceable."

Because of actions taken by Bathsheba and the prophet Nathan, the aging King David, who had ruled Israel for forty-seven years, chose Solomon as the successor to his throne over his other older sons and particularly over his son Adonijah. Young Solomon was the first king of Israel to be born to a king of Israel, and he was also the last king over the twelve tribes of Israel. He began his rule probably when he was still a teenager and ruled Israel for forty years.

According to the account recorded in 1 Kings (Old Testament), one night, shortly after being crowned king of Israel, Solomon had a dream in which the Lord God appeared to him. God told Solomon to ask for anything he desired—anything he wanted. Solomon humbly replied that he was only a child, and he really didn't know much of anything. Nevertheless, he reasoned—most likely because he now was faced with the responsibility of leading an enormous group of people—that what he needed most was wisdom; he needed to know right from wrong so that he could fairly judge the situations of the people who constantly came before him with their disputes. Solomon's words read,

> And now, O Lord my God, thou hast made thy servant king instead of David my father: and I am but a little child: I know not how to go out or come in. And thy servant is in the midst of the people which thou hast chosen, a great people, that cannot be numbered nor counted for multitude. Give therefore thy servant an understanding heart to judge thy people, that I may discern between good and bad: for who is able to judge this thy so great a people?[4]

The account in Chronicles says Solomon asked for "understanding and wisdom," instead of an "understanding heart." Nonetheless, whatever asked for, God was pleased with Solomon's selfless request and said,

> Because thou hast asked this thing, and hast not asked for thyself long life; neither hast asked riches for thyself, nor hast asked the life of thine enemies; but hast asked for thyself understanding to discern judgement; Behold, I have done according to thy words: lo, I have given thee a wise and an understanding heart; so that there was none like thee before thee, neither after thee shall any arise like unto thee.[5]

In other words, God granted Solomon's request. From that moment on, the Scriptures note that Solomon would be the wisest man who ever lived. In addition, God threw in the riches, the lives of Solomon's enemies, and fame as well—all things that Solomon did not ask for.

After Solomon's dream, the only biblical account detailing Solomon's wisdom in use occurred when two women came before him in a dispute over a baby. In this famous account, both women claimed that they were the baby's mother. Solomon listened to their differing stories.

The women lived together in the same house, and both had given birth within three days of each other. The circumstances of the women's contentions began one night when one of the babies died, "because [the mother inadvertently] overlaid it."[6] Standing before Solomon, one woman alleged that the child of the other woman had died. She further claimed that while she was sleeping, the other woman must have switched the babies because when she awoke, she realized that her own baby was missing and that the other woman's dead baby lay in its place on the bed. Of course, the woman being accused of switching the babies protested to Solomon that the first woman was making up this entire story so that she could have a living child.

Realizing that there were no witnesses to this event, Solomon listened to both stories. It was purely one woman's word against another's. Solomon (exhibiting what we would today term out of the box thinking) solved this dilemma by asking that a sword be brought to him. He suggested to both women that cutting the baby in half, giving each woman half a baby, could solve the problem. One mother evidently felt this was a fair solution. The true mother of the child, of course, immediately pleaded that the very-much-alive baby be given to the other woman so the baby would continue to live. Thus, Solomon was able to determine the identity of the real mother, restoring her child to her. Solomon's response to this dilemma is often cited as proof of his wisdom.

The Old Testament documents elsewhere the veracity of Solomon's wisdom. No other of Solomon's wise decisions is recorded, but his reputation as possessing great wisdom is noted in many places. Solomon became known far and wide. People from many lands, including the Queen of Sheba,[7] came to see him—and his extensive kingdom.

Solomon is also known as the great king of Israel who built the long-awaited temple. Originally planned by his father, King David, the temple was built and finished by Solomon, according to an edict of the Lord God. He began to build the beautiful and ornate temple in the fourth year of his reign. The temple was a sacred place to the twelve tribes of Israel and an important cultural edifice since it was to house the Ark of the Covenant, containing the stone tablets obtained by Moses on Mount Sinai. It was completed seven years later.

The Old Testament describes in detail the temple, Solomon's elaborate home, the various cities he built for his army and for his chariots, the fleet of ships he built in which he carried gold from Ophir. He used his knowledge and wisdom in commerce and industry. He has been called the Copper King because of his exports of copper and iron throughout the region.[8] The enumerations of all his riches go on for pages in the account recorded in 1 Kings.

But Solomon was not always wise. He had an enormous kingdom and strengthened it by making alliances with Egypt and by marrying the daughter of the pharaoh. In fact, he married numerous women from other cultures. The Old Testament account states that Solomon had seven hundred wives and three hundred concubines! Many of these women were born in other lands and were not Israelites; they were idol worshippers. In Solomon's later years, these foreign wives influenced him to build temples for them, places where they could go to worship their foreign gods. Solomon granted their requests. According to the scriptural account, this did not please Israel's God, and Solomon fell from his favor.

Solomon is credited with 3,000 proverbs and 1,005 songs. Some scholars believe that he is the author of the Book of Ecclesiastes, Song of Songs, and parts of Proverbs. Perhaps the proverb in Ecclesiastes 4:13, "Better is a poor and wise youth than an old and foolish king, who will no longer take advice," was in reference to himself in his later years. He also is credited with Proverbs 1:7, which reads, "The fear of the Lord is the beginning of knowledge: But fools despise wisdom and instruction."

What can we discern or judge about Solomon as it applies to wisdom? Solomon, at least in his earlier years, was faithful in worshipping and following Israel's God. From his life, we also learn that even the wise can fall from the favor of God. Thus, one concept that one can glean from Solomon's story is similar to that given by Mburu and Itani-san—that wisdom is a gift of God. Another is that even very young people can possess wisdom. Yet another is that the wise are unselfish. When Solomon was given the gift of wisdom, God said it was because Solomon's desires were directed toward others and away from himself. He thought of his people first and not of himself. We also learn that Solomon listened carefully before making judgments. He was open to new ideas—he entertained and befriended individuals of other cultures and lands, making marriages and alliances.

HIS HOLINESS THE DALAI LAMA

> No matter whom I meet and where I go, I always give the advice to be altruistic, to have a good heart. I am now forty-four years old, and from the time when I began to think until now I have been cultivating this attitude of altruism.[9]

The life story of His Holiness the Dalai Lama of Tibet (Tenzin Gyatso), the very much-alive-but-in-exile head of the Tibetan state, is well documented and recorded. More is known about the Dalai Lama's life, beliefs, and motivations than those of Solomon's. In some ways, the two men led quite opposite lives.

His Holiness the Dalai Lama of Tibet is the spiritual as well as the temporal leader of the Tibetan people. He is revered by his people and by others throughout the world as a wise leader and statesman. The name *Dalai Lama* translates literally to "Ocean of Wisdom." His life story is contained in his autobiography, *My Land and People: The Original Autobiography of His Holiness the Dalai Lama of Tibet.*[10] In addition, the Dalai Lama has written other books about his viewpoints and his advice for living a good and productive life. He freely gives interviews and appearances to illuminate the plight of his people. His goal in life is for happiness, "irrespective of religious belief."[11]

The Dalai Lama was born as Lhamo Dhondup (his name literally meaning "Wish-Fulfilling Goddess") on July 6, 1935, in Taktser, Tibet, a small village located in the northeastern part of Tibet. His father was a kind and humble farmer. The Dalai Lama was born into a large family—his mother had sixteen children, but only seven of them survived infancy. Taktser was his home until spiritual events whisked him away at four-and-one-half years of age. At this time, he was designated as the fourteenth Dalai Lama. He noted that being taken from his family and familiar surroundings created "a somewhat unhappy period of my life."

Upon taking up residence in the capital of Tibet, Lhasa, the five-year-old Lhamo Dhondup was officially made the spiritual leader of his people in 1940, when he became the fourteenth Dalai Lama. His formal education began when he was six years old, following a centuries-old system whose purpose is to "broaden and cultivate the mind by a wide variety of knowledge,"[12] and he was taught by renowned private tutors. He began by learning to read and write. His early education resulted in a rather isolated and lonely existence for a young child. Even though his family lived nearby and he saw them once every month or so, it was still a difficult situation for a young child who was accustomed to being surrounded by his large, warm, loving family.

How Lhamo Dhondup became the present Dalai Lama is a story dependent upon Buddhist spiritual beliefs, including reincarnation, and some amount of wisdom. The thirteenth Dalai Lama, Thupten Gyatso, died in 1933; and the search for his reincarnation as the fourteenth Dalai Lama began. Following the ancient tradition, the oracles and learned lamas (wise men) were consulted so that it could be determined where the reincarnated Dalai Lama had been born.

Several days were spent in prayer and meditation, and then the regent (appointed to rule Tibet by the national assembly until the reincarnation of the Dalai Lama was found and was mature enough to lead the country) saw the vision of three Tibetan letters—*Ah, Ka,* and *M*—followed by a picture of a monastery with roofs of jade green and gold and a house with turquoise tiles (descriptions matching the monastery in Taktser and of the home where Lhamo Dhondup was a two-year-old child).[13]

Because of these various signs and visions, by 1936 high lamas (monks) and important men, called wise men in the Dalai Lama's text, were sent out to the east, where the signs indicated the child had been born. They found the house, and they were invited in. By watching Lhamo's actions and administering multiple tests, the lamas confirmed that the reincarnation of the Dalai Lama had been found. After describing this complicated process, The Dalai Lama humbly concluded this story with the statement, "I was that boy."[14]

Beginning at the age of six, the Dalai Lama was educated extensively in the traditional systems of Tibet, which maintained "a high moral and intellectual standard . . . . By modern standards, it has the defect of entirely ignoring the scientific knowledge of recent centuries . . . The basic purpose of the Tibetan system is to broaden and cultivate the mind by a wide variety of knowledge."[15] The Tibetan system of education not only provides information but also, according to the Dalai Lama, "lays down various methods for developing . . . mental faculties."[16]

When he was twelve years old, the Dalai Lama began dialectical discussions with his tutors. He had to "study and learn by heart the treatises on the 'higher subjects,' including the *Prajnaparamita,* the Perfection of Wisdom,"[17] and hundreds of other intellectual texts. When he was thirteen years old, the Dalai Lama was admitted to the five monastic colleges at two monasteries, Drepung and Sera. There he debated and discussed the Great Treatises with "learned abbots, who were formidable contestants in debate."[18] By age twenty-four, he took the preliminary examinations, where he competed with fifteen learned scholars in public debates. A year later, he successfully completed his final examination, a series of three grueling debates held in front of hundreds of learned lamas, receiving the degree of master of metaphysics.[19]

In 1948, Tibet, an autonomous nation, experienced incursions by China onto its territory. A few years later, the Dalai Lama, still a student, received word that the Chinese were moving forces toward Tibet to attack or perhaps intimidate the small country into surrendering to them. The Tibetan army fought the Chinese soldiers briefly. Meanwhile, in Lhasa, the Forbidden City, the Dalai Lama reported,

> While these disasters were taking place in the distant eastern marches of Tibet, the government in Lhasa was consulting the oracles and the high lamas, and guided by their advice, the Cabinet came to see me with the solemn request that I should take over the responsibility of the government. This filled me with anxiety. I was only sixteen. I was far from having finished my religious education. I knew nothing about the world and had no experience of politics, and yet I was old enough to know how ignorant I was and how much I had still to learn . . . . I hesitated [but eventually saw] I could not refuse my responsibilities. I had to shoulder them, put my boyhood behind me, and immediately prepare myself to lead my country, as well as I was able, against the vast power of Communist China."[20]

The Dalai Lama negotiated with, and eventually even went to, China to try to mend fences and explain his country's point of view; but in the end, the Chinese were not listening. Mao Tse-tung, China's leader, made it known that China intended to rule over Tibet through a military and political committee. China slowly began to take over the government of Tibet. They assumed control over the religious activities as well. The situation was so grave that the Dalai Lama decided if he were to lead his people, he could not do it in a Tibet under Chinese rule. Therefore, he went to India. Later, he was persuaded to return; but after yet another attack by Chinese troops, the Dalai Lama decided he had to leave again or die. He wrote,

> It was I who had to find the answer and make the decision; but with my inexperience in the affairs of the world it was not easy. I have no fear of death. I was not afraid of being one of the victims of the Chinese attack. I honestly believe that my strict religious training has given me enough strength to face the prospect of leaving my present body without any apprehension. I felt then, as I always feel, that I am only a mortal being and

an instrument of the never-dying spirit of my Master, and that
the end of one mortal frame is not of any great consequence.
But I knew my people and the officials of my government
could not share my feelings. To them the person of the Dalai
Lama was supremely precious. They believed the Dalai Lama
represented Tibet and the Tibetan way of life, something dearer
to them than anything else. They were convinced that if my
body perished at the hands of the Chinese, the life of Tibet
would also come to an end.[21]

Thus, in the middle of night in 1959, dressed as a common soldier, the
Dalai Lama escaped out of Lhasa, and headed again toward India. After a
harrowing trip over the mountains of Tibet, dodging the Chinese soldiers,
the twenty-four-year-old Dalai Lama and his entourage of lamas and other
religious figures found refuge in Dharamsala, India, the exiled home of the
Tibetan government ever since.

Since living in exile in India, the Dalai Lama has never stopped working
for his people in Tibet, now completely under Chinese rule. In Tibet,
conditions are such that Tibetan babies are taken away from their parents
and raised and educated in China in an attempt to change the thinking of
the Tibetan people, to erase their spiritual roots.

The Dalai Lama, explaining that his ideas are not unique, strongly
advocates that people everywhere foster love, patience, tolerance, forgiveness,
humility, compassion, commitment, inner restraint or virtue; maintain
discipline; assume responsibility; cultivate discernment; and endure suffering.
Interestingly enough, the Dalai Lama wrote,

> It is also worth remembering that the time of greatest gain in terms
> of wisdom and inner strength is often that of greatest difficulty.
> With the right approach . . . the experience of suffering can open
> our eyes to reality.[22]

The Dalai Lama closed his book *Ethics* with a prayer that expressed his
thoughts.

> May I become at all times, both now and forever
> A protector for those without protection
> A guide for those who have lost their way

A ship for those with oceans to cross
A bridge for those with rivers to cross
A sanctuary for those in danger
A lamp for those without light
A place of refuge for those who lack shelter
And a servant to all in need.[23]

These words sound remarkably like the words I heard in Kenya from Muthoka and Mburu, in Japan from Itani-san, and from other wise people I met in my travels.

COMMON WISE CHARACTERISTICS?

Is there any correlation between the wisdom of Solomon, the wisdom of the Dalai Lama, and the wisdom spoken of in the present world?

In spite of the differences of epoch and culture, both Solomon and the Dalai Lama seem similar in that

1. there is a written record of their actions as well as an orally presented story;
2. both men were remarkably young when they became the leaders of their numerous people/nation;
3. both, humbled at being called to rule at such young ages, sought for spiritual guidance;
4. while the education of Solomon is not documented, based on his skills and accomplishments, he undoubtedly, like the Dalai Lama, received the best education available at the time;
5. both men expressed concern for the common good of their people;
6. both lived disciplined and principled lives, lives that conformed (at least, for Solomon, until his old age) to the precepts of a spiritual belief;
7. both were willing to make changes in their lives and encouraged their nations to do the same.

Like Solomon and the present Dalai Lama, all individuals, regardless of culture or epoch, vary in personality and life situations. Becoming wise is not a guaranteed outcome in anyone's life. The American philosopher Robert Nozick noted that "wisdom in itself is certainly no guarantee that one will achieve 'life's important goals.' But just as a high probability does not guarantee truth, the world must cooperate too. A wise person will have gone in the right direction, and, if the world thwarts his journey, he will have known how to respond to that too."[24]

If wisdom is, as I am suggesting, an attribute that does not change in its manifestation over time, over culture, or over socioeconomic status, then it should be the same and will be as recognizable in people today as in people of the past. The characteristics that seemed to define Solomon (as far as can be conjectured) as well as the Dalai Lama are qualities found in many wise people. As I met wise individuals in various cultures and asked them to tell me their life histories and their thoughts about life and about wisdom, I found these qualities in abundance.[25]

Endnotes

[1] Webster's Dictionary defines sagacity as "a keen and farsighted judgement." *Webster's Ninth New Collegiate Dictionary* (1984), 1036.

[2] Robert Sternberg, "Intelligence and Wisdom," In *Handbook of Intelligence,* edited by R. J. Sternberg (New York: Cambridge University Press, 2000b), 645-646.

[3] *Holy Bible, King James Version*, Old Testament, I Kings 4:29-30.

[4] *Holy Bible, King James Version*, Old Testament, 1 Kings 3: 7-9.

[5] *Holy Bible, King James Version*, Old Testament, 1 Kings 3: 11-12.

[6] *Holy Bible, King James Version*, Old Testament, 1 Kings 3: 19.

[7] Werner Keller, *The Bible as History* New York: William Morrow and Co., 1956. The Queen of Sheba learned of Solomon's fame and riches and was curious about his wisdom. She traveled from the ancient land of Shebans (said to be located in the southern part of modern Yemen) to question Solomon. She was duly impressed by his words and his riches. (p. 209.)

[8] Werner Keller, quoting Glueck, *The Bible as History* (New York: William Morrow and Co., 1956), 197.

[9] These words are those of the Dalai Lama, reported by Clint Willis in *A Lifetime of Wisdom: Essential Writings By and About the Dalai Lama* (New York: Marlowe and Company, 2002), 39.

[10]   The Dalai Lama XIV, His Holiness, *My Land and People: The Original Autobiography of His Holiness the Dalai Lama of Tibet* (New York: Warner Books, 1962/1977). The Dalai Lama's autobiography was originally written in 1962 in Tibetan and was then translated into English. The 1977 edition is a rerelease of the book, with comments by the Dalai Lama about the intervening years.

[11]   Ibid., back cover.

[12]   Dalai Lama, *My Land and People: The Original Autobiography of His Holiness the Dalai Lama of Tibet* (New York: Warner Books, 1962/1977), 22.

[13]   Ibid., 8.

[14]   Ibid., 9.

[15]   Ibid., 22.

[16]   Ibid., 23.

[17]   Ibid., 25.

[18]   Ibid., 25.

[19]   Ibid., 28.

[20]   Ibid., 62-63.

[21]   Ibid., 156.

[22]   Ibid., 140.

[23]   Dalai Lama, *Ethics for The New Millennium* (New York: Riverhead Books. 1999), 237.

[24]   Robert Nozick, *The Examined Life: Philosophical Meditations* (New York: Simon and Schuster, 1989), 269-270.

[25]   Paul B. Baltes, U. M. Staudinger, A. Maercker, and J. Smith, "People Nominated As Wise: A Comparative Study of Wisdom-Related Knowledge" *Psychology and Aging, 10,* 1995), 155-167. Some psychological research has attempted to identify wise individuals in an effort to determine various psychological and demographical facts about them. Paul Baltes, Ursula M. Staudinger, Andreas Maercker, and Jacqui Smith (1995) conducted a study where journalists in Berlin were asked to nominate people that they were aware of who exhibited wise characteristics. The purpose of their study was to apply the researchers' own wisdom paradigm (ideas of what wisdom comprises) to real, living people. In the end, the wise people selected (Germans, all under age eighty) were noted to be equally as wise as the clinical psychologists who made up the comparison group. The researchers posited that psychologists have become the wise men and women of a modern age.

Chapter Four

All Our Relations

We are all related; we are all of community.
—*Mitakuye Oyasin*[1]

No matter what our culture, our race, or our language is, we humans are, deep down, the same. One significant way we are alike lies in our almost-universal appreciation and reverence for our ancestors—to those who have gone before us. True, we show that appreciation in different ways, but even though it sounds simplistic, we realize that we would not be here on earth were it not for our ancestors.

At least since the beginning of recorded time, and undoubtedly before that, humans of all *tribes* have sought to know how best to live their lives. The truths that our ancestors learned about living a successful life, or just surviving, have been handed down from generation to generation so that each succeeding generation, and humankind in general, might benefit from the accrued wisdom. This wisdom was both orally transmitted and preserved in writing. It took the form of stories, myths, proverbs, rituals, and even fairy tales. All cultures have evidence of this process. When preserved in written form, it is known as wisdom literature. Familiar themes occur in oral and written wisdom regardless of cultural source.

We know the importance of wisdom to the people who inhabited the ancient world because the early written texts were almost miraculously preserved.[2] Our ancient ancestors prized wisdom. It was regarded in most of the texts that have survived as something *some people* grew into. So instruction or rules were written to guide the way. In Egypt acquiring wisdom was the best that "a nonroyal aristocrat or a common intellectual" could hope for.[3] Wisdom sayings, knowledge that makes one wise, were very popular and continue to be so today.

In ancient Egypt, an Egyptian named Ptah-hotep[4] was the chief justice and vizier during the reign of Djedkare-Isesi toward the end of the Fifth Dynasty (2450-2300 BCE). *The Instruction of Ptah-hotep* is claimed to be the oldest book in the world that has a distinct author.[5] Ptah-hotep set forth a collection of proverbial maxims (wisdom writings) that survived on papyrus copies—*The Instruction of Ptah-hotep*. The book begins with an explanation of why Ptah-hotep wrote this treatise; he stated that he was getting old and feeble and he wanted to retire from his job. He wrote,

> Oh sovereign, My Lord!
> Old age has occurred, and Age has arrived
> Feebleness has come and weakness is renewed
> One sleeps in discomfort every day
> The eyes are dim and the ears deaf
> Strength perishes, weary-hearted
> The mouth has become silent, and cannot speak
> The heart is finished, not even remembering yesterday.
> The Bones have been ill a long time
> And Good has turned into Evil
> All taste is gone
> What age does to people is evil in everything
> The nose is stopped up and does not smell
> Sitting and standing are difficult.[6]

Ptah-hotep's description of his old age has a familiar ring to it.[7]

Ptah-hotep wrote *The Instruction of Ptah-hotep* primarily for his son whom he hoped would take over his position of advising King Isesi. He explained, "That I may say to him the words of the judges, the counsel of those from ancient times, heard from the gods . . . teach him what was uttered formerly, then he can set a good example for the Children of the Nobles . . . No one is born wise."[8]

The maxims included in his writings deal primarily with human relations and "the peaceful virtues of kindness, justice, truthfulness, moderation and self-control."[9] These virtues were considered essential for an advisor to the king. Much of Ptah-hotep's wise advice seems relevant to modern times. It represents the lessons learned by an experienced old man over his lifetime. It also points out that human beings have not changed much over the millennia. Some of the sayings from *The Instruction of Ptah-hotep* are the following:

- Do not be arrogant about your knowledge, nor trust that you are one who knows.
- Take counsel with the ignorant as with the knowing.
- Wealth does no good if one is glum!
- If you want perfect conduct, free from every evil, guard against the vice of greed, a grievous sickness without cure. There is no treatment for it. It embroils fathers, mothers, and the brothers of the mother. It parts wife from husband. It is a compound of all evils, a bundle of all hateful things.
- That man endures whose rule is rightness, who walks a straight line; he will make a will by it.
- The greedy has no tomb.
- Be generous as long as you live.
- Kindness is a man's memorial.
- People's schemes do not prevail; God's command is what prevails.
- Wise words are rarer than precious stones and yet may come even from slave girls grinding the corn.
- Be prudent whenever you open your mouth. Your every utterance should be outstanding, so that the mighty men who listen to you will say, "How beautiful are the words that fly from his lips."
- Do not boast at your neighbor's side. One has great respect for the silent man.

Wisdom and the wise man are frequently represented in the surviving papyrus scrolls and literature of Egypt.

Early Egypt was not the only place where wisdom was a topic of conversation. Many cultures have contributed to the ancient literature of wisdom. Another important group of early writings stems from the Near East civilizations.[10] Known as the Mesopotamian wisdom literature, these writings include fragments from Sumerian and Babylonian cultures. They contain prescriptions for conducting life—mostly in the form of parables, fables, proverbs, anecdotes, and short stories that "epitomize principles of correct living, embody moral pronouncements, and contain crucial information about their society."[11]

The ancient Greeks believed that "wisdom outweighs any wealth"[12] in bringing happiness to people.[13] Philosophy, the love of wisdom, was once an all-important field of knowledge. In fact, ancient Athens was called the seat of wisdom.[14] The five hundred years before Christ was a period where many different conceptions about wisdom occurred, and traces of these views are found in the ancient writings.[15]

Much of the early literature from other ancient Middle Eastern groups, such as the Canaanites and Phoenicians, did not survive the Dark Ages although these peoples are also known to have used parables, fables, and other stories to extol what is good in life. Homer's *Odyssey* and *Iliad* are not just good stories; they were among the first documents to extol rationality and wise actions in man.[16]

Today, we still look to those who have lived before us—parents, grandparents, ancestors, leaders, and prophets—for guidance. Thus, it was not surprising that one of the common characteristics of the wise people I met was their universal admiration and gratitude for their families, their tribes and communities, and their "roots"—their cultures and their ancestors. Certainly the Navajo individuals I met were inspired by their ancestors. Each person was grateful for his or her heritage and the teachings of traditional Navajo culture. Navajo beliefs and teachings revealed to them the purpose of life and helped them maintain balance in their lives.

The Navajo comprise one of the largest Native American tribes in the United States. Approximately 330,000 individuals are enrolled members of the Navajo Nation, placing the Navajo Indian tribe as the largest federally recognized tribe in the United States. It represents about 15 percent of the entire Native American population of the United States.[17]

The Navajo Nation, a vast reserve located in the Four Corners region of the American Southwest, encompasses portions of the states of Arizona, Utah, Colorado, and New Mexico.[18] Its area is larger than the combined states of New Jersey, Rhode Island, Connecticut, and Massachusetts! A sovereign nation within the borders of the United States, the Navajo Nation has its own government, located in Window Rock, Arizona, with an elected president and council. Nine major tribal groups represent seventy or eighty different Navajo clans. The Navajo clan system represents one of the major roots of the culture.[19]

Since the Navajo lands encompass scenic marvels, historic ruins, and recreational facilities, tourism is encouraged. Places such as Monument Valley, Canyon de Chelly, Chaco Canyon, and Shiprock are familiar to people around the world. The topography of this vast land is varied, ranging from low elevations to dry deserts to beautiful high mountains. Revenue for the Navajo Nation comes from a wealth of natural resources, including coal, oil and gas, and uranium. Other sources of income are presently being developed, including a long-protested casino, Fire Rock Casino. Navajo people have been concerned for several years about the problems that a gambling casino will bring to their society.[20]

Long ago, the Tewa-speaking Pueblo Indians referred to the Navajo people as *Navahu*, a word meaning "the large area of cultivated land." Picking up on that, the Spanish who came early into the area called them *Apaches de Nabahu*, "Apaches of the Cultivated Fields." The word *apache* means "enemy." The Spanish considered the *Apaches de Nabahu* to be different from the rest of the Apaches, however. Alonso de Benavides wrote a book in the 1630s that changed the name to "Navajo."[21]

Western anthropologists believe that the Navajo are a seminomadic people who share a common ancestry with the Apaches. Both groups are Athabascan, coming out of Northwestern Canada and Alaska thousands of years ago. It is theorized that, as these people traveled south and west, they met up with people who were farmers. These people, the Anasazi, were the ancestors of the present-day Pueblo Indians. The early Navajo people settled near the Pueblos, learning from them how to plant beans, corn, squash, and melons; weave; and make clothing and artistic objects. The Navajo people, however, have quite a different view of their beginnings.

The Navajo believe that their language is sacred. It is another of their "roots." One wise Navajo man whom I met believed that the Navajo language itself enables people to be wise. Given the name *Ni'hookaa Diyan Diné*, which translates to "Holy Earth People" or "Lords of the Earth,"[22] Navajos today call themselves the people, or the *diné*. In the Navajo creation story, thought preceded speech, and then speech brought the world into existence. Their creation story tells of three previous underworlds from which the Navajo people consecutively emerged before arriving into this world. Although many Westerners believe that God created a man (Adam) first, traditional Navajos say that Talking God, *Haashch'eelti'i*, created a woman first. For that reason, everything on earth is in respect to the woman.[23]

As a people, the Navajo still struggle to maintain their traditional beliefs, ceremonials, and rituals. Those who choose to adopt the traditional philosophy strive for balance in all aspects of their lives—physical, mental, social, and spiritual. This became apparent as I met with the Navajo wise ones.

One charming and thoughtful Navajo woman whom I was privileged to interview taught me much about the importance of the traditions, stories, and ceremonies to the Navajo. Since she prefers to remain anonymous, I will call her *Shandiin*, a Navajo word meaning "first sunray." I first met

Shandiin on July 22, 1999, when she graciously invited me to her home on the Navajo Nation for an interview.

I drove to the Navajo Nation on Interstate 40 and, thanks to Shandiin's excellent instructions, easily found her home. I knocked on the front door and soon found myself introducing myself to the epitome of a traditional Navajo woman, beautiful and strong yet humble and modest. Shandiin, a great-grandmother in her sixties, was dressed in typical Navajo fashion—a deep turquoise long-sleeved blouse and a long full-gathered multi-colored skirt accented by traditional Navajo jewelry crafted in silver and turquoise. Her graying dark hair was pulled back into the traditional Navajo bun, which was wrapped with bright turquoise cording.

Shandiin gestured for me to come into her living room and invited me to sit down in one of her comfortable chairs. Her voice projected an inner strength and confidence. She introduced herself to me in Navajo fashion, saying, "My mother's clan is Folded Arms People, *Bit'ahnii*. And I am born to Salt Clan, *Ashiihi*. My maternal grandfather's clan is Towering House, *Kinyaa'aanii,* and my paternal grandfather's clan is On Water's Edge, *Tábaahi*. And that's who I am as a person—as a Navajo person."

She then explained the custom of naming one's clan in introductions. "That's how an individual identifies himself or herself when they are introducing themselves. They always mention their clan. Then people know who you are—because our clan is our root, you know. It's within us, so it comes down the line."

David Suzuki and Peter Knudtson, cultural researchers, explain that most members of indigenous societies, including the Navajo, have traditionally believed that wise individuals, whom they call *elders* or *elderlies*, fulfill an important role.

> Throughout human history, *elders* have occupied a special position in society. They have painstakingly accumulated reservoirs of personal experience, knowledge, and *wisdom*—or compassionate insight and a sense of the enduring qualities and relationships around them. They freely offer this wisdom to living generations of their people in an effort to help them connect harmoniously with their past, present, and future.[24]

Even though all elderly individuals are respected for what they have learned through their life experiences, "only a few have the specialized knowledge of the cosmos that uniquely equips them to provide wise counsel to the community and the world."[25]

As spiritual leaders, guides, and counselors to those who are searching for peace and harmony in their lives, the elderlies, especially the designated medicine men and women, guide individuals toward a positive personal growth through the performance of rituals as well as through wise counsel. They have a deep reverence for life—all forms of life. Although regarded as unique and gifted by people in their communities, they retain a profound humility.

When I asked Shandiin about wisdom, she referred to ancient Navajo teachings and practices. She articulated her immense respect for the wisdom of the Navajo people, especially its designated wise—the elderlies—telling me, "The elderlies way back had a lot of wisdom—a lot of knowledge. The elderlies taught their children to listen and to obey. There was no talking back."

She further explained that children are not as knowledgeable as adults. "The children are in the process of growing up. When they get to adulthood, then they'll know right from wrong . . . . In past times, every evening would find conscientious parents gathering their children into the hogan, where important traditional stories would be told to them before they went to bed. Children were always taught to get up at the break of dawn—and to run. Run as far as they could, and then come back."

Shandiin put her head back against the chair and laughed, and then continued to explain, "You don't go back to bed! The purpose of running was to gain wisdom and to gain knowledge—to gain inner and outer strengths."

The first interview with Shandiin ended after an hour since she had to go to work, but she invited me to return the following day to continue our interview. The next day, as I drove to her home, I marveled at the beauty of the high mountain desert of the Navajo Nation. That July morning, the sky was a brilliant New Mexico blue. The air was dry and crisp.

When I arrived at Shandiin's home, she was waiting for me at her front door, dressed in an attractive deep-purple blouse and coordinated Navajo broom skirt. A deep turquoise pin accented her blouse. Her hair was pulled back from her round face in the traditional Navajo bun, wrapped this day with purple cord.

After setting up the recording equipment once again, the interview continued from where we left off the previous day. Shandiin began, "According to my mother, my maternal great-grandparents always talked to their grandchildren about how to carry themselves as individuals: they were encouraged to be well respected, to help people out, to not be selfish, and to share whatever they had with others."

Although Shandiin never knew her great-grandparents, she was extremely close to her maternal grandparents. Her grandfather was an important man. He was a Navajo Council delegate, and he had many sheep—the symbol of Navajo wealth. Like many wealthy men of his time, Shandiin's grandfather practiced polygamy; his two wives were sisters. Shandiin's grandmother (wife number two) never learned to write her name, but she became an excellent and exceedingly skilled weaver. Herds of numerous sheep and goats supported the family with its twenty-four children. At a time before the United States government mandated compulsory education for Navajo children, most did not attend school. Only three of the twenty-four children in the family went to school—one of the three was Shandiin's mother.

Speaking of her grandfather, Shandiin explained that he did not agree with the white man's style of education. "He believed that staying home, weaving, taking care of livestock, doing silversmithing—just doing things at home—was also education."

Life on the reservation was difficult. For instance, most of the children of wife number one died from tuberculosis. However, as Shandiin described it, life on the *Rez* (the present colloquial term for the Navajo reservation) also taught many important lessons and principles for living well.

Shandiin's father had gone to school until the ninth grade, but then he dropped out because he wanted to earn some money. Her mother, prizing education, finished her high school education at the Indian school in Albuquerque, New Mexico. After her mother finished high school, Shandiin's parents married. The first of their five girls arrived the next year. Shandiin was the middle child in the family.

Both Shandiin's parents worked for the government school system, and of necessity, they traveled around the Navajo Nation from school to school and community to community. An aunt, her mother's fourteen-year-old sister, became the family's nanny. She cared for the children while the parents worked.

Shandiin noted, speaking of formal schooling, "Our parents spoke English in our home. Since our aunt was not educated, we as children more or less educated her. So she now speaks English, even though she never went to school. She spoke in Navajo to us, and I think that's how we help each other. She educated us in learning our language and then vice versa."

At that time it was mandatory that Navajo children, scattered all over the Navajo Nation, attend the white man's boarding schools during the normal school year. Shandiin's maternal grandfather was adamant, however, that all of his grandchildren spend their summers with him so that they could be educated in traditional Navajo ways.

When Shandiin began to describe her childhood summers with her many cousins at her grandparents' hogan, she settled back into the chair, smiled, and laughed as she remembered how influential her grandparents were in her life. Her hands moved back and forth expressively as she spoke, "My parents would take us out to Grandpa's in the summertime, so you got to learn the Navajo way of life—not just always the white man's way of life . . . . We learned to do many things. My grandpa and grandma would teach us, 'This is the way you herd sheep; this is the way you take care of sheep . . . . There's some dogs there, and they're your helpers. They're the ones that guard. Make sure the coyotes don't get the sheep . . . . Now you kids can play, but don't really concentrate on playing—because the coyotes will steal from you. You have to be alert!' So there'd be a whole bunch of us kids herding sheep all summer."

Shandiin's grandparents guided their grandchildren with discipline and loving care—building inner strength for the difficulties they knew the children would face someday. Laughing again, Shandiin described her experience, saying, "They'd make us get up at the break of dawn. And then we'd run. And we'd come back and they'd say, 'You're not running far enough. You are running to obtain knowledge—to obtain wisdom—to have inner and outer strength and to build your self-esteem, your self-image, your self-worth, and all that goes with it—you know, you as an individual. And honestly, you know, when you grow up that way, you will never be sorry—you'll be able to go through hardship; you'll be able to go through turmoils and tribulations and whatever may come across. You'll go over the hurdles.' And so, rain or shine, we got up in the morning and ran—then we'd let the sheep out."

The summer days with the cousins at Shandiin's grandparents' place were filled with responsibility, fun, work, explanations, stories, and example. The children herded sheep and goats, learning how to protect the herds from coyotes. They also learned to wash, card, spin, and dye the wool sheared off the sheep. They spoke Navajo all summer. In order to conserve family resources, shoes were rationed. The children went barefoot. Shandiin explained, "So in the summertime we all went [to grandpa's] and that's how we were able to keep our traditions and our culture, and to learn to respect them." She and her siblings speak fluent Navajo to this day.

When Shandiin became old enough, she attended a one-room public school. Speaking Navajo was forbidden at this school. When the one-room school became so crowded that the students could not fit into the classroom, Shandiin's parents decided that they must send their daughters to a better school situation—so they sent the children to a Presbyterian boarding school nearly a hundred miles away. They would take their daughters to school in September, traveling over dusty rutted roads that turned to impassable mud after rain or snow. They would gather the children back home each May.

The only day off from the boarding school was Christmas. Fortunately for Shandiin, her parents wrote to her and her sisters weekly, and they came to visit every other week "when the roads were passable," bringing with them fry bread and picnics that were generously shared with those girls whose parents were not able to visit. "These girls became our sisters," Shandiin related.

I asked Shandiin if she ever got lonely being away at school. She pondered my question for a few moments. She then replied that she didn't remember being lonely—probably because her sisters were also at the school. But she did have other memories of the Presbyterian school.

She recalled, "I always remember that we prayed a lot. The school was very, very strict. We weren't allowed to talk our own language. And we weren't allowed to dance—it was a sin to dance! . . . All our letters were censored."

Shandiin laughed a bit as she contemplated the situation, remarking, "You wonder how in the world we weren't brainwashed!"

She didn't regret her attendance at the boarding school, however. She continued, "Even though the school was very strict . . . in a way I'm thankful that I went there. Because, you know, you think back and there are times when maybe you don't want to do things—things that aren't healthy for you—but yet you do it. And since I'm at this age now, I have overcome the hurdle. I was able to stand up to the hardship."

Through it all, Shandiin remembered the constant reassuring and loving message she received from her father—a message that continues to influence the family to this day. "My father always emphasized, you know, 'You pray every day. Pray to the Morning God and you'll always be taken care of. Always remember that you are a Navajo. Always remember how you were brought up—what we have taught you. That's going to remain with you for the rest of your life . . . . If anything should ever happen to me, then you have to go on. You can't look back.'"

Shandiin continued, "I used to always wonder what he meant by that. But today my teaching is the same as what my father had taught me. I always tell my grandchildren, whether maternal or paternal grandchildren, 'Always remember who you are. Remember you are Navajo. Remember what your Navajo name is—what it means. And always remember who your relatives are. Don't just bypass them. Always shake hands with them.'"

Then addressing one of the questions about wisdom that I had asked her previously, Shandiin said, "When you first asked me, 'What is wisdom?' I had to think about it. But I feel that that's what it is. It's knowing who you are and where you came from."

After graduating from high school, Shandiin was encouraged by her father to get a job. "My dad always encouraged us to work. He'd say, 'You know, I can't be supporting you forever—and remember what I told you.'" Shandiin smiled broadly, saying, "He always brought that up!"

Shandiin found work in a small town, assisting a woman who was a social worker. Her job was to check on the people who were receiving welfare. About nine months later, Shandiin was transferred to a city in the Midwest to work as an instructional aide—she was one of only three individuals asked to do this by her superiors. Shandiin and the other two aides, without training, began to teach adults, age eighteen and older, to learn to speak English, to write their names, and to do basic arithmetic.

Shandiin remarked, "They were people much older than I was, and I was scared to death."

Although Shandiin had been promised that she could finish her college education if she took the job in the Midwest, that promise never came to fruition. After three years, the program was disbanded; the students were sent back home; and Shandiin, age twenty-two, was sent "crying all the way," as she described it, to work at another Indian school in another Western state.

When Shandiin arrived at the newly assigned school, it was not in session. Consequently, she had nothing to do. She was lonely. She wrote home, telling her parents that she didn't think this school was the place for her and she'd like to come home.

Her father and mother wrote a lengthy reply. Shandiin smiled as she recalled that letter. "I remember my dad writing, 'Remember what I always told you.' That statement was beginning to sound like an old record! He told me, 'You can come home as long as you can look for a job and get a job. You are going to have to have a vehicle, and you've got to have a roof over your head. You can't come and depend on us to support you and all that. I did not teach you that.'"

Shandiin petitioned her employers to let her return to the Navajo Nation. They complied, and she was given a position at a school in a small town about an hour and a half from her parents' home. It was at that school where she met her future husband, a Navajo man who was also working at the school. The two of them fell in love and were married one year later in a Navajo chapter house. They began their family a year after that.

Shandiin has tremendous respect for her mother-in-law, a traditional Navajo woman from whom she learned a lot. She credits her with teaching the importance of Navajo ceremonials in acquiring a balanced harmony in life. Her mother-in-law's wisdom helped Shandiin adopt a new way of being and seeing her world.

For instance, when Shandiin's first child was about to be born, her mother-in-law brought the traditional red sash and wool to the hospital[26] to aid in the delivery—much to the chagrin of the Western doctors at that time. Difficulties arose a year later with her second baby—a child who exhibited failure-to-thrive tendencies. The Western doctors couldn't diagnose what was wrong, nor could they cure this tiny baby.

Shandiin was encouraged by her mother-in-law to seek out a hand trembler.[27] She agreed, and when it was arranged, Shandiin checked the baby out of the hospital and went to a location where her mother-in-law had a hogan ready for the hand trembler, who came immediately to help. A traditional ceremony was performed in which her frail six-month-old baby was blessed, given herbs, and prayed over. Shandiin put the little one back on the traditional Navajo cradleboard; the hand trembler told her to get him some milk, which she did—and he was returned immediately to the hospital, where, being much improved, he was marveled over by the nursing staff.

Shandiin explained, "Today you would never know he was the same person. I always tell him, 'Never, never turn away from your traditional way. This ceremony is what we had for you. Always remember that.' And to this day, he hasn't been in the hospital for anything . . . . So we learned a lot from my mother-in-law."

When her third son was born, Shandiin's husband began to drink; and unfortunately, it became a considerable problem for the family. The situation was resolved somewhat when he was, as Shandiin put it, "saved by the Pentecostal Christians." He joined with them, and Shandiin went along with him in his new religion—for twelve years.

She spoke of this change, "It was a big switch. In those days, the Pentecosts, Evangelists, and other preachers really encouraged the Navajo people to burn their traditional paraphernalia. But I never had any such things—only my mom and dad did. So it was easy for me to 'give myself up'—to say, 'I believe.' Whereas for my mother-in-law and my husband, it was hard.

Twelve years later, circumstances led Shandiin to return to her traditional Navajo beliefs. Following the death of her father, she became very ill. Shandiin believed her illness was the result of her going against the traditional Navajo thinking that women should never hunt deer—and as it happened, she and her husband had gone deer hunting together.

Shandiin laughed as she recalled that her father begged her not to go deer hunting. "My dad just begged me—went up and down and sideways. He was so much against it. But then I would say, 'Well, Dad, you know I don't believe in the Navajo way now. I believe the Christian way. He [God] will take care of it.'"

"I don't care how Christian you are, honey," Shandiin's father replied. "You will always be a Navajo, and you will come back. No matter what, you are going to come back to your traditional ways. I feel sorry for you, my dear."

Shandiin's illness continued, but at the time, she was still torn between Christianity and her traditional beliefs. Her condition became severe, and she was hospitalized. She was thin, anemic, and depressed; yet during her illness, none of her Christian friends came to visit her, nor did they offer to help. Finally, Shandiin's sister, exasperated with the situation, came to the hospital one day and said to her, "Where are those damn praise-the-lord Christian people? Where in the hell are they?"

At that point, the Navajo ladies at the hospital joined in the conversation to say that they had tried to get Shandiin to take some traditional herbs. Shandiin finally decided to have several traditional ceremonies performed by Navajo medicine men. Her sister quickly got her out of the hospital, arranged for the ceremonies, and Shandiin eventually was restored to full health.

Sometime later, tragically, Shandiin's husband died prematurely and unexpectedly, leaving her to raise their children by herself. She found work at the Bureau of Indian Affairs and the Indian Health Service. She was well trained in social work and was working toward a bachelor's degree at a university.

One semester before her scheduled graduation, another tragedy struck. This time one of Shandiin's children was killed in an accident. She quit attending her university classes. She spent five years grieving. She again became incredibly thin. She was angry with everyone. "I was even angry at my sisters and my mother. I refused to visit them. I just stayed here at home. I'd go to work and then come back here—and cry at night when the kids were asleep."

Finally, a cousin took Shandiin to a Navajo crystal gazer,[28] who diagnosed her problem and prescribed a five-day Evil Way ceremony[29]—to be performed right away. Following that ceremony, Shandiin became stronger and was soon returned to her full health. Since then, she has had this ceremony performed several times. As a consequence, according to Navajo customs, she now cannot attend funerals—but she credits the ceremony with helping her overcome her grief and depression. With time, Shandiin, relying on her traditional Navajo beliefs and ceremonies began to understand and come to terms with the events of her life, including all her disappointments and losses. Shandiin was becoming a wise elderly.

A strong Navajo woman, Shandiin is now a mentor to many, helping others learn about themselves and about their own strengths. She teaches all aspects of Navajo culture to young people who aren't fortunate enough to have had grandparents and others who set Navajo standards for them to live by. She credits her tenacity and strength to the discipline and adherence to principles she learned in her youth. Taking what she has learned from her grandfather, her grandmother, her father, her aunt, and her mother-in-law, Shandiin blends them together with the Western style of teaching.

She declared, "I really learned a lot from going to school. And then also putting in the traditional teaching that I got, and then going to workshops, listening to the traditional people, giving talks—I have put all that together from my grandfather's teaching, my grandmother, my dad, and then my mother-in-law, and then the Western way of teaching, and then also the traditional people teaching. I have put all of that together . . . . I feel I have kind of put it all in a gunnysack and I just take a little bit out at a time. And so, I'm really thankful that I have gone back to the traditional way—and that's what I teach my children and my grandchildren."

Retired from her career, Shandiin now finds herself busier than ever. She spends time educating the young—and not just her own grandchildren. She tours the country giving presentations on traditional Navajo ways of medicine or beliefs, contrasting them to Western medicine. She gives presentations at universities and all other types of institutions, trying to educate others as to how her ancestors, the wise elderlies, conducted their lives. At home on the Navajo Nation, she works to educate her people to the dangers of the diseases and problems many of them face—like alcoholism, diabetes, drug abuse, and violence.

This humble yet convincing and wise spokesperson for the traditional way of life loves living within the Navajo's four sacred mountains and helping Navajo children learn about the importance of their clans and language. She is a strong advocate for teaching all Navajo children their traditional language, believing it to be a crucial part of their identity.

Shandiin is also an innovator. She worked with others to organize weekly "sweats"[30] for Navajo women. "The sweat lodge is a place of spiritual refuge and mental and physical healing, a place to get answers and guidance by asking the Creator and Mother Earth for the needed wisdom and power."[31]

Firm in her convictions and protective of her grandchildren as well as other young people, Shandiin believes that there are some things that children should not participate in or experience until they are adults. Also, she believes that children must be kept busy—and especially that all teenagers need responsibility and jobs.

On my first visit with Shandiin at her home, I witnessed Shandiin's wise philosophy for children in person. While we were talking, the doorbell rang. Shandiin went to the door and opened it to greet a handsome Navajo young man of about fifteen. She cordially greeted him by name. He asked if Shandiin's granddaughter—a beautiful young woman of fourteen who lived with her grandmother—was at home. Shandiin smiled and graciously said to him, "Yes, [her granddaughter] is at home, but you won't be allowed to meet with her. She is too young to be meeting with young men privately. Nothing good would come of that." Her granddaughter was not allowed to date, and it would be several years before that would happen. Shandiin also explained to the young man the problems that can arise from dating too early. Her words of wisdom were delivered with love and kindness, and the young suitor left her doorstep quietly and respectfully.

Shandiin practices what she preaches. She believes that good communication, affection, caring, respect for others, and friendliness are important examples for parents and grandparents to set for their children. "I feel we have a lot to give, and a lot to take too. It works both ways."

Her final words to me reflected her concern for young people everywhere, not just among the Navajo. "Wisdom, I feel, is learned from a young age—as a toddler—and the family (the extended family) is very helpful. Parents must learn to discipline their kids and tell them what life is all about and how to carry themselves as individuals. When people learn their values at a young age, their wisdom will grow as years go by . . . . But nowadays, you know, . . . a lot of that learning is dying out. There are some of us who are trying to say, 'We've got to keep it alive. We've got to keep going so that we can instill the wisdom into these young people—so that they can go out into the world knowing who they are and where they come from.'"

The influence of the family—of "all the relations," as the Navajo are fond of saying—in childhood is obvious. The cultural heritages of the wise individuals in this book are obviously important factors as well. Thus, the evidence that wisdom is passed down through the millennia and has an application in our present lives is strong.

Endnotes

1   *Mitakyasi oyasin* is a Lakota phrase that is loosely translated in English as meaning "all my relations." It is used as a salutation or a prayer for balance and harmony among all the elements of the universe, animate and inanimate. Suite 101.com. www.suite101.com/article.cfm/ caring_soul/80730 (23 May 2007).

2   Thomas Cahill, *How the Irish Saved Civilization: The Untold Story of Ireland's Heroic Role from the Fall of Rome to the Rise of Medieval Europe* (New York: Doubleday, 1995).

3   http://www.humanistictexts.org/ptahhotep.htm#Introduction (15 March 2007). Pharaoh, as the only god on earth, could be deified beyond the mere limits of wisdom. Humanistic Texts, Authors Born Before 1000 BCE.

4   Ibid. The tomb of Ptah-hotep is located within a group of mastabas west of the Step Pyramid at Saqqara, Egypt. Saqqara, located about twelve miles south of Giza, used to be Memphis, the capital of Egypt's Old Kingdom. Ptah-hotep's father, Akhet-hotep, held the office of vizier before Ptah-hotep in Egypt's Fifth Dynasty. Ptah-hotep's tomb is annexed on the south side of his father's tomb-making a double tomb. Ptah-hotep's tomb has beautiful well-preserved scenes and an inscribed sarcophagus.

5   Jacq Christian, *The Wisdom of Ptah-hotep: Spiritual Treasures from the Age of the Pyramids* (London: Constable and Robinson, Ltd., 2004).

6   Miriam Lichtheim, translator, *Ancient Egyptian Literature: The Old and Middle Kingdoms, 1* (Los Angeles: University of California Press, 1973).

7   Ibid.

8   Ibid.

9   Humanistic Texts, Authors Born Before 1000 BCE. http://www.
    humanistictexts.org/ptahhotep.htm#Introduction (15 March 2007

10 Aleide Assmann, "Wholesome Knowledge: Concepts of Wisdom in a Historical
    and Cross-Cultural Perspective," In *Life-Span Development and Behavior, 12,*
    edited by D. L. Featherman, R. M. Lerner, and M. Perlmutter, (Hillsdale, NJ:
    Lawrence Erlbaum Associates, Inc., 1994); Daniel N. Robinson, "Wisdom
    Through the Ages," In *Wisdom: Its Nature, Origins, and Development,* edited
    by R. J. Sternberg, (New York: Cambridge University Press, 1990).

11 Stephen G. Holliday and Michael J. Chandler, *Wisdom: Explorations in Adult
    Competence, Contributions to Human Development 17,* edited by J. A. Meacham
    (New York: Karger, 1986), 11.

12 T. H. Banks, translator, *Three Theban Plays: Antigone, Oedipus the King, Oedipus at
    Colonus, Sophocles, Antigone,* line 1050 (New York: Oxford University Press, 1956).

13 Ibid.

14 Adler, 1955, quoted in Vivian Clayton and James E. Birrin, "The Development
    of Wisdom Across the Life-Span: A Reexamination of an Ancient Topic," In
    Life-Span Development and Behavior, 3, edited by P. B. Baltes and O. G. Brim,
    Jr. (New York: Academic Press, 1980).

15 Aleide Assmann. "Wholesome Knowledge: Concepts of Wisdom in a
    Historical and Cross-Cultural Perspective," In *Life-Span Development and
    Behavior, 12,* edited by D. L. Featherman, R. M. Lerner, and M. Perlmutter,
    (Hillsdale, NJ: Lawrence Erlbaum Associates, Inc., 1994).

16 Daniel N. Robinson, "Wisdom Through the Ages," In *Wisdom: Its Nature,
    Origins, and Development,* edited by R. J. Sternberg, (New York: Cambridge
    University Press, 1990).

17 Elizabeth Hardin-Burrola, Thursday, November 6, 2008. "Public forum
    examines casino pros, cons." *The Gallup Independent.* Gallup, New Mexico.

18 Peter Iverson, *Diné: A History of the Navajos* (Albuquerque, NM: University
    of New Mexico Press, 2002). There are actually several pieces to the Navajo
    "reservation." The main Navajo Nation (comprising 13,989,222 acres) is
    found in the states of Arizona, New Mexico, and Utah There are three separate
    bands of Navajos that are connected to the main land area—all located in
    New Mexico: the Alamo Band (63,109 acres), located about thirty miles west
    of Magdalena; the Ramah Band (146,953 acres), located about forty miles
    west of Gallup; and the *Tahajiileeh* (formerly *Cañoncito*) Band (76,813 acres),
    located about twenty-five miles west of Albuquerque.

19 Harrison Lapahie, Jr., http://www.lapahie.com (12 January 2007). At
    birth, Navajo children belong to their mother's clan, and the clan name

(like the western surname) passes on through each mother to her children. Marriage between individuals of the same clan is frowned upon. Thus, in meeting another individual or a public group for the first time, a Navajo person introduces himself or herself by announcing his or her maternal and paternal clans so that people will know. The clan system enlarges one's family network.

[20] Elizabeth Hardin-Burrola, Thursday, November 6, 2008. "Public forum examines casino pros, cons." *The Gallup Independent.* Gallup, New Mexico.

[21] Alonso de Benevides (1630), reported in James I. Hesser, "Navajo Migrations and Accumulation in the Southwest," *Museum of New Mexico Papers in Archaeology* 6 (Santa Fe, NM: Museum of New Mexico, 1962).

[22] Harrison Lapahie, Jr. http://www.lapahie.com (12 January 2007).

[23] M. A. Link, *Navajo: A Century of Progress (1868-1968)* (Window Rock, AZ: Arizona: Navajo Tribe, 1968). The Navajo story of the creation of the world is rich with detail. It is helpful in understanding how the Navajo view the world and their relationship to it. Briefly, it relates that the people of the first world (or black world) were different from people today, but First Man and First Woman were two of the beings from this world. Talking God, *Haashch'eelti'I,* gave the specifications for building a hogan, where the people met and organized their world, and setting their boundaries within the four sacred mountains. The Navajo deities, the Holy People, organized the earth—with sun, moon, and stars, clouds, trees, and rain. Eventually the Holy People created the four original clans. The first clan, *Kiiyaa'aanii,* or Tall House People, were made from yellow and white corn. Other clans joined with them. Changing Woman created four more clans, who traveled from the western sea to join with the people at *Dinetah,* the *Diné* traditional homeland, located in multiple canyons draining into the San Juan River, thirty miles east of Farmington, New Mexico.

[24] David Suzuki and Peter Knudtson, *Wisdom of the Elders: Honoring Sacred Native Visions of Nature* (New York: Bantam Books, 1992), 224.

[25] Pam Colorado, a Wisconsin Oneida of the Iroquois Confederacy. Quoted in David Suzuki and Peter Knudtson, *Wisdom of the Elders: Honoring Sacred Native Visions of Nature* (New York: Bantam Books, 1992), 224.

[26] Personal conversation with Shandiin in 1999. The red sash is part of the Navajo birthing process. It is hung from the hogan ceiling. The expectant mother holds to the sash during birth pangs. The newborn is delivered onto the new wool remnant.

[27] A hand trembler is a Navajo medicine man who possesses a special healing skill.

28   Trudy Griffin-Pierce, *Earth Is My Mother, Sky Is My Father: Space, Time, and Astronomy in Navajo Sandpainting* (Albuquerque, NM: University of New Mexico Press, 1992. A crystal gazer or stargazer, *deest'ii'ii'lini*, is a diagnostician—a medicine man who determines the cause of an illness, the source of misfortune, or the location of lost objects while in a trance state. A crystal is often looked through to find what specific ceremonies are needed for the patient.) (p. 143).

29   Gregory Cajete, *Native Science: Natural Laws of Interdependence* (Santa Fe, NM: Clear Light Publishers, 2000). The purpose of the Navajo "sing" is to cure illnesses of the mind or body. The five-day Evil Way ceremony is one of the more well-known. Frank Waters, *Masked Gods: Navaho and Pueblo Ceremonialism* (Athens, OH: Swallow, Ohio University Press, 1950). "The sing among the Navajo is a communal ritual involving a complex process of chants, combined with the creation of sand paintings and the application of a variety of plants, based on some of the illnesses reflected through the guiding myth of the Navajo" (p. 121).

30   Richard Smoley and Jay Kinney, *Hidden Wisdom: A Guide to the Western Inner Traditions* (New York: Penguin/Arkana, 1999). A "sweat" is one of the most sacred rituals of the Navajo. Its purpose is to strengthen and to purify the individual. Within the sweat lodge, water is poured over hot rocks (called *grandfathers*), and steam fills the structure. "The sweat lodge represents the womb of our true Mother, the Earth. It is a traditional American Indian belief that the Earth is, in fact, the first Mother, and we are, therefore, direct descendants of Her. There are many things in the sweat lodge which help to reinforce this relationship" (p. 178).

31   Bernice, 2005, Canyon deChelly. *Notenboomv.* 7, http://www.theculturedtraveler.com/ARCHIVES/SEP2005/Canyon%20de%20Chelly.htm (4 September 2006).

Chapter Five

Principled and Disciplined

*The man of principle never forgets what he is
because of what others are.*
—Baltasar Gracián[1]

The darkness of the night crawled slowly westward across the earth after the SAS (Scandinavian Airlines System) plane left Boston, flying east over the Atlantic Ocean toward Europe. Six hours later, as the plane neared the British Isles, the red and yellow morning rays of the sun were stretching over the horizon. Looking out through the oval window by my seat on the left side of the plane, Ireland became visible, appearing as a lush green carpet in the vast ocean below—with occasional patches of white clouds dotting its surface. This flight was the first leg of my international quest to find wise individuals among the Saami people living in northern Norway.

The Norwegian county of Finnmark is located near the top of the world above the Arctic Circle. Finnmark, meaning "Land of the Saami," is the largest and most northerly county in Norway. It borders on Russia, Finland, and Sweden.[2] The name *Saami* derives from the word *sapmi*, which denotes both the land (the geographical area) of the traditional Saami as well as the people themselves. Although they have never had their own state or nation, the Saami represent the oldest surviving indigenous people in northern Europe. They inhabit areas of Norway, Sweden, Finland, and the eastern Kaelia and Kola Peninsula of Russia. There is evidence that the Saami have lived in these far northern climates for numerous millennia—five thousand years or more.[3] They survived in the inhospitable environment of the Arctic primarily as fishers or reindeer herders.

Of the more than thirty-five thousand Saami who presently live in Norway, approximately 10 percent of them reside in Finnmark. Historically, the most important industry on the coasts of Finnmark has been fishery, whereas inland it has been reindeer herding and some agriculture. Living in a subarctic and arctic climate, where agriculture is difficult, the Saami have adopted a modest lifestyle and by maintaining contact and a deep respect with nature. Spiritual and religious traditions, especially in past days, played a role in their survival as well.[4]

Traditionally, the Saami were seminomadic reindeer herders and hunter-gatherers, but in more recent times, they have become a settled people. Not so long ago, they lived in small family or closely related groups called *siida*. Such groups would cooperatively herd reindeer and participate in other aspects of Saami social life.[5] Some of the siida were large and powerful, but all of them were tightly bound together socially, spiritually, and by tribal law. Some of their success depended on their belief in their spiritual leader, a person called a *noaidi*—a shamanic figure.[6]

Over the past several hundred years and until relatively recently, the Saami people and their unique culture have been oppressed and subjugated into political territories without regard for their unique way of life.[7] Among the Saami, private ownership of the land was unheard of, and they held the reindeer grazing lands in common. However, in 1902 the Norwegian government passed a law stating that no one could own or sell land unless they spoke Norwegian. This law effectively disenfranchised the Saami people. The Saami language was prohibited everywhere in Norway at that time. It could not be spoken—let alone taught in schools. Saami religious artifacts were burned, and their shaman killed. "The Sami were forced to adapt to the cultural system of each country."[8] This encroachment by outsiders made life difficult for the Saami.

After World War II, the lifestyle of the Saami[9] changed dramatically. Advancements in technology changed reindeer herding for many. One is more likely to see a reindeer herder keeping track of the reindeer herds on a snowmobile, a scooter, or even a helicopter, than seeing a Saami person on skis. Today only approximately 10 percent of the Saami raise and herd reindeer.[10] In Norway and Sweden, reindeer herding is a somewhat protected occupation; it is considered the *exclusive* right of the Saami.[11] Over the past thirty years, the Saami have been able to establish advisory parliamentary bodies in Norway, Sweden, and Finland. Cooperation across national borders has increased due to the efforts of a Nordic Saami council.

Following our flight to Norway in late May of 1999, my daughter Katrine, a recent graduate in anthropology from the University of Utah, and I drove inland from the coastal town of Alta[12] to the village of Guovdageaidnu (also known in Norwegian as Kautokeino), an important Saami town near the Finnish border. The frosty air that day was pristine and clear; the skies were azure blue. There were no clouds. As we left the *Altafjord* (Alta Fjord) on the Norwegian coast, with its rugged coastline framing the exquisite waters of the Baltic, slivers of green grass were beginning to emerge from under the three or four inches of snow that still covered the ground. The highway eventually followed the meandering *Altaelva* (Alta River), avoiding the steepest parts of a deep-walled canyon named Sautso (the largest canyon in northern Europe). Where the walls of the canyon were visible, the bedrock appeared to be comprised of quartzite and shale.

As our rented car climbed higher and higher in elevation, the breathtaking scenery—the canyons, the river, the tundra, and the landscape—was magnificent. Hundreds of newly formed waterfalls, fed by the snowfields high overhead, cascaded down the steep canyon walls, running over the highway into the river. A layer of snow lay at least five inches thick on top of the ice-covered river, but everything was melting fast. The Alta River used to be the major transportation route for the Saami. In the winter (March), while the river was still frozen over (before the dam was constructed), the Saami loaded their unique reindeer-pulled sleighs with meat, hides, and other things to market and trade in Alta. They used the frozen-over river as their road.

Katrine and I occasionally saw small herds of reindeer in the distance. The tundra had only a few deciduous shrubs although what I thought to be shrubs actually could have been trees stunted by the cold. When we returned three days later, the river was flowing freely, and almost all the ice and snow on its banks had melted. This happens yearly in the Land of the Midnight Sun—when the sun never sets!

Upon our arrival at Guovdageaidnu/Kautokeino, Katrine and I checked into the Norlandia Kautokeino Hotel. Our room was small by American standards, but the view of the town from our hotel room window was absolutely exquisite. Our hotel window framed the famous Kautokeino Saami Church.

At this point in my journey, I had no idea which wise Saami persons I would be able to interview. With help from the Institute for Urban and Regional Research in Alta (Norut NIBR Finnmark), I had a list with me of several Saami people who were considered wise by people in Alta, Norway. One Saami man headed my list—Ole Henrik Magga, a professor of Saami linguistics at the Saami University College in Guovdageaidnu (Kautokeino).

Guovdageaidnu is a small village, and I easily located the college. I inquired at the school office about Professor Magga, and I was promptly escorted down a short hallway to his office. Ole Henrik Magga, a man in his early fifties, was seated at the desk in his modest office, grading final papers. He is a gracious man with a winning smile, and he speaks excellent English. He was most cordial to me, especially considering I had arrived unannounced. He agreed to be interviewed on the following day. He also told me he was quite used to being interviewed and videotaped. His statement should have been a significant clue to me about the accomplishments of this incredible man, but at that time, I had no idea of his importance to the Saami people and the other indigenous peoples of the world.

The following day, Ole Henrik Magga and I met at the Saami College. He escorted Katrine, who handled the video and audiotaping of the interview, and me to a bright and pleasant conference room at the Saami College. We sat facing each other across a conference table. Katrine helped with taping the interview. Ole Henrik always dresses in traditional Saami clothing. This day he was wearing a royal blue coat lined with red fabric and decorated with bands of yellow and white trim. His brown hair was slightly out of place, and his dark piercing eyes danced whenever he smiled—which was often. He was willing to share his life story with me.

When I asked him about wisdom, Ole Henrik mentioned his grandfather and then his mother. Both of them, he explained, exemplified wisdom in their lives. They conveyed their wisdom, he said, through the telling of stories.

"Storytelling happened more often in our culture when I was young than it does now. All the people told stories. They didn't say, "Do this!" and "Do that!" In a way—in the stories—a kind of wisdom was hidden there. This is not only true in our culture. It is well-known that many cultures have these kinds of small stories—the kind of silly moral stories that are important. There are stories about children and animals and that kind of thing—even grown-up people. But deep inside, there was something, a wisdom, that you learned little by little—what it's all about. I think that was the older generation's way to try to teach us what wisdom is like. I think that wisdom has much to do with your relationships to other human beings and animals—and the rest of the world."

Ole Henrik Magga lived his formative years with his grandparents. He was born in 1947 in the heart of Saami territory, thirty kilometers from Guovdageaidnu. "My family has been in reindeer herding for generations."

His mother was not married when he was born. She did marry later, and young Ole Henrik went to live with her and his stepfather when he was about twelve years old, but until that time, his grandparents raised him.

Ole Henrik's grandfather chose to farm rather than be out with the reindeer, however, and Ole Henrik grew up on a small farm—but he was also able to participate in reindeer husbandry. He explained, "Everything, every transport and every kind of transportation, had to be made with reindeer. That was the only form of transportation in this area. So everyone had to learn to have a very close relationship with reindeer—since you depended on them . . . . It's like having a car now."

Ole Henrik' maternal grandfather, whom he affectionately admired, was a deeply religious man—a Christian. His grandmother was not as active religiously, and she enthusiastically supported Saami culture. She taught her grandson the traditional Saami stories and the Saami way of life. Ole Henrik described his grandmother, saying, "Her thing was the living culture—the music, the stories, and all that. I think her heart was always with the reindeer, because she didn't actually accept having to live on the farm. She was always, her whole life, out on the mountains."

Ole Henrik's grandmother lived a very hard life. Her father died early—probably of alcoholism—and she also lost two of her brothers when they were young—fourteen and twenty-one years old. Life on the tundra was hard and often short. Nevertheless, Ole Henrik had the support of a big family—uncles, aunts, and eventually eight brothers and sisters. The whole family became involved with the reindeer at certain times of the year—and still does.

Since the Saami families were so scattered throughout the area, the Norwegian government mandated that Saami children go to boarding schools. Thus, when Ole Henrik was seven years old, he went to boarding school in Guovdageaidnu/Kautokeino where he remained for eight years.

Ole Henrik remembered the experience vividly because at this school, he only heard the Norwegian language from his teachers—a language that he did not understand at that time. "It was very difficult. That is why I remember it very well—because it was a sad thing, both for me and for the other children as well. We were crying and very upset. When we went to the school, we didn't know one word of Norwegian, and we were taught *only* in Norwegian—*all the time*. And that meant that I spent three or four years in school before I understood what the teacher was saying. And many of my fellow students never learned one word, and they never learned how to read and write. And afterward, I used to say, 'It's not thanks to the school system but despite it that I learned to read and write and do all those things—to manage.' It was really very bad."

In his third or fourth year at the boarding school, Ole Henrik finally had a teacher who spoke Saami. It helped him make the transition to Norwegian. In fact, he recalled the day that he finally began to understand what he was being taught in school. During a lesson on paleohistory, the teacher was explaining about the mammoths that had lived in the Arctic long ago.

Ole Henrik recalled the experience, saying, "He showed us pictures of a kind of elephant with hair, and it was so fantastic! I have never forgotten it. Because that was the first time—the very first time—that I had an idea about what the teacher was telling us. Probably, the others had told us many nice stories, but I wouldn't know. And after that experience, I used to interpret for the other children—so the teacher said this, and this, and I'd repeat it in Saami."

As a young teenager, Ole Henrik continued his schooling in Karasjok, the capital city and a major center in Finnmark. There he lived with a family, not in a boarding school. Many Saami children did not go to school when they were thirteen, fourteen, or fifteen years old because they were needed at home to help with the reindeer herds.

Also, many Saami parents had had such bad experiences with the school system that they did not trust it to help their children. In fact, according to Ole Henrik, one of his relatives told him, "You shouldn't go to those silly schools. They're no good." But he was an excellent student, and he did very well in school. Unfortunately, the difficult part of attending school so far from his home was that he was able to return to his home only on Christmas and Easter. The trip from school to his home took several days by reindeer-pulled sleigh.

Because he was a promising student, one of Ole Henrik's teachers helped him go on to a school in Alta, Norway. Some Saami children found it difficult to adapt to living in a larger town like Alta, but Ole Henrik had already been there many times as his family moved back and forth to the coastal islands with the reindeer.

Ole Henrik explained, "After you have been away for two years, you're not so helpless anymore. You learn very much from that. It's harsh, sometimes, especially when you are a small child, but you're learning. That's the good part of it."

After two years at Alta, teachers encouraged him to attend the Gymnastic, a high school, in Oslo, Norway's capital. He did. Following that, he entered the military for his one year of obligatory service to Norway.

Upon completing his military obligation, Ole Henrik intended to become a freshwater biologist and began to study that field at the University of Oslo; however, his plans changed after he took a course in Saami and found that linguistics was the field he really loved. Changing majors to linguistics, he obtained a bachelor's degree (or a *kanmak*, as it is called in Norway). He went on to obtain the equivalent of a master's degree in linguistics. Because of his experiences with the education system, Ole Henrik chose to become an educator—one who would make a difference. He developed a student-centered philosophy, which guides him today.

While at the university, Ole Henrik met his future wife. She is also Saami and a linguist. They married and have two children. They help one another with their work—doing research and writing Saami dictionaries and grammar books. He worked on language reform from 1973-1978. He helped to establish Saami as a topic of study at the university level in Tromsø, Alta, and Kautokeino, Norway, and assisted in the development of dictionaries and a writing system. Even though Saami had been a written language since 1619, various versions of the language existed. Ole Henrik and his associates developed the form of written Saami that is used today.

As we were talking, Ole Henrik called himself an activist. He then explained that while he was a student at the University of Oslo, he headed a newly formed Saami Student Organization. That was in 1968—a time when young people all over the world felt that they should "do something" in this world. It was also the time of Vietnam War protests. Numerous political activist groups existed on all major university campuses, including Marxist-Leninist groups. The Marxists were especially strong at the University of Oslo. Ole Henrik said, "They took over the university, but they found no success with the Saami Student Organization."

Ole Henrik cautioned his Saami peers about the Marxists by saying, "Do not listen too much to these people because they . . . are too dogmatic! And many of them don't really have any experience with life." In stark contrast, most of the Saami students had had rich experiences with life. They certainly had not been sheltered from the rigors and difficulties of life.

Ole Henrik knew the course he wanted his life to take, and he worked toward that goal. He didn't believe in "revolutions" in the way that they were touted in the 1960s; he did, however, believe in processes. He has not changed his basic principles and convictions since his early college years.

Ole Henrik Magga was instrumental in the formation of the Norwegian Saami Association and became its first chairman. From 1979 to 1981 a major confrontation occurred between the Saami people and the Norwegian government over a hydroelectric dam that the Norwegian government wanted to build on the Alta-Kautokeino watercourse. The Norwegian government felt that damming the Alta River would provide needed electricity for the area in the future. Unfortunately, by destroying grazing and calving areas, building the dam threatened the livelihood of many Saami and their reindeer herds. Because of his position as chairman of the association, Ole Henrik assumed responsibility for leading the Saami people, many of whom felt threatened and angry, in demonstrations to protest the building of the dam. In one demonstration, hundreds of people chained themselves together and lay down in front of the construction equipment. The Norwegian government responded by sending more than a thousand policemen to confront, remove, or arrest the protestors. It was a tense time.

Ole Henrik noted that leading an angry group of people was not easy. "During times of conflict, everything can happen. There were many ideas, and it was not always easy to lead."

He tried to keep things peaceful and to keep the situation under control, explaining, "It's not very difficult to have people in such a situation do whatever you want them to do. They can do it. The problem is how to keep people calm and *not* have them do the wrong things."

I asked Ole Henrik how he knew what to say and do to ensure that the demonstration in protest to the building of the dam remained peaceful. He answered, "Well, I don't know. I think it was what I started with. Because even if I couldn't formulate it in words, I always had a feeling of what's the right thing to do. I had the feeling of being led in some way—what to do and what to say. The idea is to make use of all those things you have learned. In a way, you have processed many things in your unconscious mind, and they come out like this."

Ole Henrik relied on an intrinsic sense of right and wrong. Knowing what to say and do in the Alta River confrontation was a combination of experience and knowledge—as he put it, "knowledge from your own experience and from other people's experience." But he also stated that he had a firm belief in other people as well as in himself. I was struck by his ability to look at each individual and attempt to understand his or her position. He sincerely believed that people—all people—only want those things that they believe are the right things for themselves and others.

He told me, "You must have a kind of basic belief in *other* people. Even in people you disagree with. You should not seriously doubt their motives. Their motives can be good—as good as yours. Therefore, you shouldn't define your opponents as evil people."

Eventually, a much smaller Alta dam was built over the protests of the Saami people. Later the Norwegian prime minister Gro Harlem Bruntland confessed that the dam "wasn't really worth the political trouble."[13] The government expressed regret about the whole affair.

Here again, Ole Henrik offered generous understanding for the position taken by the Norwegian government in the conflict. "The Norwegian government is really a democratic government based on human values. It is not that difficult to deal with them. They had to make a choice in that case [Alta River Dam], and while it was not a good choice . . . they *believed* that to run Finnmark, they had to have so much electricity for the coming years."

Even more remarkably, Ole Henrik saw positive aspects stemming from the Alta dam confrontation. The conflict brought a new consciousness and a new awareness about the Saami's plight in Norway and the rest of the Arctic. The Norwegian government had learned, and so had the Saami people. Two commissions were subsequently established—one for the Saami's cultural rights and one for their land rights. The first commission developed regulations on education, language, and a constitutional amendment. Ole Henrik drafted these documents.

The documents ensured that the Norwegian government provided the means so that, in Ole Henrik's words, "the Saami can keep and develop their language and culture—even if the parliament doesn't give any specific rights to individuals. It's a kind of 'in principle' legislation."

In addition to teaching and researching Saami, in 1989 Ole Henrik helped to establish the Norwegian Saami parliament. Working closely with the government of Norway, Ole Henrik served as its first president for eight years, trying to establish Saami rights, which included teaching the Saami language in the schools. Many Saami do not speak their language anymore. Today the Norwegian government is cooperating in strengthening the indigenous Saami people and their cultures—thanks in many ways to Ole Henrik's determination and his commitment to fairness. Today Saami is taught in Finnmark schools, using textbooks written in Saami; there is a Saami radio station, Saami newspapers, and a healthy Internet community. The Saami people are proud of their heritage once again. The wisdom inherent in the Saami culture has not been lost.

Ole Henrik Magga has demonstrated his leadership and his courage over and over. Assuming the preeminent role of a leader in the Saami community, he fully understood that in the Arctic environment, the balance between the condition of the land, the reindeer herds, and human population has oftentimes been precarious. All elements are intertwined in a kind of symbiotic relationship. When Rio Tinto, an international mining company, with the Norwegian government's approval, moved into Finnmark to begin strip mining, Ole Henrik did not hesitate to courageously confront them about their operations on that fragile landscape. He explained, "A couple of years ago, I went out when Rio Tinto Company came up here. You know, that huge international mining company, Rio Tinto. It's a very well-known international mining company, with much *dirt* on their hands. So I went to them, saying, 'You know, even if you have formal permission from the Norwegian authorities, you don't have any permission and certainly no moral permission from our people, the Saami. You are on our land. I ask you to stop these activities.' And they actually did!"

Ole Henrik's respect for all people, his desire to work for justice and fairness, tolerance for everyone, and his courage to stand up for his convictions are certainly laudable.

Possessing many talents that he uses in positive ways, Ole Henrik is a musician, playing the flute and the guitar—but his basic musical feelings are with the traditional Saami musical form, called *joik*. He grew up singing Christian hymns morning and night and joiked with his relatives out on the tundra during the day.

The early Christian missionaries discouraged joik. They called it music of the devil; it was closely associated with the Saami shaman. The shamans were persecuted and sometimes even killed by those early Christian clergy who tried to eradicate Saami traditional practices. Here again, instead of criticizing the missionaries, however, Ole Henrik respectfully sought to understand their motives. He sympathized with them, saying. "And you have to respect them for that [their stand on joik and Saami beliefs]—because that was their belief. You shouldn't question that—because it was sincere."

Ole Henrik quoted the first Saami missionary, Thomas Van Weston, as saying, "My wish is that all the Saamis go into the paradise before me." He then added, "You shouldn't doubt him on that. I think he was serious, and he did a wonderful work with that in many ways. Of course, he was also too harsh. He actually had a kind of interrogation with people. And part of this was condemnation of Saami religion—and its music."

Even though Ole Henrik's grandfather was a devout Christian, wisely he never conveyed such ideas to Ole Henrik or spoke in a derogatory manner of Saami customs. In fact, he noted that his grandfather was always singing, and "sometimes I was not sure about it—was that a hymn or a joik? And

I don't think he cared." Today Ole Henrik, ever the peacemaker, works and cooperates with the church to try to mend any bad feelings on either side—"to try to settle these things."

When I asked Ole Henrik why he thought he had been nominated to be interviewed about wisdom, he humbly conjectured that it was because he was well-known for his work with the Saami parliament. "As you know, when people see you on TV sometimes, people start to believe that you are something of importance. That's not always true—because not everything in the media is so wise."

Before I left, Ole Henrik Magga honored me by singing a joik—his grandfather's joik. Although I hadn't understood the words, the haunting, sad melody, the pure pitch and poignant syllables carried by Ole Henrik's baritone voice conveyed great emotion and transcendent love. His grandfather's death had been tragic and unexpected.

Ole Henrik's understanding of international issues and indigenous people is profound. He served as a member of the United Nations World Commission on Culture and Development, developing policy for indigenous cultures.[14]

Following my visit to Guovdageaidnu/Kautokeino, I learned that Ole Henrik was selected in 2002 by the United Nations to preside over the indigenous peoples of the world at the United Nations.[15] This is a forum representing the social, cultural, and economic interests of nearly 500 million indigenous peoples worldwide—and one that he had a significant role in persuading the United Nations to form. While each country has representation in the United Nations, the many indigenous peoples living around the world have not had such representation—until May 2002 when the UN organized them. Now these peoples—the Maori, the Native Americans, the Saami, the Ainu of Japan, and others throughout the world—have a voice in the United Nations. As the first chairman of the indigenous peoples of the world at the United Nations, Ole Henrik Magga made sure that their voices were heard. He served in this position until 2004.

People possess virtues and vices in differing degrees. Most of us act virtuously at some time during our lives. Most of us have acted at some time or another from the position of our vices as well. What we need is the judgment, the common sense, and the wisdom to determine what is moral and right in each situation we face. The life of Ole Henrik Magga reveals the principled life he has lived.

Like Ole Henrik, William Olotch, a Kenyan man, lived his life by a strict ethical code. A successful Nairobi businessman, William was the director of the Pan Africa Insurance Company, Ltd. I walked through the crowded streets of downtown Nairobi to the impressive Pan Africa Insurance Building from my hotel in downtown Nairobi in September 1999. A receptionist quickly paged William.

A tall, handsome, and kind man, William Olotch ushered my husband and me into a large well-appointed conference room. He was most cordial as he tried to answer my questions about his life. The strength of his commitment to ethical and moral values became evident. He spoke slowly in his deep resonant voice as he told me his story.

William Olotch was born in 1944 in a small town, Singida, in central Tanzania. His parents had been born in Kenya—in the Staya district, about one hundred kilometers from Kisumu and about five kilometers from the Uganda border. He was the second of seven children—four boys and three girls. He has one older brother.

One of the highlights of William's youth occurred when he lived for a time with a widowed grandmother from whom he learned many traditional stories and customs. He told me his story.

"As far as the culture where I come from is concerned, I was *privileged*—and I'm saying *privileged* deliberately—to have lived with my grandmother. My father was out working elsewhere in Tanzania, but he left me with my grandmother—just the two of us. She was an elderly lady at the time—must have been seventy plus. I was eight or nine years old. So I lived with this old lady, doing most of the things she couldn't because she was old—drawing water from the wells, grinding millet or maize. So most of the time, we stayed at the same house—same room. And the whole night was stories—about her own life and what people used to do when they were children—the traditions and the customs. So what I know about our culture, as it was, is from this old lady."

William used the term *old lady* with such reverence and respect it was clear that he loved her deeply and that he gained not only information about the culture from her but a sense of its power and importance as well. He also described his grandmother as "a lovely, lovely lady"—one who was "a very wise lady." This revered grandmother loved children. She had had sixteen children, but twelve of them died around the ages of one or two. Of the four children who survived, William's father was the only son.

William's grandfather had converted to Catholicism, and his parents raised their family to be Catholics as well. William Olotch remained true to this faith. In an Irish seminary school, he was influenced by Father Lynch, an old Irish principal. He recalled, "Once a week, Father Lynch called us to talk about many things, such as, what's life all about? how to carry yourself in life—topics that I don't think many schools addressed. So we had quite a good grooming in commonsense living by an early age from the priests that we had—and particularly Father Lynch."

After attending lower primary school in Tanzania, William went to upper primary school in Kenya. He attended secondary school and went on to study economics and business administration at Kenyan colleges. After graduation, he joined a firm of insurance brokers. His employment has taken him to various places, including Nigeria, London, Zurich, China, India, Toronto, and even New York City. "I have been all over the place."

William is married, and he and his wife have two sons and four daughters. He spoke of his gratitude to his teachers, who were able to help him get into the "right" schools and encouraged him to excel. He did more than was expected of him in school—a trait that carried over to performing his duties at work. It was also a common trait among all the wise individuals I interviewed.

Friends and mentors from William's school have assisted him along the way. "It is a very select group of people who have come from that school. I was encouraged there. We didn't have prefects—or people to oversee what you were doing. No. In this school, you are given the rules—the rules of the school—and you kept them. We were trained to be responsible. We were also disciplined—taught how to look after your affairs. So we didn't have a problem with people shouting at us, 'You must do this!' We were taught how to do things without being told to do it. 'See It and Do It.' That was the motto. We were motivated to do things without being pushed to do them."

When I asked him about the most meaningful accomplishment in his life, William briefly mentioned his career in insurance and his struggle to pass the necessary exams to become a fellow in the insurance business. He then stressed the importance of honesty. He told of the times that he lost business opportunities and promotions because he maintained a high standard of honesty. Yet he told me, he could not do differently, declaring, "I find the hardest thing to overcome is to cheat or pretend. To put up a face and tell you 'I like this' when I don't. To be honest, I think I missed a lot of opportunities in life in terms of jobs just because I tell people what I think is right. And I don't know how to stop. That has been my problem really . . . particularly in this country because of what I have said accidentally—and which I believe in—taken to be anti-system or anti-whatever . . . . But I have no regrets."

Explaining that living virtuously is not always easy to do, William said, "I think society has really changed over the years. All along, people look for a profession. You work hard to qualify and to get into a profession that you know you can manage and that you know pays you well. But things have been distorted in the sense that knowledge and determination alone may not really put you anywhere. At least that is the distortion that this country has seen. I'm sure that this discourages some young people from what they would have done best, and therefore, they have gone into other things and done things that gave them fast money. Because people here, in the young population, want money. The goal seems to be to get money fast and become rich. Everyone here wants money. The concept that education gives you many other good virtues and opportunities is not there. It is not there. Now, it is how you can get money as fast as you can."

William shifted uncomfortably in the chair in which he sat. He continued, "There are certain things that don't give rewards to individuals immediately—we don't see it. Just being good and doing good for everybody doesn't seem to be enough of a reward anymore. Human beings want to get something out of whatever it is."

When asked about wisdom, William remarked, "Wisdom is knowledge, acquired through reading or talking to people that are wise. Honesty in expressing that knowledge and being an honest man. It is a style of living. So you have the knowledge acquired through reading, associations, or whatever, and you are respected because you are honest. You have more to offer in terms of what you know than other people. To me that is wisdom . . . . But those with wisdom don't seem to go very far in life. Those who are wise do not succeed politically—they don't succeed in anything. Wisdom and honesty don't take you very far in the world."

As to what was important to him, William listed first his family. He then mentioned that he felt it was important to also help others to succeed. He happily helps children from poor families, providing them the financial support to go to school, and enabling them to improve their lives.

Are there certain fundamental rules of human conduct that are similar from culture to culture or tribe to tribe? Obviously people have varying notions of what has value in their lives—and what does not. Yet the wise ones valued and lived principled and self-disciplined lives. Somehow they acquired a commonsense kind of knowledge—one that exceeded anything learned through normal educational institutions. They were not only lovers of truth but also displayed remarkable virtues. For instance, Ole Henrik Magga, William Olotch, and other wise ones exemplified courage in their ethical and moral actions. Courage, a virtue often associated with wisdom,[16] is admired in all cultures. All fundamental virtues are. It is as the philosopher John Locke stated, "The most general rules of right and wrong, the most general rules of virtue and vice, are kept everywhere the same."[17]

Endnotes

[1] Baltasar Gracián. Martin Fischer, translator, "A Man of Principle," *The Art of Worldly Wisdom* (New York: Barnes and Noble, 1993), 280.

[2] Sunna Kuoljok and John E. Utsi. Translated by Thomas Rutschman, *The Saami: People of the Sun and Wind* (Jokkmokk, Sweden: Ajtte, Swedish Mountain and Saami Museum), 59. Although the Saami are located in Norway, Sweden, Finland, and the Kola Peninsula of Russia, for this study I chose the Norwegian Saami because various researchers have worked with the Norwegian Saami and written extensively about their unique traditional beliefs.

[3] At the end of the Ice Age, about ten thousand years ago, people began to settle in Finnmark. They were hunters, fishers, and gatherers and were probably the ancestors of the Saami. Stone engravings in the area date from 4200 BC.

[4] www.sqc.fi/--ylikuka/scnordic/sami/. Long ago, Genghis Khan wrote that the Saami—or *Fenner*, as they were then known—"were the one nation he would never try to fight again. The Saami were not warriors in the conventional sense. They simply didn't believe in war and so they disappeared in times of conflict. The Saami remain one culture that has never been to war. They are known as peaceful retreaters—able to adapt to changing living conditions whether they were caused by nature or by other people."

[5] Nils Aslak Valkeapää, *The Sun, My Father*, translated by Ralph Salisbury, Lars Nordstrom, and Harald Gaski (Guovdageaidnu, Norway: DAT O.S., 1998).

[6] www.bewt.org/servlet/GetDoc?/meta_id=1539 (15 January 2005). The *noaidi* had a distinctive role within the Saami *siida* and was able to interpret events for others. Traditional Saami shamanism as practiced by the *noaidi* was a very serious issue, connected to the interrelationships of the human, natural, and spiritual worlds. Some of the skills of the *noaidi* included being able to travel outside their own bodies—a type of out-of-body experience, or "astral travel"—and working with one's "power animal" and other shamanistic techniques. "A *noaidi* was capable of visiting the *sájvva*" (the Saami paradise where the deceased live) and people from far away would come to him/her for wise advice.

Eutopia Adventures 16 (2004). http://www.eutopia.no/Poetry.html (25 February 2005). "The *noaidi* is a person who by means of personal power is able to collect and further present knowledge to his family or *siida* members . . . . The *noaidi* could play the role of a doctor, a priest, a mediator in conflicts, and an adviser [sic] in difficult questions. By means of his *goavdi*, the drum, he [or she] was able to keep contact with the society and gods." Kari Yli-Kuha, 1998. www.sqc-fi/-yikuka/scnordic/sami/ "The *noaidi's* special drum, the *goavdi* or *runebommen*, was important symbolically and spiritually. It was central to the practice of the *noaidi*. The lightweight drum was held in the noaidi's hand, painted with symbols in a different pattern unique to each *noadi*. The drumstick was carved from reindeer bone, and a ring of brass or silver was placed on the skin of the drum. When the drum was drummed, the noaidi was able to gather certain knowledge and "keep wisdom" by observing how the ring moved on the drum face." Stein Jarving, "Sami Shamanism." "The drum was both a map and a compass. The shaman also used a hammer, he joiked [a traditional Saami song form] and could, through the rhythms of the drum, enter a trance. "The primary use of the drum is for the shaman to go into trance and travel in the spirit world."

[7] Knut Helskog, *The Rock Carvings in Hjemmeluft/Jiepmaluokta* (Alta, Norway: Bjørkmanns, 1996. The Saami were not Vikings. Thousands of years before the Vikings, as the polar ice caps began to recede, according to one theory, humans, who were probably hunters, began to push into the northern environment. Another theory suggests that people were already living in the far northern areas of the earth, and the ice age trapped them, isolating them from the rest of the world. In any event, these early humans lived and flourished. They left their stories carved on the rocks of Finnmark. People learned to survive in this harsh cold climate by hunting, fishing, and herding reindeer. One four-thousand-year-old rock carving even depicts a person on skis.

[8] Kari Yli-Kuha, "Sami Mythology." *The Sami,* 12 (1998). http://www.lysator.liu.se/nordic/scn/faq23.html (25 February 2005).

[9] In Norway, one is considered Saami if at least one grandparent spoke Saami—a language that the various ruling governments tried to eradicate from about 1700 until 1963.

[10] JoAnn Conrad, "Sami Reindeer-herders Today: Image or Reality?" *Scandinavian Review,* Winter 2000).

[11] Einar Niemi. In Harald Gaski (ed). "Saami History and the Frontier Myth: A Perspective on Northern Saami Spatial and Rights History." *Sami Culture in a New Era: The Norwegian Sami Experience.* Karasjok, Norway: Davii Girji OS, 1997), 77.

12   *Visit Norway.* http://www.visitnorway.com/templates/NTRarticle. aspx?id=41775 (10 May 2005). Alta is the largest city in Finnmark, with 17,000 inhabitants representing various nationalities. Alta has been known for its mining and slate industries and its fisheries; the Alta River is famous worldwide for its salmon fishing.

13   R. Paine, *"Dam a River, Damn a People? Sami (Lapp) Livelihood and the Alta/ Kautokeino Hydro-electric Project and the Norwegian Parliament,"* *IWGIA Document* 45, International Work Group for Indigenous Affairs, Copenhagen. 1982).

14   Ole Henrik Magga, "Cultural Rights and Indigenous Peoples: The Saami Experience, United Nations Educational, Scientific and Cultural Organization," *World Culture Report: Culture, Creativity, and Markets* (Paris, France: Darantière, 1998), 76-84.

15   Permanent Forum on Indigenous Issues, First Session, 17th and 18th Meetings. United Nations Press release 24 (May 2002).

16   Suresh Srivastva and David L. Cooperrider, editors, *Organizational Wisdom and Executive Courage* (San Francisco: The New Lexington Press, 1998). This text addresses the wisdom and the courage that is necessary for executives in an organization to initiate change.

17   John Locke, 1690, "Essay Concerning Human Understanding," edited by Peter H. Niedlich, *The Works of John Locke* (New York: Clarendon Edition, 1982).

Chapter Six

Honed By Adversity

Adversity is the foundation of virtue.
—*Japanese Proverb*

My daughter Katrine and I flew into Alta, Norway, aboard an early morning Scandinavian Airlines flight from Oslo, on Saturday, May 15, 1999. With no appointments planned until Tuesday, I spent the time in Alta talking with the local citizens whenever I could. Although most Norwegians do not attend church services on Sunday morning, Katrine and I did. I had called ahead for directions to and the meeting times of the Church of Jesus Christ of Latter-day Saints (the Mormons). They were meeting at that time in the home of Kristian Kristensen, the local church leader in Alta. Driving north from the center of Alta, we easily found the yellow frame farmhouse with its large barn set back from the local lane exactly as described to me during my phone call.

I found a spot to park our rental car. Katrine and I nervously approached the front door of the house and knocked. Linnea Kristiansen, Kristian's wife, opened the door, greeted us warmly, and welcomed us into her living room.

A small group of children and adults gathered for the church service, among them two young American Mormon missionaries. Fortunately, these two young men volunteered to translate the Norwegian service into English for us. Katrine and I took our seats on the comfortable living room couch.

A handsomely rugged Norwegian man in his early seventies—Kristian Kristensen entered the room, greeting us. His deep, resonant, friendly voice and welcoming smile immediately put me at ease—even though I didn't understand one word of what he said. In his gentle yet in-charge manner, he conducted the meeting.

Following the church service, Linnea Kristensen invited everyone to stay for rice porridge—a Sunday tradition for the Alta church. I enjoyed the delicious pudding that was accented with cloudberries, a Norwegian delicacy that was new to me. Linnea serendipitously asked me why I had come to Alta. I told her that I was looking for Saami individuals who would be considered wise by their peers. She then laughed and said, "Oh, you are in the right place!" She clarified her statement by informing me that her husband knew many Saami people. They were his friends. He grew up with them.

Norwegian by birth, Kristian spent most of his life in the far northern Norwegian city of Alta. A true Renaissance man, he had many occupations and quite a few "hair-raising" adventures throughout his lifetime. Widely known in Alta, Norway, as a friend of the Saami, he has a deep appreciation for the Saami people, their way of life, and their ability to survive far above the Arctic Circle, in the Land of the Midnight Sun.

When Linnea told her husband of my quest to interview wise Saami individuals, he immediately disappeared into a back room of the house, where he made a few telephone calls. Half an hour later, he and I, along with the two Americans serving as translators, were on our way in my rented car to meet two Saami individuals. Although Kristian did not speak English, he was fluent in Norwegian, German, Saami, and Finnish. One of the men Kristian introduced me to lived in Alta itself and is discussed in a later chapter, but the other man lived out of town on top of a snowy high mountain ridge overlooking the majestic fjord.

We drove north out of Alta on a steep winding mountain road; snow was deep on the sides of the highway. Close to the top of a ridge, Kristian indicated that I should pull off to the side of the road, which I did. I could not see anything but snow, trees, and the fjord that lay in the distance, far below the steep mountainside to our left. Everyone but Katrine, who chose to stay with the car, climbed out.

Unprepared for hiking in the snow, I was wearing black church shoes with two-inch heels. Kristian led the three of us up a steep snowy slope. Nevertheless, I found my shoes very useful. I dug my heels into the snow for traction as I struggled up the slippery slope. Near the top of the ridge, a small wooden house appeared. Smoke from its chimney was visible, circling white into the blue Arctic sky. Outside, hanging from a nearby tree in the frigid air, was a skinned reindeer carcass with several pieces of the carcass missing.

We were at the home of a Saami reindeer herdsman, Jørgen Klementsen Büljo. When Kristian knocked at the door, Mr. Büljo answered. Then he and Kristian stepped inside the house, and the door closed behind them. I'm sure that Kristian was inside doing his best to explain why a grandmother from New Mexico in the United States was standing outside the door—and why Mr. Büljo should care. After several minutes, the door opened, and Mr. Büljo cordially invited all of us inside. The wood fire in a corner stove warmed the room. It felt good. We sat down in the comfortable chairs of the living room. Jørgen Büljo spent more than an hour answering my questions and, through the translators, explaining his life and livelihood as a reindeer herder. He and Kristian tried their best to help me understand the culture and lifestyle of the modern Saami person.

As we left Mr. Büljo's home, I asked Kristian if he considered Jørgen Büljo wise. He laughed and, shaking his head from side to side, diplomatically replied, "He's a typical Saami man."

I cautiously made my way down the slope to the car, once again digging the heels of my shoes into the deep snow for traction. Safely reaching the car, the five of us then returned to Alta, and along the way, Kristian pointed out many local sites of historical interest.

Throughout the next week, as I was talking to the townspeople of Alta in my search for nominations of wise Saami individuals, Kristian's name was mentioned several times. In fact, he received more nominations for being a candidate for wisdom (six) than did anyone else in my search for the wise. (Most Norwegians did not understand the word *wisdom*, and so I mentioned the wise characteristics of such persons.) When Kristian was selected, I was hesitant to include him in my study of the wise—since he and I belonged to the same church, and I wanted to remain as unbiased as possible when it came to who was identified as wise. Yet I did not nominate him, and in actuality, specific religiosity did not seem to make a difference among the wise I had interviewed. I called him and asked if he would tell me his life story. He reluctantly agreed.

A week later, on Monday, May 18, 1999, I interviewed Kristian in the comfortable living room of his home, with the same two American translators helping us to understand one another. The reasons why Kristian had been hailed as wise by the townspeople of Alta were varied but became readily apparent to me as I learned of his attitudes toward people, animals, the land, the sea—and of his extraordinary integrity.

Kristian's adventurous life had been filled with events that would discourage many. Yet at age seventy-three, he was full of youthful enthusiasm and a yearning to live his life to the fullest.

The Kristensens ran a successful farm outside Alta, Norway, in the harsh Arctic climate of Finnmark. Kristian obviously cared for and had compassion for the earth and the living creatures it sustains. He told of how ducks in the area began to realize that they would be safe from the hunter on their farm and how, over the years, the flock that regularly congregated at a pond on his property had grown from two ducks to fifty or more.

"They might be safe from hunters," said Kristian, "but not from the fox or the lynx—who get their share of the ducklings."

He also spoke of the local forests and how they needed care—something that isn't happening much anymore in the region. Walking out his farmhouse door and into the field next to his barn, Kristian would call out. Upon hearing his voice, the wild deer living in the forest would come to him. He was trusted by his many farm animals and the wildlife alike—not to mention the people of the area. Indeed, he went out of his way for me—a complete stranger who showed up at his doorstep. I later learned that his kindness to me was not unusual, for he generously gives of his time and means for friends and strangers alike.

Kristian M. Kristensen was born in Elvebakken in the Alta area. As the fourth child of eleven children, he had seven brothers and three sisters. Two brothers and a sister were born before him, and five brothers and two sisters were added to the family later. Kristian's parents were also born in Alta. His early ancestors were among the first Scandinavians to come to Alta, which for centuries was well-known as a Saami trading post. One of his grandmothers was Finnish and arrived in Alta when she was nine years old, but the other three grandparents were born and raised in Alta.

When Kristian was three years old, his family moved from Elvebakken to a farm just south of Alta, close to where the Kristensens' farm is now located. Kristian grew up and was educated in Alta. There is much to do on a farm; he learned about hard work. At seven years of age, he went to school, but he learned the skills necessary to survive in the harsh Arctic climate from his family and his Saami friends.

"School!" Kristian exclaimed. "I didn't have a whole lot of interest in school. I learned from my family to work and do more practical things. So I was more bent toward working. It could have resulted a little from the fact that school wasn't the main focus of my parents."

In school, he showed an interest in drawing and painting. His drawings, paintings, and art objects were displayed in the school more often than any of his peers.

When asked about individuals who had been influential in his life, Kristian mentioned his father. "I really admired my father, and my father had respect for the children and their own personalities. So I had no difficulty in being obedient to my father."

During the winter, his father worked with slate—making shingles and other products. The quality of Alta's slate was known throughout Europe. When the children were not in school, they helped their father with the slate. Young Kristian learned to drive a team of horses pulling a wagon, and he worked hauling construction materials and supplies while still a boy. In the summers, his father install telegraph and telephone lines, and Kristian helped him.

Kristian's parents maintained a religious home. They were both leaders in a sect of the Lutheran Church known as Laestadianism. Laestadianism,[1] founded by a Swedish man named Lars Levi Laestadius, began in the middle of the nineteenth century as an opposition movement to the prevalent Norwegian state-governed Lutheran Church. It became quite a strong influence in many Saami communities. Its tenants were promoting the equality of all people, believing every person is a child of God, and denouncing the materialism of the world.

Kristian expressed gratitude and appreciation for both his parents. He spoke of his mother's abilities to lovingly care for her eleven children. "She watched out for her children. She always made sure that everything was put in its place," he related. "She worked hard to provide the necessities of life for her family. A talented seamstress, she sewed most of our family's clothing and constructed most of our bedding. She learned to make her children's leather shoes from her father who had been a shoemaker."

There was much to do in the days before washing machines, dryers, and other such modern conveniences; for instance, his mother baked dozens of loaves of bread at a time for the family without the use of an electric or gas oven.

Kristian's parents were generous and hospitable individuals. They always invited Saami families to stay with them during the several times a year when the Saami traveled from the interior to trade meat, reindeer skins, and their handmade goods in Alta. Kristian remained good friends with many Saami individuals who, as children, stayed in his family's home.

In 1939 Germany's war of conquest (under Adolf Hitler) in Europe, which became World War II, changed the normal way of life for most Scandinavians, including the Kristensen family. The details of World War II are well-known, but they are briefly reviewed here as they relate to Norway.

In England, prior to World War II, Prime Minister Neville Chamberlain pursued a policy of appeasement with Germany's Adolf Hitler. Chamberlain believed that the problems posed could be settled without military force. Because the blockade of Germany in the World War I had been so effective, he felt that a blockade would be sufficient once again to defeat the Germans. But this time, in contrast to World War I, all of Scandinavia was neutral and, in fact, was delivering oil and other supplies to Germany, along with the Balkans and the Soviet Union.[2] In the end, the English blockade was not effective at all. Chamberlain's ideas were further eroded when war broke out in September of 1939 in France. The French armies quickly collapsed.[3] Yet at sea, the British were still dominant.

At that time, Adolf Hitler wanted to make sure that he maintained control of the supplies of nickel and iron coming from Sweden—shipped through the city of Narvik, located in northern Norway.[4] Even though Norway had assumed a neutral position to keep Hitler from invading their country, Hitler needed to secure Norway. Poland fell, followed by Finland (March 12, 1940). Norway was next, in spite of its attempt to remain neutral.

The invasion of Norway began with the arrival of a small German force on April 3, 1940, followed by the main Wehrmacht[5] forces during the nights of April 7 and 8. By April 9, the Germans occupied most of Norway's major ports, including Oslo. The king of Norway and his family, along with certain members of the government, escaped to England. The Norwegians resisted the invasion, and some Germans were killed at the invasion of Oslo; but within a few months, Germany succeeded in occupying the whole of Norway.

When the German Wehrmacht invaded Norway, Kristian was fourteen years old. He remembered the event well. "I was in the ninth grade in 1940. We knew that there were problems. One day, I was sitting in school when the brother of the teacher came into the classroom to let us know that the German Wehrmacht had invaded Oslo."

I asked Kristian, "How did you and your classmates react to this news?"

Kristian answered, "We continued with school after that announcement. We weren't very scared, but we were a little bitter about it"

Eventually, about four hundred thousand troops—members of the German army, navy, and air force—occupied Norway. Even at the end of the war, with the collapse of the German Third Reich in 1945, there were still 360,000 German and Austrian soldiers in Norway.

The defeat of Norway was a serious problem for the Allies. The deep fjords on the coasts provided safe harbors for German submarines. The submarines were a major threat to the allies because they were able to cut off supplies that were coming on transport ships across the Atlantic from America. The situation became grave.

Hitler's Wehrmacht rapidly spread from Oslo up the Norwegian coast to Finnmark, arriving in Alta, Norway, about six months later. The Germans tried to force Norwegians to join their ranks. By April 1945 there were two thousand Norwegian men forming an armed alarm unit. Germany had planned to enlist ten thousand men to assist their occupation. These Norwegian men in German uniform were scattered about the country, acing as Norwegian SS units who fought against small groups of the courageous underground Norwegian "peace fighters."

Throughout this time, Germany was intent on keeping the far northern areas of the Atlantic Ocean open to ensure that the supply of nickel would continue to flow to the German arms industry. That meant the occupation of Norway was crucial to their war efforts. Although the German navy was no match for the British, the German battleship *Tirpitz*, known as the "Lonely Queen of the North," spent her entire career (1941-1944) in the waters of Norway and was often based in Kåfjord at Alta. The fjord offered good protection for this sister ship of the Bismarck and the largest warship built in Germany.[6]

In Alta, the Wehrmacht, including German and Austrian soldiers, established a camp close to the Kristensen family farm, on the spot where Kristian's farm is now located. They built barracks for their troops and garages to house vehicles and equipment. Later, when Germany went to war against Russia and invaded them, Operation Barbarossa, the Alta camp was turned into a camp for Russian prisoners of war.

The Wehrmacht captured an enormous number of Red Army Russian soldiers. By the end of 1941, three million Russian soldiers had been captured by the Germans. These prisoners were often "denied adequate food, shelter, and medicine. Soviet POWs died by the hundreds of thousands."[7] These conditions also existed for the Russian prisoners of war in Alta. The Kristensens, living within one-half kilometer (three-tenths mile) of the camp, were well aware of the conditions in the POW camp.

Kristian described the deplorable circumstances existing in the camp. "There were about seven hundred Russian prisoners here. Some of them lived in the insulated barracks, but there were so many prisoners that all of them could not be housed in the barracks. So some of the prisoners were held in an uninsulated garage. The prisoners were mistreated. It was terrible! They froze in the winter. The conditions were extremely bad."

In the frigid, dark Arctic winter weather of Finnmark, getting fresh drinking water from the frozen rivers could be problematic. Holes drilled into the thick ice covering the rivers would quickly freeze over in the bitter Arctic cold. The Germans had difficulty maintaining a water supply for themselves and their prisoners. On the other hand, the Kristensens, skilled at survival, had no problem getting fresh water. Consequently, the German authorities approached the Kristensens' farm to get water from the family's hole in the river ice for the camp staff and the prisoners of war.

When the Russian prisoners came to get water, they would put the water in containers, which were then loaded on a sled and taken back to the camp. Because the Russian prisoners used the family's water hole, the Kristensen's compassion and generosity enabled them, whenever possible, to also provide food to the cold and starving Russian men.

Kristian explained, "We were really glad that the Germans came and asked us for the access to water because we were then able to help out the prisoners by giving them extra food. There were a lot of boys in our family. We would go out and fish in the ice off Rafsbotn [a place located at the bottom of the Alta Fjord]. All of us were really expert fishermen. Every morning my mother would cook very large pots of fish stew. Then she would store the fish by putting it into large pots. Often my mother would prepare the fish just so we could give it to the prisoners."

The family quickly learned which of the camp guards were lenient and which were harsh. When a lenient guard was with the prisoners as they came for water from the family water hole, members of Kristian's family set pots of cooked fish on their front porch. Seeing the food, the guard would ask if the prisoners could have some of the fish. The Russian prisoners would then run to the porch, eat, and then stuff fish into their pockets.

"When the guards were of harsh temperament," Kristian explained, "we were more careful about how we gave the prisoners the fish."

Members of the family would often surreptitiously slip cooked fish into a prisoner's pocket. They also hung fish to dry in the trees along the river. These dried fish were intended for the Russian prisoners as well.

The Kristensen family became clever with their altruistic offerings for the prisoners of war. Kristian related the following:

"There was one occasion when the boys in the family caught a lot of herring under the ice in traps. We got so many herring that it was really difficult to pull the traps out of the water. We had to drive the horses down onto the ice in order to pull the fish traps out. After we gathered the herring from the traps, we salted them. We then laid the herring all over the snow and ice—there were so many herring!"

Kristian smiled as he continued his story.

"Since the German guards saw all that good salted herring spread all over the place and the prisoners of war were hungry, they came and asked us 'What's going on here?' We told the guards, 'We have so much herring that we cannot eat it all. So we've just spread the herring out on the snow over there. It will decompose there and become fertilizer for next spring.' We really couldn't tell them that we caught the herring, salted it, and put it out on the snow so that the Russian prisoners could have food. After all, not all the guards were generous and kind."

The Alta prisoner-of-war camp operated next door to the Kristensen home for more than two years. Kristian was a teenager between fifteen and sixteen years old at this time. He got to know the German and Austrian soldiers and also the Russian prisoners. It was during this time that he learned to speak both German and Russian. He wasn't afraid to go to the camp since, as he put it, "I hadn't done anything wrong!" But one might raise the question, Why was this young boy allowed to move so freely among the guards and prisoners at the camp?

Kristian noted, "I was only a teenager, so I wasn't seen as a threat by the German guards. A grown man had to be careful—but a teenager could go to the camp and talk to the prisoners and could talk to the guards. I was a comrade of German soldiers and the Austrian soldiers as well." Obviously, he was not perceived by the soldiers at the camp to be a threat. In fact, he became close friends with one of the Russian prisoners at that time.

The Kristensen family's survival depended on their farm livestock—cows, chickens, sheep, and horses. One of the German soldiers stationed at the POW camp had an out-of-control dog. Unfortunately, the dog attacked and killed two of the family's lambs. Kristian, who was only sixteen at the time, believed that the dog was a threat to the family's income; he decided to complain about it. Several of the neighbors had also lost animals to this particular dog, but these neighbors were too frightened to complain to the Germans. However, Kristian was a courageous young man. At first, he went to the Norwegian police about the matter, but they couldn't, or wouldn't, help. So he decided to go to the German camp commandant.

When Kristian reached the office of the commandant, he explained the situation and then courageously demanded, "I want two hundred kroner each for the lambs that were killed, and I want the dog shot or destroyed so it cannot kill other livestock."

The commandant asked him, "Whose dog is it?"

Kristian did not know the name of the soldier, but he did know where he worked in the camp. Kristian and the commandant then went to the place where the man was working—Kristian on his bicycle and the commandant on a motorcycle. The soldier who owned the dog was pointed out, and the commandant ordered him to pay Kristian the four hundred kroner—which he did. The soldier was also ordered to kill his out-of-control dog. Kristian's courage and commitment to doing what is *right* began early in his life.

The Germans lost many battles in Russia during the fall of 1944. When Finland and Russia joined forces, the Germans feared that Russia would attack them (coming at them down from the top of Norway) if they stayed in Nord-Trons and Finnmark. Therefore, they chose to retreat—at least as far down the Norwegian coast as Lyngen in Tromsø County, where a defensive front against the Russians had been planned.

On October 17, 1944, the Germans announced the evacuation of all the civilians from Finnmark as part of this retreat. Everyone was ordered to leave, including the indigenous Saami peoples. At first, the request to evacuate was voluntary. The Kirkenes, an area in the extreme northeastern portion of Finnmark, was first on the list. But the first evacuation ship, the D/S *Alta* left there, headed south, on October 22, 1944, with only twenty-two individuals, Norwegian national socialists and sympathizers, on board. The Soviet forces crossed the Norwegian border into Finnmark that day. By October 27, they had liberated east Finnmark. The next day, October 28, the German evacuation order was no longer voluntary.

The German army was retreating, and every person and domestic animal in Finnmark was to go with them; remaining animals would be slaughtered and people shot. A deadline of November 10, 1944, was mandated for the complete evacuation of northern Norway.

The German Wehrmacht wanted to make sure that there would be nothing left in Finnmark that the Allied forces (the Russians and Finnish) could use for survival over the approaching Arctic winter. A scorched earth policy was instituted, destroying all food supplies and resources—the livestock, telegraph and telephone lines, houses, barns, etc. The German occupying forces took all the horses in Finnmark (including the Kristensens') to carry equipment and supplies as their army retreated toward Tromsø. According to Norwegian author Anne Merete Knudsen,

> people were only allowed to take the property with them that they could carry. The rest was to be burned. People therefore hid the things [buried or stashed in coastal caves] that they were particularly afraid of losing.[8]

With most of the local population hiding family treasures and even food supplies in secret places, the German soldiers and others often went hunting for such treasures. When found, they dug them up and took them with them as "spoils of war" as they retreated to the south.

As the Wehrmacht retreated, scorched earth tactics were employed. They destroyed all the communications—the telegraph and telephone lines. Special forces of commando units systematically burned or destroyed homes, businesses, barns, bridges, roads, wells, lighthouses, power stations—everything. At the end, even the magnificent Altagård Forest was leveled, with the large felled timber being freighted south. Many new minefields were laid, adding to the mines that had previously been installed by the Wehrmacht. All of this was done in an effort to prevent the Allies from occupying northern Norway.

It is estimated that seventy thousand people in Finnmark and Nord-Troms became refugees from their homes—forty-five thousand of them by force! All families were forced to board buses or boats, and they were taken south as refugees. Most people left on boats. There were few cars left in northern Norway—they had all been commandeered by the German forces. Some people rode their bicycles south on Road 50. Fishermen were often allowed to take their own vessels south to Tromsø. Soldiers and Russian prisoners of war walked south in a steady stream, day and night.

> The prisoners of war tottered and staggered along on the National Road. They walked slowly. On good days, they could walk 30 km [19 miles]. In addition, approximately 600,000 horses, mules, military vehicles, guns and other military equipment were transported southward.[9]

The Norwegian city of Alta was a major gathering spot for evacuees from Finnmark. Most civilians left by boat from there.

Some German soldiers remained in the area up until the liberation; however, they were ordered to look for those who were hiding and to complete the destruction of the area. At least twenty-five thousand residents tried to avoid being evacuated by hiding in caves, tents, and turf huts along the shores or inland. The Saami were experts at hiding.

During these days of "madness," Kristian and his father were actually in the mountains, ordered by the Germans to watch over the telegraph lines. If there were any problems or acts of sabotage to the lines, Kristian's father was ordered by the Germans to fix them. However, according to Kristian, "one day, we received orders to leave our assignment and to go home. We went home on our bicycles."

In the meantime, Kristian's mother and the other children had been ordered to evacuate their home. Kristian explained, "But instead of doing that, my family got some supplies together—some bedding and other necessities—and escaped into the forest."

Kristian and his father returned from the forest to find their farm and the city of Alta virtually deserted. They had no idea what had happened. Kristian related the events that then transpired.

"A man came down the street on a bicycle. We called out to him, "What's happened here?" He explained that the Norwegian members of the Nazi Party, the supervisors, had come by and told everyone that they had to evacuate. He said that everyone was taken by bus to Alta to the boats that would carry them south."

Kristian's father knew that his wife would not have evacuated their family with the others. He and Kristian headed back into the mountains to search for the family. Eventually they found them. The family stayed out in the woods in a concealed turf hut for nearly a week. There were many families doing the same thing.

It was a dangerous risk, but thousands chose to take it. Many chose to hide in caves, under rock formations, or in the mountains in turf huts or rock crevices. Some Russian prisoners of war escaped from the prison camps and were among those hiding out until the Allies could liberate them. German soldiers used airplanes, local fishing boats, speedboats and trained dogs to search for them. When these individuals were found, they were forcibly evacuated to southern Norway—or they were shot.[10]

Even though the Wermacht burned most of the buildings and houses in the area, a few were left standing to house a small military force that was left in Alta until the liberation of Norway. Empty houses were also used to attract those who were hiding from the German authorities. The Kristensen family farmhouse was one of them. It was not burned.

With the Kristensen family hiding in the mountains, the few animals left on their farm went unattended. Kristian said that they tried to care for the animals by sneaking down into the barns to feed and take care of the animals. However, every night, the house was filled with German soldiers on their way south, fleeing from the Russian front. They came and spent the night in the house, and then continued their journey.

But one night, there weren't any German soldiers in the house. Kristian continued, "So everyone in the family came down out of hiding. My mother started to make preparations to make bread so that we could take it to our hiding place in the woods. However, about five o'clock in the morning, three German soldiers came with machine guns. They kicked in the door and ordered my family to get their things together. We had one hour. We could only take what we could carry—mostly clothing. My sister had the sense to take some of the family silverware; she put the cutlery in her pocket. It was the only luxury we took with us. All the family pictures, all the other memories and family heirlooms were just left. There was a horse and wagon waiting outside. The smallest children rode in the wagon, and the rest of us walked down to the Bossekop [the center of the city of Alta]. The Germans subsequently destroyed the farmhouse and barn."

The following day, the Kristensen family and other captured escapees were put onto a ship that had come to Alta from Murmansk in Russia. It was carrying German troops. After the ship again set sail and was about a half hour into its journey to the south, an alarm on board sounded. Allied submarines were in the area, and the ship was in danger of being attacked.

Kristian explained what happened next. "All of the evacuees were ordered out onto the deck, and we started singing Norwegian songs quite loudly to alert the Allies ships to the fact that our ship was an evacuee transport that carried Norwegian citizens. So fortunately, we weren't attacked."

When the ship finally reached Tromsø, a coastal city 150 miles south of Alta, the refugees were expecting to disembark, but instead, the German authorities ordered everyone to stay on board. Those in charge had hoped that the presence of civilian refugees on board would once again protect the ship and the German troops aboard it from attack. However, while the boat was docked for a few hours in Tromsø, several hundred people left the ship anyway, including the Kristensen family. The vessel started out again, and a little south of Bodø, it was torpedoed and sunk.

Finding housing for the thousands of evacuees from the north stressed the facilities of those communities of mid to southern Norway. The thousands of evacuees from Finnmark were to be housed in the homes of Norwegian citizens. The German occupying government mandated that all families who had any spare room in their homes take in refugees. The formula used to determine if a place had spare room was to measure all the dwellings in a district—including churches. Five meters square (fifty-four square feet) was determined to be the amount of living space required by one person. So after deducting five square meters per person in the family, if a house or building had any room left, evacuees were assigned to live there.

As people from northern Norway streamed into Tromsø and other cities, they were allowed to choose the city in which they would like to go live. Since Kristian's father was familiar with the city of Harstad, the family went there. The thirteen-member Kristensen family was so large that they had to be housed in two homes. The people with whom they stayed gave the family their living rooms. Most of the Kristensens lived under these conditions for about a year although Kristian returned to Alta as soon as he could.

German forces left Norway on May 8, 1945, and Norwegian men began to return to Alta. They mostly returned on small boats, hoping to begin the process of rebuilding. Deciding to return to Finnmark before the Norwegian authorities had deemed the area safe and could oversee and regulate the return of the population was risky, however. Returning was considered an act of civil disobedience. Mines set deliberately as the Wehrmacht retreated from northern Norway existed everywhere—in the sea and on the land. Because of this fact, the return to Finnmark and Nord-Troms was banned for a year. In spite of this, more than twenty thousand people returned to their homes during the last seven months of 1945.

Kristian was the first from his family and among the first group of men to return to Alta; he returned in June. He discovered that everything in the region had been destroyed. He recalled, "The only thing left was the old Alta Church. I had to reorient myself when I reached Alta because the bridge over the Alta River had been blown up. The houses were gone. There was nothing else standing."

Kristian, however, was not to be stopped. He returned to Harstad and used money he had saved to pay for a boat that returned him to Alta.

When he returned, he brought twenty-one horses back with him. "I knew that the horses taken by the German forces were being held in the area between Tysfjord and Narvik. The Norwegian military was going to auction them off. I went there and bought seven horses. I also found as many of the family's horses as I could. I found fourteen of the horses that had been my uncle's."

Even though the rebuilding of Alta was underway, getting building materials to Alta was difficult. Kristian stayed in the area, living in a tent. There were no building materials available in the region. The bridges were all gone. Most materials available during the summer and fall of 1945 were brought to the area by ship, dropped into the sea, and floated to the land. Horses, cows, and sheep were put into the water from ships and boats and were obliged to swim to land. Because the forests were gone, the only wood in the area consisted of small planks salvaged from the German's airplane runway in Alta. From these short planks, small houses, only three to four meters (ten feet) square, were constructed.

Kristian related, "The German army built an airport in Alta during the occupation. The runway was made of wooden planks. The first people to come back to Alta used these boards to build small houses. We were able to cut out the planks and transport them from the site of the airport over the river to our homesite on horseback. We had problems getting over the Alta River because the planks of wood were so dry that they floated extremely well. And the current was strong enough that the horses and wagons loaded with the planks all couldn't get over the river. So we had to wait until the tides were right, and then the horses were able to swim over, pulling the wagons. Because a wagon and its cargo was so light that it would float, we sat on the wagon—or stood in the wagon—and were pulled by the horses across the river."

Many of the men in Kristian's family eventually returned to Alta and began to rebuild the house and the barn, living in tents in the Land of the Midnight Sun. Kristian's mother and the family's small children returned at Christmastime, bringing with them two cows, some calves, and some sheep. Slowly, the Kristensens began to rebuild their lives in Alta.

During this rebuilding process, Finnmark remained a dangerous and desolate area. Even though Herculean attempts were made to clean up the mines of northern Norway, and even though the Germans left quite good records as to where mines were located, not all of the thousands of land mines were discovered, and tragically, many deaths occurred because of them.

One day, when Kristian was about nineteen years old, he and his friends were out in the mountains. They stopped to prepare a meal. Kristian somberly described what happened, "Two of my friends and I were out in the mountains preparing our meal. One of them sat down in one place to eat, and the other friend sat down in another place. They both got up to prepare a little bit more of the meal, and after doing so, one of them sat down where the other had been sitting. Although we didn't know it, on that exact spot was a mine left over from the war. I think that my one friend sat down a little harder than the friend who first sat in that spot. The mine went off, killing my friend."

Tragedy, loss, and death were ever present, even after the war was over.

To earn some money (*nkroner*—Norwegian kroner), Kristian went out on ships to the North Sea for two or three months every year. "We were after seals. The last time out we had over 22,000 skins; about 250 were even hanging on the deck because all the holds were full of sealskins." The seals were taken to the factories to be processed for meat and fur coats.

Kristian earned enough money that, upon returning to Alta in 1950, he bought his own farm. It was the land where the German prisoners of war had been located. He started to raise mink and ermine on the property.

Kristian continued to sail, however, even traveling to the Grand Banks in 1952-1953. His last time out to sea to gather seals was in February of 1956. This time, a new dangerous adventure—depending on how you view it—occurred. On the coast of Iceland, the ship he was on encountered an iceberg, collided with it, and sank. Fortunately, the crew was able to make it to land but, shipwrecked, found themselves marooned on an isolated sheep farm in Iceland.

The sailors were finally rescued, and Kristian returned to Alta. He then took up a land-based occupation—raising ermine and mink full-time. That lasted for fourteen years, until 1970, when the market value of mink became so low that he had to find another way to make a living. He was broke and without a job, but in spite of this, he kept his sense of humor.

Describing his plight, Kristian laughed as he told me, "I didn't know exactly what I should do after I stopped raising mink. The last payment I got was so little money that I thought I was going to lose everything. I had to do something. But I said to myself, 'At least I have my shirt—they can't take that away. I get to keep the shirt. And that's enough!' It went better than I thought. I just worked and worked and worked. I began with farming, and I invested small amounts. A successful farmer in a land that is hard to imagine being farmed, Kristian built the house on his farmland in 1960, and an addition to the house in the 1990s.

Kristian's father had always said that Kristian was too busy to find a wife. However, in 1984, Kristian married Linnea, a lovely Finnish widow. Instantly, he acquired a family of four boys and one girl. They were young children, and one of the boys had special needs for schooling but was a musical genius. Linnea and Kristian complemented each other. Both of them were recognized as stalwarts in the Alta community.

Katrine and I were in Alta for Norwegian Independence Day, May 17. The entire city seemed to turn out for the celebrations, which included a parade through the town. The streets teemed with people wearing flags or badges that displayed the bright national colors. Individuals waved small red, blue, and white Norwegian flags. Small children were dressed in traditional costume. We stood with the crowd on the main street as the parade of celebrating individuals passed by. Everyone sang, cheered, and clapped. As the end of this parade came into view, we saw a horse-drawn buggy driven by Kristian with Linnea by his side. Both were dressed in traditional Norwegian clothing. The one-hundred-year-old buggy belonged to Kristian and was pulled by one of his magnificent horses. The crowd on the streets cheered as they went by. I asked several people standing nearby about Kristian. Everyone respected and admired him. This respect was well deserved.

Kristian Kristensen was a humble farmer/fisherman/entrepreneur. His wisdom, although recognized by those who knew him, was not rewarded with accolades, awards, or appointments to political office. He represented one of unnumbered and unrecognized wise individuals living among us today. He humbly balanced the values of honesty, hard work, truth, moral sensitivity, spirituality, gratitude, compassion for people and creatures, and ethical behavior in his life.

Certainly, Kristian lived a life of wisdom. John Kekes, the philosopher, wrote the following statement about wise people, like Kristian and other wise ones, "The more wisdom we have, the more likely it is that we shall succeed in living good lives."[11]

Kristian was called a good man, a man of action. He looked for the positive in all situations. He faced many difficult situations, yet he did not believe that his life had been particularly difficult. When comparing the one-hour-evacuation order given to his family by the Germans with the situation then (in 1999) ongoing in the Balkans, Kristian noted that in the Balkans, people who were displaced were only given three minutes to leave their homes. "We were given an hour," he said in grateful comparison. "The people of the Balkans had it much worse than my family and I did."

Like his father, Kristian was a deeply religious man. He joined the Church of Jesus Christ of Latter-day Saints later in his life. An accepting and generous man, he lamented that the people of Norway specifically and the world in general did not seem to recognize the divinity of Jesus Christ and the hope of his gospel. Kristian, like other wise ones, was concerned about the way humans everywhere are treating each other and the earth.

Kristian befriended people of all walks of life, and those who knew him considered him their friend. His compassion and concern for the Saami people was profound. They have often faced severe discrimination. He gratefully recognized the contributions that this indigenous group of people made to the environment in the past, when they would care for the forests—since their livelihood came directly from a healthy tundra and mountainous terrain. Reindeer herding with helicopters, scooters, and snowmobiles has made life easier for the Saami, which is in many ways a good thing. However, Kristian worried that the land would not be able to sustain the increasing number of reindeer.

Kristian believed that the Saami people give up a rich and rewarding heritage as they abandon their old traditions. He said, "There is a lot of worth in the way that they have lived and handled life. The way they have lived is fantastic—they have developed unique clothing and can make all the things they need to live. They are able to live in balance with nature."

Kristian tried to live in balance with nature as well. In addition to his vast survival skills, he had constructed his own Saami sleds, sewed his own Saami-style clothing from reindeer hides, including gloves and shoes. He was also a talented artist. In fact, he mentioned that if he was no longer able to farm, he would like to spend his time drawing and painting. He possessed an expert knowledge of the people, animals, and plants of the Arctic region. He was optimistic about the future of Norway and the rest of the world.

Then, in 2003, life handed Kristian another unanticipated situation; he suffered a stroke and lost most of his eyesight. Linnea wrote me a letter, explaining that Kristian has faced this latest "adversity" as he has all others in his life—with courage and determination to do whatever he can to contribute. He insisted on feeding the animals on the farm every day. She ended her letter by saying, "Kristian is an incredible man, even now!"

By 2009 Kristian was completely blind, but he continued to be (as Linnea recently told me) "the type of person who would plant a tree today, even if he knew he was going to die tomorrow."

Like Job in the Old Testament, Kristian experienced one adversity (my word) after another in his life; and again, like Job, he did not complain about his life, nor did he "curse God." Actually, he gave no indication to me that he thought his life had been particularly difficult. He positively pursued living the best life he could and, in the process, eventually overcame every difficulty that he encountered. In the process, Kristian has helped and befriended friends and strangers. Is he truly wise? I came to believe he is.

I am reminded of the lyrics from an old 1940s song, originally performed by Ella Fitzgerald and the Ink Spots. "Into each life some rain must fall, but *too much* is falling in mine." Almost everyone, at some point, could sing this lament; nevertheless, one of the most surprising discoveries that I made as I interviewed wise individuals like Kristian was how much adversity—losses, hardships, and sorrows—they experienced in their lives without complaint. I was not expecting such a finding.

To greater or lesser degrees, all the men and women I interviewed faced adversity in their lives. As I talked to more wise people and learned how they dealt with the circumstances of their lives, it became evident that their reactions to what I term adversity (and they called life)—whatever its cause and whenever it occurred—were, in fact, similar. They faced their difficulties with courage and resolve, and like Kristian, they did not even consider tragic or unfortunate events in their lives as adversities. On the contrary, all of the participants looked on their problems as a normal part of life—something to be overcome or accepted.

Adversity, suffering, and loss are part of life. We all experience it. How we react to it marks one of the differences between the wise and the foolish. As Sally Taylor, a university professor, noted,

> Although some adversity may be self-inflicted by foolish behavior, much suffering comes regardless of anything we have done. No matter our age or situation, we will experience suffering in this life. It can be physical suffering, or it can be mental or emotional suffering—or both at once. But suffering is a necessary part of the human experience.[12]

Not one wise person that I interviewed felt sorry for himself or herself because of the numerous problems and afflictions in his or her life. Like metal honed in a refiner's fire, the wise ones were strengthened and became more brilliant after overcoming pain, personal hardship, abuse, discrimination, or tragedy.

Endnotes

[1] Sunna Kuoljok and John E. Utsi, *The Saami: People of the Sun and Wind* (Jokkmokk Sweden: Ájtte, Swedish Mountain and Saami Museum, 1993, 32). Laestadius was born on January 10, 1800, in Jäckvik, Sweden. Since his mother was Saami, he understood the Saami way of life. An ordained Lutheran minister, he became proficient in many languages, including all the Saami dialects, Finnish, Swedish, and Latin. Although best known as a religious leader, Laestadius was also an ethnologist and botanist. He began the Laestadian revival with his preaching. He preached in both the Saami and Finnish languages. That is why Laestadius was one of the first priests who could communicate the message using images and language, which the Saami could relate to. This was one of the reasons why his preaching had an effect on the Saami, both as a revival preacher as well as a supporter of the temperance movement. He appealed to the often-discriminated-against Saami. Laestadianism's tenants encouraged individuals to have faith in providence. It was believed that a truly devoted Christian would reject material wealth and would adopt an ascetic approach to life. Denouncing the idols that human beings create and worship, Laestadianism also taught that people are, in spite of all other conditions, equal as children of God. One's ethnicity did not matter, but membership in the congregation would separate one from the sinful outside world. Although still functioning as a sect of Lutheranism in Norway, in more recent years, Laestadianism has replaced much of this ascetic viewpoint with values more oriented toward pursuing achievement. However, the Laestadian religious belief in the equality of all men and women still prevails.

[2] Tor Dagre, *The History of Norway* (1995). www.reisenett.no/norway/facts/History/The_history_of_Norway.html (16 February 2005). The Soviets, although proclaiming neutrality, were supplying Germany with oil, grain, and war materials from September 1939 until June 1941 and, thus, were considered aligned with Germany. The Soviets occupied the Baltic regions in 1939 and 1940—without war—but when Finland refused to allow Soviet naval bases on its land, a three-month war between the two nations ensued in Finland (November 30, 1939, to March 12, 1940). The Soviets began to fear that Germany would overtake the Balkans, and in November of 1940, relations between the two countries turned sour. Hitler did plan to invade Russia, and when the Wehrmacht invasion, called Operation Barbarossa came (June 22, 1941), Stalin and the Soviet military were totally unprepared. Accordingly, the Soviet Union was forced to enter into an alliance with Britain and, later, with the United States.

[3] J. A. S. Grenville, *A History of the World in the Twentieth Century* (Cambridge, MA.: The Belknap Press of Harvard University Press, 1994). Although they

were aware of German plans, the British were quite unorganized. Chamberlain's cabinet fell, and Winston Churchill was made prime minister on May 10, 1940. "Britain now had a war leader who was at last a match for Hitler. Churchill more than any single man, sustained national morale and hope in the future."

[4] Tor Dagre, *op. cit.*

[5] The name used to refer to Nazi Germany's and Austria's armed forces from 1935-1945.

[6] http://ourworld.compuserve.com (13 August 2009). The Tirpitz weighed approximately fifty thousand tons. The crew that ran the ship numbered 2,608. The presence of the Tirpitz in Alta forced the Allies to divert three battleships (much needed naval power) to guard Russian convoys. Many attempts by submarines, destroyers, and planes dropping bombs were made to sink this ship—to no avail.

[7] William C. Fuller, *Russia: A History* (London: Oxford University Press, 1997), 320.

[8] Anne Merete Knudsen, *Refugees in Their Own Country*, Alta Museum Pamphlet No. 2 (Alta, Norway: Alta Museum, 1995) 11.

[9] Ibid., 16.

[10] Ibid., 11. Colonel Gunnar Johnson, a medical doctor and a Norwegian intelligence officer, as early as winter of 1944, was helping rescue Norwegian cave dwellers. His report included the following descriptions of conditions: "There is much misery in the district . . . . but people did not give up."

[11] John Kekes, *The Examined Life* (University Park, PA: The Pennsylvania State University Press, 1992), 145.

[12] Sally T. Taylor, "The Fellowship of Christ's Sufferings as Reflected in Lear and Life," *Brigham Young Studies* 43:2, (Provo, UT: 2004), 47.

Chapter Seven

A Thirst for Understanding

We can be knowledgeable with other men's knowledge
but we cannot be wise with other men's wisdom.
—*Michel Montaigne (1533-1592)*

The wise individuals I met persistently sought to learn new things and gain more information. They showed a curiosity about the world. Learning transformed their lives. Hiroshi Shimoguchi (hereafter referred to as Shimoguchi-san) and Walter Krause developed a mature understanding of how the world works and what is important in life because of their ongoing quest for knowledge—tempered by their experiences and common sense.

Born on opposite sides of the earth, Shimoguchi-san and Walter epitomized those who intuitively sought knowledge and were lifelong learners. Both men were soldiers in World War II—Shimoguchi-san in the Japanese army and Walter in the German army. Both men experienced and deeply understood human suffering and loss. Open to new perspectives and ideas, they intuitively were able to see the "big picture"—developing the optimistic viewpoint that perceived the world as a positive place. Yet these two men came from almost antithetical cultures.

Hiroshi Shimoguchi is a highly respected wise Japanese man living in Wakayama Prefecture of Japan. Kunio Hatanaka, one of the individuals who assisted in locating wise individuals in Japan, arranged for me to meet with him. On June 20, 1999, Hatanaka-san, my son Steven, who served as translator, and I drove to Tanabe (the small town described in chapter 3), where I met Shimoguchi-san for the first time. At that time, he was serving as the director of the Tanabe City Art Museum. The museum featured the paintings, drawings, and sculpture of talented and gifted Japanese artists.

Shimoguchi-san respectfully greeted us as we entered the lobby of the impressive museum. A distinguished-looking man with graying and slightly thinning hair, he was casually yet impeccably dressed in a knit sports shirt and casual slacks. He ushered the three of us into his office at the museum, to the left off the main entrance hall. His well-appointed office offered us comfortable seating but, more importantly, an aesthetic experience. Shimoguchi-san's office was filled with beautiful paintings and shelves of books; in fact, two of his own impressive paintings hung on the walls. He sat down behind his desk, and I sat down across from him. As we became acquainted, he spoke with passion and humor and was extremely polite and cordial. He told me his life.

Born April 21, 1925, in Tanabe, Japan, Shimoguchi-san was the last of four children in his family. His Japanese given name, *Hiroshi*, means "generous" and fits him well. He had two brothers and one sister, born quite a few years before him. By the time he entered elementary school, his siblings were out on their own.

His father was not around much either. According to Shimoguchi-san, "my father traveled around a lot, and he was a soldier in northeastern China in the late 1930s during the Sino-Japanese War [1931-1945]."[1] Shimoguchi-san greatly admired his mother, saying that she "had a fair way of looking at people—she did not judge them." He never knew his grandparents.

As a young child, Shimoguchi-san was drawn to learning, especially to the arts. He loved to draw and paint. He could read and write before he entered elementary school.

When I asked him how he learned to read at such a young age, he replied, "My teacher was the newspaper. When I found something that I could not read, I would ask around the neighborhood for anyone who could teach me how to read it. So the neighborhood was my teacher—but primarily it was the newspaper."

Shimoguchi-san went to elementary and junior high school in Tanabe, Japan; and then, as a fifteen-year-old, he enrolled at the university in Yamaguchi Prefecture. He chose to major in Japanese literature. He loved school and was a promising artist even then. He also enjoyed the sport of swimming. He seemed insatiable in his quest for learning. But war would soon bring hardship and horror into his life.

When the Sino-Japanese conflict erupted again in 1937, the Japanese began conscripting young Japanese boys, sending them to fight in China (where millions of soldiers and sailors were needed). In 1940, fifteen-year-old Shimoguchi-san was forced into the Japanese army. He had to leave the university [2] and was sent to fight in Mongolia, where Japan required a force of nearly a million men to combat General Chiang Kai-Shek's Chinese forces. [3]

Shimoguchi-san was reluctant to remember or even talk about this life-shattering event, but he did say, "What I experienced there was different than I had ever imagined. It was different from what the Americans believe happened. The leaders of the country didn't want soldiers to think; they just wanted us to fight. You didn't need to know how to study or think, and how wise you were was not of any importance—it was just the work of fighting! I was very shocked. Everything that I had become and developed—all the study and the thinking over fifteen years up until that time—was irrelevant. The only thing I was taught was the *appropriate* way to die. They did not teach me how to live at all. When those things [thinking, learning, and knowledge] aren't valued, it is just like you have already died."

The second Sino-Japanese War claimed about 1.1 million Japanese military casualties, wounded, or missing; 35 million Chinese casualties; and as many as 20 million civilian deaths. [4] The war ended soon after the American attacks on Hiroshima and Nagasaki when atomic bombs were dropped on August 6 and August 9 of 1945, respectively. On August 15, Japan's emperor Hirohito addressed the Japanese people in a recorded radiobroadcast, the *Gyo Kuonhoso* (Jewel Voice Broadcast) telling them that Japan was surrendering and that "the unendurable had to be endured." [5] The Allied powers began the occupation of Japan on August 28. The formal surrender of Japan occurred on September 2, 1945, on board the USS *Missouri*. The Japanese Instrument of Surrender was signed by Mamoru Shigemitsu, Japan's foreign affairs minister. Japanese soldiers began to return to an "occupied" Japan.

It was evident that Shimoguchi-san had difficulty talking about what happened to him and his companions during the war. He covered his mouth often with his hand to hide his grief and sadness. He said, "I feel that my past, the person I had been, died with the war. Many of my friends died in the war. I felt lucky that I could come back, but I also felt some responsibility to work for some of the people who could not come home."

Shimoguchi-san returned from Mongolia in late 1945. Life back in Japan was extremely difficult. There was no food. He said, "I spent most of my days just trying to find something to eat."

He clarified his situation, saying, "It wasn't a matter of whether you had money to buy food; it's just that there was no food! I worked at five or six different jobs, including becoming a fisherman. I learned to barter with the Allied troops from New Zealand, who occupied this region of Japan [Wakayama]. The Allies had food, including chocolate bars."

Soon after his return from China—as soon as he could—he enrolled in the university again to continue his studies. At this time, he related that his thinking was transformed.

"When I came back and enrolled in college again," Shimoguchi-san reminisced, "the first movie that I saw was *Casablanca*. I was very moved by it. I had no idea that there was a world like that. I couldn't imagine it. The things I saw in the movie were something that I couldn't imagine. I was impressed by the movies because they portrayed a different world from what life was like in Japan at that time. It was like a dream."

He continued, "My dream was when, or if, I would ever be able to own and drive a car myself. When I started working, I couldn't buy a bag or a piece of clothing with my monthly salary, and I used to contemplate the time when I would be able to buy such things with a month's salary. It was a very difficult time. I was impressed and awed by American army jeeps. They could go on unimproved roads and through rivers. It was incredible. I felt that I would never be well-off enough to have a car."

Times were difficult in Japan until about 1960, when the Japanese economy began to improve. Automobiles, televisions, refrigerators, washing machines, and other electrical appliances finally became affordable. Shimoguchi-san bought his first automobile in 1964 or 1965. He eventually married. He and his wife have two daughters and two granddaughters.

After college, Shimoguchi-san began his career as a civil servant. He worked for Wakayama Prefecture from 1951 to 1977, at which time he retired, at age fifty-two, to move on to other interests. Strongly influenced by Kamagusu Minakata,[6] an incredible man from Wakayama Prefecture, Shimoguchi-san worked for a year at the Minakata Memorial Hall in Tanabe. He was the first director of the Kinan Cultural Center and also was the deputy director of a group of people who were working to preserve the actual home of Minakata-san. The director of that project happened to also be the mayor of the city of Tanabe, and when the art museum was built in the 1980s, he asked Shimoguchi-san to leave his second retirement to become the director there.

Looking to the future, Shimoguchi-san expressed concern that Japanese young people were not being taught to know about or respect those people who were an important part of Japanese heritage. "In Japan we used to be taught about famous and noble people . . . . Teachers used to be revered. But in 1945, when the war ended, they stopped teaching that in schools. People who were considered wise or noble in the past were no longer talked about. So all authority was lost at that time. There wasn't anyone to respect in general . . . . As a consequence, I don't know who to look up to in Japan."

Shimoguchi-san continued to voice his concerns about the future of Japan and its children. "I don't think the current state of things in Japan is good," he said. "Take the national flag; they raise it at Olympic events, but there is still a debate within Japan about whether or not it really is the national flag. True, it is the flag that we use internationally, but within Japan, it is not accepted as the national flag."

He added, "There seems to be nothing that you can really depend on these days. Small children don't even know the national anthem, 'Kimi ga yo.' They think that it is a sumo song—played only at wrestling events. They see it on TV at the sumo events, and they think 'It's sumo!' I don't think that's good. I think that the Japanese have lost important things they can depend upon. They don't have a guiding path."

Shimoguchi-san continued to explain his point of view, saying, "More and more people are taking a neutral position and are in the middle—'on the fence'—and the number of people who have strong beliefs and a willingness to act on those beliefs are becoming fewer and fewer. I also think that the Japanese can be characterized as a people who, when someone has an idea to do something, everyone kind of jumps on the boat."

Shimoguchi-san concluded by saying, "In that respect, we [the Japanese] may be similar to the Germans before World War II."

I asked Shimoguchi-san, "How can that problem be resolved?"

He answered, "Education is the only way! We certainly cannot trust politicians to make the needed positive changes in Japan. But," he added, "the necessary changes will be difficult unless Japan's educators truly become educators—when that happens, they will be respected and revered as more than common laborers."

On the other hand, Shimoguchi-san expressed his abiding faith in the strength and abilities of the Japanese people. He admired their ability to "make a heroine or a hero out of even drastic situations." He also noted that the Japanese have an inborn ability to make simple and even "drastic" (unattractive) things into beautiful objects and ideas.

"So in Japanese history, people such as Toyotomi Hideyoshi in some famous stories exemplify this characteristic of Japanese," he explained. "For example, when a battle is lost or someone in the family is killed, this person is made into the heroine of the story—even though they lost. There's no such thing as a happy ending in Japan! We think better of the person who is unlucky."

Shimoguchi-san wisely noted that the younger generation was taking a more modern view of things and trying to view "things the way they are," whereas the older generation in Japan was clinging to their "same old ways" of thinking about things.

He spoke of the generation gap that exists in Japan. "No one is trying to close the gap between the elderly and the younger people. The older people do not try to understand the younger, and the younger people do not try to understand the older people. I think that if we can close that gap, Japan will become even stronger."

When I asked Shimoguchi-san about his personal goals for the future, he replied, "Life is almost over for me; there is not too much left to do. When I die, I want to look back on my life and be satisfied with it. I have had a good life. For me, I think that my life already ended once—in 1945. Now I am living a second life. Everything since 1945 is just a bonus . . . . A good life for those in my generation is not measured by honors or wealth but by whether one has strived and made continuous efforts while they are alive to do everything that they could for others. It is as in the following poem:

Tomo no himei ni ware ha naku,
[I cry with a friend's adversity]
Ware no yorokoi ni tomo ha naru
[A friend rejoices in my happiness]

The essence of this poem is that when your friend cries, you also cry with him and also that when you have something that you are very happy about, your friend also rejoices as if it is his own happiness. I want to be surrounded by this type of people. I think this is the best way of living one's life."

Clearly, people were more important to Shimoguchi-san than position or wealth. His experiences brought him compassion and a deep respect of people.

A week later, I again met with Shimoguchi-san at his office in the museum. It began to rain after I arrived. He explained more about his concern for the future. "Before the war, everyone had a global objective, or something to look to for guidance, such as the emperor and so on. But since Japan lost the war [World War II], the people don't have much to look toward to, and the people have lost their direction . . . . There is no common objective or sense of guidance. Today's leaders, whether they be politicians or otherwise, what they need to do is to not think about themselves, but to be more altruistic in thinking about things. Without that, true wisdom will not come about. I think that leaders who exhibit wise qualities are becoming fewer and fewer in Japan. Most leaders have no backbone!"

Shimoguchi-san noted that not only had Japanese values changed, but the basic philosophy about the purpose of life was changing as well. He used the Japanese word that means "pragmatic"—*enjitsuteki*. It isn't enough to accept things just because they exist, but rather, one needs to "delve deeper . . . and question why things had come about."

Shimoguchi-san also believed it was important for individuals to ponder life's important questions, such as the purpose of life. Contending that the time was soon coming when the Japanese people will be forced to rethink things, be more philosophical, and do away with the materialism that has gripped the nation, Shimoguchi-san stated, "People in Japan must be nice to one another. They should help others in distress, and if one is in distress, others will help them. In return for doing something good, people will be happy. When these types of caring relationships come about, Japan will be a much, much better place."

According to Shimoguchi-san, the concept of freedom that Japan received from the United States after the war sixty years ago is even now not well understood in Japan. Shimoguchi-san commented, "People have forgotten that freedom is a concept that exists within controlled bounds. The same applies to personal rights. One has responsibilities that have to be carried out with regard to receiving those rights. I think that to resolve these difficult issues, Japan needs to get rid of politicians who do not understand this. Americans seem willing to go around the world to stand up for their country—they think it is the right thing to do for freedom. But among the Japanese," Shimoguchi-san lamented, "there is no one who would stand up for their country. For example, even though we once had a strong military force that went to war, most of the current soldiers would leave the army before they'd go to war. They have no principles or objectives . . . . The number of people who have strong beliefs and act on them is dwindling, even though there are still some people who are always looking ahead to the future—to how they should live."

As a people, the Japanese are diligent and hardworking. But Shimoguchi-san felt that these qualities would not be enough for the future. He felt that Japanese people needed to learn to express themselves in the world arena more effectively. That transformation too, he said, would come about only through education.

As I left Shimoguchi-san and the beautiful Tanabe art museum that day, I walked out into an oppressing humidity. The darkening clouds overhead suddenly unleashed a torrent of rain. Noticing out the large museum windows that I, without an umbrella, had not planned ahead and was getting drenched in this downpour, Shimoguchi-san quickly ran out of the museum front entrance, into the pouring rain, bringing me a white umbrella. Steven and Hatanaka-san had already left the museum to get the car, and without interpreters, Shimoguchi-san and I couldn't say much to one another. However, I sensed his genuine concern and generosity toward me. I accepted his generous gift of the umbrella, saying, "Arigato gozaimashita" (thank you), using my limited Japanese vocabulary. We both bowed, and Shimoguchi-san ran back into the museum.

That was the last time I saw Hiroshi Shimoguchi. He retired from the museum in 2003. For me, Shimoguchi-san is the ideal model for all that is *noble and wise* about the Japanese character and culture.

In October the same year (1999), I found myself on the other side of the world, in Prenzlau, Germany. Prenzlau is a small city near the Germany-Poland border in what had been the Russian-controlled German Democratic Republic (the DDR) until the reunification of Germany on October 3, 1990. Twenty-five years earlier, the wall dividing West and East Germany had been erected through Berlin and onto the countryside, sealing tiny Prenzlau behind it in Communist-controlled Russian territory.

I went to Prenzlau in order to interview a man called a legend in his own lifetime[7]—Walter Krause. When he was nominated as someone fitting the description of a wise man, I was unaware that part of his story had already been published.[8] At about the same time, by chance, I discovered that my husband had known Walter forty years earlier. I communicated with Walter's wife, Edith, who speaks English (Walter did not), by telephone and later by e-mail to arrange an interview with Walter in Prenzlau.

Driving northeast from our hotel in Berlin on the efficiently engineered German autobahn, my husband and I reached the Krause home in about two hours. It was Sunday, and the traffic was light. My husband, a transportation/highway engineer, enjoyed comparing America's interstate system with the German equivalent. We both enjoyed the scenery—and the smooth efficient roads.

Upon our arrival, Edith and Walter greeted my husband (who speaks German) and me (with my poor German) graciously and invited us to attend church with them. The church, built by Walter almost single-handedly during the bleak years behind the iron curtain in Communist East Germany, was located in a large building behind the Krause's home. A congregation of about thirty individuals gathered. Ninety-year-old Walter had had health problems and walked with a cane, but his voice was strong and his intellect sharp. In fact, Walter delivered a short sermon during the service.

After church services, Robert and I walked with the Krauses to a local Chinese restaurant. It was located beside a beautiful lake near their home. When we finished our meal, we returned to the Krause's home, and Walter told me the story of his life. Robert recorded the interview, and Edith Krause interpreted between German and English.

Born July 5, 1909, in Schneidemuehl, a city now located in Poland, Walter was the first child and only son born to his parents. His parents were not married yet when he was born, but they married shortly afterward. His father was a *brunnenbauer*, a well digger. His mother worked full-time for another family; therefore, Walter lived his first six years with his maternal grandparents.

Many changes occurred when Walter turned six years old. At that time, he went to live with his paternal grandparents, who were relatively wealthy. His grandfather owned a factory. Not only did Walter change his living conditions; he also began attending a Lutheran school. Many of the children at the school were poor, and their families were certainly not as well-off as the Krauses. Walter felt sorry for the children who were poor. Each day before leaving for school, young Walter would beg his grandmother to give him extra food in his lunch, which he, in turn, later gave to the children in his class at school. He not only gave the children vegetables out of the family garden but he also shared his grandmother's delicious cookies and candies. Even when he was quite young, Walter showed a generous nature—one that was evident throughout his life.

When I learned these things about Walter's nature, I was reminded of my interview four months earlier with Itani-san in Japan. She had similar sentiments about giving food to people in her neighborhood. I began to wonder if generosity was a trait common to all wise people.

Walter explained his motivations further, saying, "The children did not have enough to eat. They were from poor families. And my grandma gave me enough for them to eat. If I see that someone needs something that I have, I ask myself, 'Do I really need this?' Usually I don't. Then I will give it to them. We had a wonderful garden at my grandfather's house, and when children were out of their houses on the street, I would bring vegetables, cookies, or candies to them."

Walter's childhood memories reflect a normal boyhood. He had many adventures. "Our neighbors had two boys, Martin and Richard," he related. "They were Polish people, and they had no food or anything. To survive, they had to steal. I would bring rabbits home from the forest for them to eat. In return, they taught me how to steal. This happened when I was a little older than seven. There were lots of fish in a pond located in front of a rich farmer's house. At a time before Christmas, the fish were stolen from the pond—we boys just couldn't wait! We took a boat out one night for the fishes. I was very happy about being able to help poor people with these fish. However, when Martin and Richard wanted to steal a goose, I didn't dare to do that. Eventually, my grandfather put an end to our adventures, telling me, 'I won't allow you to go with those boys anymore.'"

When twelve years old, Walter briefly joined the Communist Youth, thinking that it would allow him to help people. When the boys in the group began to smoke cigarettes, Walter stopped attending their meetings. He had become ill from a previous experience with smoking when he was six or seven, and he wanted nothing more to do with it.

When Walter was thirteen years old, his beloved grandfather died. His life was turned upside down. He told me, "It was quite a shock. It happened at a time when inflation was high, and the family had to leave our wonderful big house because my uncle, the one who should have continued the factory, was in the military, in action in France. Therefore, my family was destroyed financially. We were no longer rich people. I had to do chores! I had to clean the yard around my father's house. I tried, but my father was unsatisfied with my work. He spanked me. So I went to my grandma crying. She protected me."

Walter spent one last night, Christmas Eve, with his grandmother. After that, she moved away to live with her daughter in another city. Walter confided that being without his grandmother was a catastrophe in his life at that time. She had done her best to protect him from life's painful consequences.

Walter then went to live with his parents, who had long since married. He joined his three younger sisters, one of whom was blind. Walter's father wanted his only son to be a strong boy, not coddled by his grandmother. According to Walter's wife Edith, "He wanted to have a boy and not a *waschlappen* [a dish cloth]."

Although Walter's father was strict, he was also proud of his son. Walter had a good intellect and did very well at school; however, he often had no interest in the topics the teachers were presenting. He said, "I liked to go to school, but we were beaten at school, and I didn't like that. I had a good mind and was eager to learn. I had a good singing voice. I wanted to learn, but not always the things that the teachers wanted us to learn. I knew many things as a child, and I enjoyed learning things on my own."

Consequently, Walter left school when he was fourteen years old, primarily because he didn't like being beaten by his teachers.

When Walter was sixteen years old, he became an apprentice carpenter, and his life was transformed again. Missionaries from the Church of Jesus Christ of Latter-day Saints, the Mormons, came to Schneidemuehl. Walter described what happened then.

"When I was sixteen, the German missionaries from the Mormon Church came to our town. They were going door-to-door through town. Seeing them one day, the boys on the street said, 'Let's go home and get our dogs so we can chase those missionaries with our dogs!' I did not go for my dog. I had an Uncle Karl who had lived in America for a few years. He knew some about the Mormons, and he told my father, 'These are fine people. They have very good thoughts and teachings. Let them come to your house.' So my father invited these people into our house because he felt that he was well-enough versed in the Bible that he could confound them."

After the missionaries' first visit, Walter's father felt he hadn't done as well as he could, so he invited them back a second time so that he could be better prepared for their presentation. He still, however, could not confound them. He told them not to come back to his home; however, he and his brother asked Walter to go to the Mormon services on Sunday to see what it was the two missionaries were really up to.

Walter went. He felt comfortable being there. He soon wanted to go every Sunday. Walter's father gave him more and more chores to complete, making it difficult for him to attend church. But the men from the church would come and offer to help Walter finish his chores. Walter wanted to join this church, but his father emphatically forbade him from doing so. He was an obedient son.

By Christmastime, Walter became very ill. He was so sick, in fact, that everyone, including Walter himself, thought he was going to die. Walter pleaded with his father to let him be baptized a member of the unpopular "American" church. His father, of course, was frantic with worry about his son. Thinking he was granting Walter's dying wish, he gave his permission for his son to be baptized and join the Mormons.

Although it was February 1926, and bitterly cold, Walter was baptized by the Mormon elders, being totally immersed in the icy water of a local lake. He did not even bring a towel to his baptism. Arriving back home, he immediately thanked his father for allowing him to join this church; and furthermore, he promised never to disappoint his father. Nevertheless, when Walter recovered from his illness, he was disowned from the family because he had joined the Mormons.

But as Walter wryly stated during the interview, "In the end, it didn't matter because there was nothing left to inherit—no land, no jewelry . . . nothing."

The family lost their position, their wealth, and their lands because of the war and the economy. The Krause family name retained its honor, however.

The joining of this foreign church influenced Walter's attitudes, thoughts, and actions for the rest of his life. He actively supported the Mormons in every way he could. Once, Walter wanted to attend a church conference in Berlin, 300 kilometers (184 miles) away. He had no means of transportation. He decided to walk. His employer gave him the time off because he admired Walter's earnestness and willingness to walk all the way there.

"I walked from city to city—generous people gave me food—and I went on," he said. "Eventually I came to Berlin, but I didn't have an address for the conference I was going to. I only knew that the meeting was at the Lehrer Vereinshaus at Alexanderplatz. The whole church mission became alarmed when I didn't show up on time . . . . Everywhere in Berlin, there were Mormons who were told to be on the lookout for Walter Krause."

This story is a good example of Walter's tenacity. He didn't let obstacles stand in the way of what he felt he must do. He would always, throughout his life, go and try to do what he could, even when he had no idea of how he would accomplish it.

Shortly before he turned eighteen, Walter went what he called wandering for six to eight months throughout Germany. He earned money by playing the violin at dances and other gatherings. It was a time of deep depression in Europe. Walter considered immigrating to Australia but was directed by a man he met on his journey to go to Berlin for work instead. When he arrived in Berlin, however, he found out that there were no jobs there. He continued going from place to place, working for various families at odd jobs. His willingness to help himself made him lots of friends and gained him much admiration.

Walter eventually found his way to his aunt's home in Bad Saarow, and he got a job there with a master carpenter. Because Bad Saarow had a large lake, that winter, Walter worked repairing boats; but by summer, he was driving people from here to there in boats. He had a wonderful time there. One day, a Mormon missionary from the city of Frankfurt, came to him and said, "Brother Krause, we need you in Frankfurt (Oder)." So Walter immediately went to Frankfurt (Oder), and since he met his first wife while in that city, he felt he made a good decision. He married in 1932.

Walter started his own business as a carpenter in Frankfurt in 1932 as well—during the European depression. He said, "It was a hard, hard time. It became better when Hitler came into power. Things became better then because people got jobs. With one word, the industry bosses helped Hitler prepare for the war with their money. Young men could get work; they were given uniforms and food and lodging. The citizens of Germany were happy to be earning money again as the government geared up to prepare for war."

In 1940 Walter was conscripted into the German army (about the same time that Shimoguchi-san was conscripted into the Japanese army), and his carpentry business ended. Because he had befriended so many American and British Mormon missionaries, he was torn in his thoughts about fighting the Allies. Assigned to a panzer division of the German Wehrmacht, Walter served for six years, first in France, then in Poland, and finally in Russia.[9] He was grateful that he was given a duty where he wouldn't have to shoot anyone—he was assigned to be a cook.

During a war, however, even a cook in the army can be injured or killed. Near the end of World War II, Walter found himself in Russia, where he was wounded. He was placed on the last train out of Russia and Poland just before the Germans surrendered. When he reached Chemnitz, Russian officers took him by another train to Cottbus, the town on the German-Polish border where his wife and three children were living in a refugee camp. There Walter recovered from his wounds.

Cottbus had a small branch of the Church of Jesus Christ of Latter-day Saints. For a few months in 1946, Walter provided strong leadership for these people. Subsequently, he was asked to become an official missionary for the church. In this assignment, he spent years following World War II rebuilding homes and churches in many German towns. People throughout the small towns of East Germany knew Walter as a helpful person who was always available in times of need. He spent the years following the war as a carpenter as well as a leader in his church.

Early in the 1950s, Walter's wife asked for a divorce and left him. Walter was devastated. He became severely depressed during this difficult time in his life. Years later, in December of 1957, he married again. Edith Krause was helpful to him in his church callings, acting as his scribe and translator for many years.

Before the wall between West and East Germany was erected, many members of the Mormon Church escaped from Germany and headed for America or other areas. Walter and his family could have left as well—they were often in Berlin. But Walter counseled his family that they should stay in Prenzlau, behind the iron curtain in East Germany. He convinced many to stay.

Edith Krause explained, "I want to say that we all hated the Communist government—not the people—well, with the exception of those with the government. But then Walter said to us, 'Why should we not stay in Germany under Communism? We live only among the children of God. Everyone is a child of God. Many of them do not know that they are children of God—but we know it. Let us show them what it means to be a child of God.' I think it was so wise for him to say, 'Don't hate them, but show them how we can live as children of God. So be friendly to them!' I think that was the greatest thing. We tried to do it, and it gradually became better, and eventually it was wonderful."

By remaining in the DDR, members of the Krause family were denied many privileges. Because of church membership, religious people were denied certain positions and occupations in Prenzlau. They could not work as teachers of the youth. Nevertheless, Walter and Edith persevered. Walter continued to build homes and chapels, brick by brick. It was difficult to obtain building materials, but somehow he succeeded. He rebuilt his own home in Prenzlau—it was originally built over one hundred years ago.

Walter traveled many miles to minister to the needs of other church members—not only those living in East Germany but also in all the countries making up the Soviet block. In 1999, when ninety years old, he continued to inspire and serve others.

Although he did not claim to be wise, Walter had his own ideas about wisdom, explaining, "Wisdom does not mean to philosophize (to talk and discuss), but rather it means to *do* things."

I asked him, "How does one become wise today?"

He replied, "First, think about it—then do it. And then speak about it—or be silent."

Walter Krause, a heroic and legendary individual, became knowledgeable about the world and its peoples through experience, but also through educating himself. Even though Walter had only six years of education, those who knew him well credited him with being an intellectual giant. He was an avid reader of good books and a philosophical thinker as well. Edith commented, "When you meet people in Dresden and Leipzig, or maybe Wolgast and Neubrandenburg, and you asked them about Walter Krause, they will tell you that he is a wise man, but they may not be able to tell you why."

Walter passed away on April 14, 2004, at the age of ninety-four.

When it comes to wisdom, perhaps the most important *learning* involves the personal development of an inner moral core—one that serves as a firm foundation for the courage to do what one believes to be right. The lives of the wise ones reflected upon in this chapter—and this book—point out the strength that cultural differences and individual effort can bring to knowledge and learning. Shimoguchi-san and Walter gained their knowledge through experiences and years of formal and informal schooling that differed yet gave both men similar understandings about what is actually important in life.

Endnotes

1.   www.worldwar2database.com/html/sinojapan.htm (Sept. 20, 2008). The Sino-Japanese Conflict actually began when Japan seized Manchuria in 1931. Heavy fighting broke out, and the fighting extended the war to include the Chinese Civil War. That conflict was stopped through the influence of the League of Nations, but Japan would not return Manchuria to China. The conflict started up again on July 7, 1937, when the Japanese were attacked at the Marco Polo Bridge. The fighting then extended across all of western China. By December 1937, Japanese forces captured the capital city of Nanjing. "The city would be punished harshly when it surrendered. As many a 300,000 Chinese soldiers and civilians would be executed, and rape, theft, and abuse was rampant."

2.   J. A. S. Grenville, *A History of the World in the Twentieth Century* (Cambridge, MA: The Belknap Press of Harvard University Press, 1994), 272. In the 1930s a small group of military, naval, and political leaders held a centralized power in Japan. Prince Konoe, Japanese prime minister (1937-39), and others believed that

Japan should be considered equal to the other great powers. They also believed that only a courageous show of force would bring respect to their country from the Western powers. "No Japanese must accept the insulting, inferior role the western imperialists assigned to him." Confrontation was inevitable as Japan sought to become the foremost power in Asia.

3   Samuel Eliot Morison, "The Rising Sun in the Pacific." *History of United States Naval Operations in World War II, 3:* (Boston, MA: Little, Brown and Co., 2001) 16-18. China was "still far from conquered . . . nothing but the scorched earth was left for the invaders." Thirty million Chinese have become helpless refugees, "and among these millions, Japan has already imposed forced labor, the first stage in her plan for China's permanent enslavement."

http://www.moreorless.au.com/heroes/rabe.html (Nov. 10, 2008). In 1940, Japan joined the Axis alliance with Germany and Italy in September, signing the Tripartite Pact, an agreement to carve up the world following victory in World War II. The Japanese made Nanjing the capital of their Chinese government. Later, Japan and the Soviet Union signed a neutrality pact, which effectively allowed the Japanese military to concentrate its forces in the South Pacific areas. Japan's forces were stretched thin, and after attacking Pearl Harbor on December 7, 1939, the United States and Britain declared war on Japan. "Over 60 million people have died during the Second World War, including over 11 million Chinese and nearly two million Japanese. The Second Sino-Japanese War has claimed between 30 and 35 million Chinese."

4   World War II database Web site: www.worldwar2database.com/html/sinojapan. htm (4 January 2006).

5   J. A. S. Grenville, *A History of the World in the Twentieth Century* (Cambridge, MA: The Belknap Press of Harvard University Press, 1994), 322.

6   Informational Pamphlet from Minakata Museum in Tanabe, Japan, 1999 Kamagusu Minakata was born in the same city as Shimoguchi-san (Tanabe, Wakayama Prefecture). An extremely well-educated and knowledgeable man, Minakata-san was a biologist, ethnologist, and folklorist. He had lived in Europe and the United States for fifteen years. He discovered many types of new fungi and mold and contributed numerous articles in scientific publications. He was also a civic leader in Tanabe. He and Morihei Ueshiba led a protest movement around 1909-10 in Tanabe against the shrine consolidation policy of the Meiji government—a policy that sought to reorganize and eliminate thousands of shrines throughout Japan.

7   Garold N. Davis, and Norma S. Davis, *Behind the Iron Curtain: Recollections of Latter-day Saints in East Germany, 1945-1989* (Salt Lake City, Utah: Deseret Book Co. 1996), 49.

[8]   Walter Krause's life was discussed in Garold N. Davis, and Norma S. Davis, *Behind the Iron Curtain: Recollections of Latter-day Saints in East Germany, 1945-1989* (Salt Lake City, UT: Deseret Book Co., 1996) and Thomas Monson, *Faith Rewarded: The Personal Account of Prophetic Promises to the East German Saints* (Salt Lake City, UT: Deseret Book Co., 1996).

[9]   A panzer division was synonymous with an armored division. The Germans had many panzer divisions, each having both armor and infantry. *Panzer* means armed fighting vehicle.

Chapter Eight

"Know Thyself"

This above all, to thine own self be true,
And it must follow, as the night the day,
Thou canst not then be false to any man.
—William Shakespeare, "Hamlet"

Many who have written about and researched the topic of wisdom associate the acts of self-reflection and meditation with those who are *wise*.[1] Self-reflection and meditation are similar although there are subtle differences between them. Self-reflection, often termed critical reflection, is the act of pondering, contemplating, and considering one's personally held beliefs and motivations. Meditation is a method employed to quiet the mind and is often affiliated with spiritual contemplation. Both self-reflection and meditation have been linked with the path to wisdom.

The reflective process begins with the assumptions.[2] Assumptions are those taken-for-granted ideas, commonsense beliefs, and self-evident rules of thumb that guide and inform our thoughts and actions. Most assumptions about life are formed in childhood. They are the heuristic mechanisms through which we account for the events in our lives. They confirm and shape our perceptions. We are able to make sense of events because assumptions underlie our understanding. Assumptions can constrain our learning, however. We are often so comfortable with our assumptions that we are unaware of them, and we certainly resist changing them.

The critical reflection process begins with the questioning of prior assumptions.[3] Most of the time this occurs in adulthood. That is the usual time for reassessing the assumptions of the formative years that may have resulted in distorted views of reality. The question *why* is often asked. Such a question invites self-reflection and often forces a person to examine previously unexamined assumptions. Reflection on prior assumptions usually broadens a person's worldview.

This critical reflection process is often precipitated by what Jack Mezirow (who named the process) called a disorienting dilemma[4] or what I have termed *adversity*. Events such as the death of a loved one, divorce, health problems, financial losses, and wars qualify as disorienting. These are situations that often lead people to change, to transform their assumptions, thoughts, and/or behaviors. Often, though it is difficult, people implement new paths or directions following such an event, wherein they try out a new role in life, acquire a new skill or knowledge (for instance, a person returns to school), and begin to reintegrate new perspectives into their lives. Critical reflection can lead to an empowered sense of self.

Critical reflection is essential to the development of wisdom. John A. Meacham, a psychologist who has researched the topic of wisdom, stated,

> The challenge of wisdom . . . is to continually discover the new doubts, uncertainties, and questions that are presented by a critical evaluation of one's current knowledge level . . . . Those people who become wise, then, would have adopted a mode of critical reflection that leads them to continually discover both answers and questions and new forms of knowledge.[5]

Meacham noted that while it is relatively easy to gain knowledge, it is more difficult to know what that knowledge is worth. Wise individuals continually reassess what they know—expressing their doubts and uncertainties.

This quality is not automatically associated with the formally educated. As Mihalyi Csikszentmihalyi (an imminent psychologist and prolific writer) noted, education can bring individuals to their own untapped potentials, but "*magnis magnos clericos non sunt magis magnos sapientes*" (the greatest scholars are not the wisest men).[6] This statement stands as a caution for those who would hope to find wisdom at a university!

Eastern philosophies claim that meditation enables one to reach enlightenment or wisdom. Meditation leads one along the path, the path of wisdom, to *nirvana. Zen and the Brain,*[7] written by neuroscientist James H. Austin, MD, describes how the brain functions in meditation. This book explains Zen as a means to facilitate change—or personal transformation.

Zen's meditative techniques emphasize training one's attention and bare awareness, and it stresses self-reliance, self-discipline, and personal effort. It describes an inner journey, but only as a prelude to the "going out." As a result, selfishness decreases and selflessness increases in a person. One is said to possess "a good heart." According to Eastern views, the self, such an important concept in the West, becomes increasingly absent as a person's wisdom increases according to Eastern views.

Cultures other than those of the West have also adopted a form of reflecting on and questioning basic assumptions. Most of the wise ones I interviewed reflected on their lives (although they didn't use that term) and found a way to make their lives eventually conform to the standard that they believed "right" for them. One Navajo man did so in his life. Like other wise ones, his path in life was not easy.

I assigned this respected Navajo medicine man the name White Elk.[8] He agreed to be interviewed for my research only if he could remain anonymous. I drove for three hours on Interstate 40 from my home just north of Albuquerque to meet with him. Crossing miles of picturesque high mountain desert and entering the Navajo Nation, I found White Elk's home within a beautiful piñon and juniper landscape—scenery so common to northern New Mexico and Arizona. As I drove onto his homestead on that sunny afternoon, White Elk emerged from his house and directed me toward his hogan, a large rounded wood-sided structure located in front of his Western-style house.

As I entered the door of the hogan, my eyes slowly adjusted to the semidarkness. There were windows, but simple cotton curtains covered them. The floor was formed from the compacted red-colored earth. In the center of the hogan sat a fifty-gallon black oilcan heater. Circling about the floor by the walls, cushions and pillows, obviously meant for people to sit on, offered comfort. A table was situated against the southern wall, and three wooden chairs were positioned at various places in the room.

White Elk, a friendly and gentle man, spoke very softly and calmly as we introduced ourselves. His voice reflected experience and authority. He immediately informed me, however, that he found it difficult to be interviewed about his life. He worried that stories from his past could negatively influence those individuals who presently looked to him for guidance. He had elements in his past that he had overcome—things that he feared might offer excuses to those whom he counsels. He did not want events in his life story to stand in the way of or to be a stumbling block to the progress of anyone else. Also, he mentioned that since he has made dramatic changes in his life, going back and thinking about the things he had moved beyond was not "healthy" for him. Although he found it difficult, he still wanted to help me with my research because he felt his life story might be of help to someone. He invited me to sit down next to him at the table in the hogan.

Although in all the other interviews with wise individuals I was able to record what was said, White Elk would not allow me to tape-record or videotape our conversations. He asked that I leave a tape and the tape recorder for him to use so he could record his life story privately. He told me, "I cannot talk about my life with you here." Some of this position was in respect to his role as a Navajo medicine man.

I left the tape and a tape recorder with White Elk. We agreed to meet again after he had recorded the events of his life.

I saw White Elk again two months later when I returned to pick up the audiotape that he had recorded about events in his life. The drive to his home once again was pleasant and easy. The mesas and arroyos of the western New Mexico landscape, reflecting the fall beauty of the high mountain desert, seemed to fly by. As I drove on the highway near White Elk's home, I immediately recognized the hogan. Pulling into the driveway, I honked once and waited in the car—as White Elk had instructed me to do. I waited a while, then honked again—rudely (I realized later) demonstrating my Western impatience. White Elk emerged from his house and graciously motioned me toward his hogan.

The hogan sat large and solid in the warmth of a morning sun, its entrance on the east, where the doorway stood to greet the sun every morning. I was beginning to realize the importance of the east-facing door. I had just returned from my trip to Kenya. I remembered that the round huts of the Kikuyu in Kenya also had east-facing doors. I had slept in a Kikuyu hut and had been awakened by the sounds of the stirring and chirping of the birds shortly before the sun showed its face on the eastern horizon. I realized that there is a sort of magic when the early morning rays of the sun reach into the space where you are living. The Navajo and others have always been aware of this blessing.

As I entered the door of White Elk's hogan, White Elk again invited me to sit down by him at the table. We conversed about wisdom and other things. White Elk suggested I take written notes for that conversation, which I did.

Our conversation about wisdom began with my question, "What is wisdom?"

White Elk's head lifted somewhat at that question. He answered, "Wisdom comes when one is completely matured. A person can become mature at an early age, in middle age, or in later ages—or not at all. Maturity is the ability to rely on one's self."

White Elk believed that self-sufficiency is a significant part of wisdom. He explained, "To be wise means that one must plan ahead—think of possibilities and plan for them. It is knowing what to do and what not to do. It involves making choices. If one is dependent on one's parents for help, one cannot obtain wisdom."

White Elk noted that in the West, wisdom is often thought of as a mental activity. But traditionally, wisdom is only possible when the mind and feelings come together. "Nature," he told me, "is wise. Nature itself has a wisdom, and thus, traditionally, we pray to elements of nature. We believe in 'nature over mind,' but just the opposite is the case in the Western way of thinking. There it's 'mind over matter.'" For that reason, White Elk believed that Westerners don't know what wisdom is.

White Elk believed that the Navajo language enabled people to be wise. He said, "Navajo enables people to know immediately what things are, because it uses, for instance, the sound or the doings of a thing to describe it."

He noted that he speaks Navajo whenever possible when counseling individuals who are in trouble and who have come to him as a medicine man to be made whole again. He counsels people with his prayers and teaches correct principles through those prayers. Lives are changed when he teaches traditionally because the mind and emotions are intimately involved. Balance is the key to life. "To be wise one must balance the mind and body together—otherwise you are off balance."

Because many people come to him for help with their physical, spiritual, and mental problems, White Elk gave me an example of how he works with them. He told me of a young man who had recently attempted suicide. The night before our meeting, the boy's mother brought her troubled son to see White Elk, following the third time the boy had tried to kill himself.

White Elk described how he tried to help this young man. "We entered the hogan. The traditional process started with a prayer that I said in order to enlighten the young man's mind. I immediately and directly addressed the boy's problem, asking him, 'Why are you here?' I then said to him, 'You are my brother. Your mother is my clan mother, therefore, I am her son also. You have a father and a mother. You were made from your father's sperm and your mother's egg and nurturing in her body. Even though your father is no longer present, he is still your father. You have brothers and sisters in your family. When your mother and father came together, you were made. God chose from the thousands of cells in the sperm of your father, just one cell—he trusted only one sperm cell—to become you. God trusted in you. His door is open. He calls for you. He knows you are coming and wants you in his arms. He says, 'My child, I want your help. You are an angel. Work for me. You have earned it now.'"

White Elk continued to teach and guide the young man. "What you did twice and tried to do again—if you succeed at that, the door shuts. What is it that you want? The second thing is that your mother is here with you. If someone came to hurt your mother, what would you do?

"The boy answered, 'I'd hurt them.'

"I then talked about John (not his real name) and the significance of his name. 'John is your *bellihana*, your white man's name—that's not you! You are your mother's. You hurt your mother when you do these harmful things to yourself.'"

White Elk then performed a traditional ceremony to help the boy begin his healing process and to restore balance and harmony to his life. He explained that prayer and ritual reach deep inside the psyche, and they are powerful tools.

White Elk believed that wisdom is found through one's mind and by one's feelings—one's heart. "The heart can't work if the mind is not functioning. It all depends. One can be wise at anytime in life, but 'wisdom falls with the leaf.' [It dies with each wise person!] To be wise, one must balance the mind and body together—otherwise, you are off balance."

Handing me the recorded tape, White Elk again expressing how difficult it was for him to complete. He also hoped that his story would be helpful to me. I returned to my home near Albuquerque. As I listened to White Elk's recording, I found that his life story reflected not only his adversities but also his joys.

Raised as a traditional Navajo, White Elk grew up in an isolated place on the Navajo Nation, living with his mother, siblings, and a grandfather. He explained on the tape, "I was raised mostly in the traditional teaching in my childhood days. The traditional way of life was taught. How to live the traditional life. How to survive. How to live an independent life . . . . The Navajo language was spoken in our family because we come from an uneducated family. Our grandfather is uneducated. Our mother was uneducated. My father passed away when I was only three months old. Mostly every day in the evening we talked our own native language."

By using the term *uneducated*, White Elk referred to the fact that his grandfather and mother did not speak or write English. They were certainly educated in terms of the knowledge held by the traditional Navajo culture and its worldviews.

When White Elk was four years old, he remembered going to a day school. He walked to and from school every day—rain, snow, or sunshine. His memories of the school were not pleasant. "The school was about one and a half miles from where we used to live. I used to walk to school with my brother and my sister. During the winter snow, we still walked. During the school, we were taught Western teaching. We were forced to speak English. We were told not to speak our own native language. If the teacher or one of the school staff should catch us talking Navajo, they used to chase us into the restroom and give us a bar of soap to wash our mouths out. This was done to teach us not to talk our own native Navajo language."

A stepfather came into the family, but shortly thereafter, he was killed in an accident. This unfortunate event left White Elk's mother to care for the family, the large herd of sheep, and the homestead. White Elk's mother pulled him out of school, keeping him at home to help her with the sheep that represented the family's livelihood. The other children in the family continued to attend school.

White Elk became skilled at caring for the sheep. As a seven-year-old boy, he lived on his own, camping in the mountains through the summers. He learned to cook. Even though he found it hard, he stated that he learned a valuable lesson—handling hard things gives one confidence and strength.

White Elk noted, "While helping my mom during the summer and even in the winter, I took care of the sheep. There were just about three hundred heads of sheep. That was a job! You have to handle everything. You've got to be like a man. You have to think about how to raise the lamb and about how that lamb needs to be nurtured. You learn this. Sometimes the mother sheep will just walk away from her lamb, and you need to reunify the mother and the lamb."

When he was fifteen, White Elk returned to school. He attended a boarding school in another small community. He started in the fifth grade. The next year, he went to another boarding school even farther away from his home. He enjoyed participating in sports. "I played every sport. I was good in track, football, and basketball. I was good at sports."

After only three years of formal education, six months into his high school training, White Elk decided to try to join the armed services. "A number of us that took the test, and all of my high school fellow students failed. I was the only one that passed that test for the armed service . . . . I chose the army."

White Elk was ordered to go to Albuquerque for his physical exam. He thought that he would be examined and then return to the Navajo Nation to finish his education. However, out of the three hundred men given physical examinations at that time, only five passed—White Elk was one of them. He and the other four men were immediately sent to a boot camp where proficiency tests were administered. His highest proficiency was in the field of communications; he was recommended to be a radio operator, and he went to communications school in yet another state. He received top secret clearance and was put to work coding and decoding messages. Subsequently, he was sent to help army units throughout the country.

At the beginning of the Cuban missile crisis, White Elk and his unit were deployed to the East Coast, where they boarded ships bound for points unknown. They eventually discovered that they were to be involved in a confrontation with the Russians.

"I found out that there was a Cuban crisis," said White Elk. "Russian warheads were being shipped to Cuba. We spent so many days—close to thirty days out to sea—only to find the warheads were returned back to Russia. And so we came back."

Then in December of 1962, White Elk's entire battalion was called up by President Kennedy to relieve the National Guard and the marines in Vietnam. They were to be shipped out at Christmastime. But White Elk added, "The late president Kennedy gave me a Christmas present . . . . I was given a discharge—an honorable discharge."

White Elk returned home and found employment as a police officer in a large city on the Navajo reservation. In his travels, he had the opportunity to meet many people—as he said, "Good and bad." The army trained him in the communications field, but he lamented, it also introduced him to alcohol and drugs—mostly marijuana.

Like many Vietnam veterans, these substances eventually became a problem for him. Under the influence of alcohol, he became mean tempered. In the meantime, he had married and was the father of two children. His first wife and his children left him because of his addictions. They told him he was mean and not good for anything. His life was in shambles.

One night, passed out on the street in freezing weather, White Elk almost died from exposure. He recorded, "But I still didn't learn a lesson. I continued on. On another occasion, I woke up and found myself in the middle of a Native American Church[9] meeting—having no idea of how I got there. It was a long distance from the city where I lived. The church congregation was praying for me. This event turned things around for me. I realized that the only person that you can change is yourself. That day I committed to changing the direction of my life. I continue to stand by that commitment.

"I also went to the Christians. I sat down with them. They also prayed for me. They taught me the scriptures. We held the Bible; we prayed together. My late uncle was a preacher. And I told him that 'I'm going to save myself.' And he prayed, and we always prayed when we came together . . . I restored myself. It was me. I wanted to change my life. I didn't have to go through counseling. I didn't have to go through the treatment. It was me. I wanted to change. I accepted the Great Spirit. The Great Spirit had placed me on this earth for a purpose—and that was not to destroy and abuse my life. From then on, I continued to train—to learn the Christian way, the Native American church way and our Navajo belief way . . . . It took a long time.

"It is hard for me to talk about. It brings memories, but yet I accept those."

Overcoming his addictions, White Elk began the long hard road to pull his life back together. "For if a person wants to change," he confided on the tape, "the individual has to accept the higher power and keep that belief. I know it's hard to say no. It's easy to say yes when somebody says, 'Let's go to town.' It's easy to say yes instead of saying no. But you don't know what's in the future. You don't know what's going to happen to you. If you say no and you stay behind, then you know that you are not going to be encountered by anything you can't handle. The only thing is that you have to pray."

Obviously, White Elk found strength in the spiritual realm. Critically reflecting on his life, he relied on traditional Navajo beliefs and customs as well as Christian teachings.

The Native American church[10] has good success with alcoholics. White Elk learned about the effects of alcohol on his life from them. He began to realize the person whom he wanted to be—"how I wanted to be respected." He accepted hard truths about himself. He explained, "Yesterday I was born, today I'm still learning. I accept the things that I cannot change but give it to the Holy Spirit—the Creator. Let him take care of it."

White Elk stayed faithful to his commitment to become a positive influence among the Navajo people—and through much effort and hard work, he is now a Navajo medicine man. He works to help others find spiritual, emotional, and mental harmony and balance.

Eventually, his children came back to live with him. They bring him joy. White Elk married again, and he and his present wife had a son, whom they both adore. White Elk has talked to him about his past life. His son is proud of his father and, after finishing college, has a goal to become a medicine man too.

White Elk concluded his tape by saying, "What my son says to me gives me hope. I have everything that I wanted to have, and I'm what I wanted to be—I'm helping people. By telling people who I am and where I was . . . I can just teach them, but I cannot change them. It's for them to accept what I've said and for them to accept it—and to change themselves."

Regardless of one's culture, wisdom is an intrinsically rewarding mental experience. It seems that White Elk considered his life, past and present, and his culture quite seriously. The process of reflection helped him change his perspective and to find a different view of life.

People who have developed an outlook that takes a broader view are often seen as wise. As the philosopher Robert Nozick observed,

> Wisdom is not simply knowing how to steer one's way through life, cope with difficulties, etc. It also is knowing the deepest story, being able to see and appreciate the deepest significance of whatever occurs."[11]

Taking a realistic assessment of one's life usually results in a self-transformation, like White Elk's, that involves "changing one's character so that it will conform more closely to the requirements of one's ideal of a good life."[12] In order to transform character, a person must make a commitment (tacit or known) to act in a way that is consistent with his or her beliefs and knowledge about living a good life. It means that the assumptions of one's culture, religion, family, and tribe have been examined and accepted or rejected. It does not constitute a withdrawal from the world, but rather an embracing of the world as one has come to understand it.

Contingencies of life must be expected. Misfortune, injustice, scarcity, death, war always loom on the future horizon. Through such calamities, individuals, as seen from the examples reported in this book, maintain their sense of self and their ability to choose the right actions. As the philosopher Robert Nozick wrote,

> The process of living wisely, pursuing or opening oneself to what is important, taking account of a range of circumstances and utilizing one's fullest capacities to steer skillfully through them, is itself a way of being deeply connected to reality. The person who lives wisely connects to reality more thoroughly than someone who moves through life spoon-fed by circumstances, even if what these try to feed is reality. Whether or not he proportionally pursues the full range of reality, he is aware of that range; he knows and

appreciates reality's many dimensions and sees the life he is living in that widest context.[13]

The wise ones are aware of, and accepting of, themselves and others. In other words, they know themselves and are empowered by that self-knowledge to change, to adapt to the reality in which they live, and to strive to become a person with integrity.

In both Eastern and Western traditions, reflection and meditation consist of making the mind and the body quiet, to try to remove oneself from the rigors of the day and the noise and cacophony of our lives, so that one "sees" what is important in one's life. "Wisdom involves seeing, but a special kind of seeing—seeing deeply, seeing the essence."[14]

Many people are virtuous and helpful to others. Most (but certainly not all) religions advocate tolerance and love for all people. Yet when the goal is to consistently behave in a way that shows respect for self and others that requires wisdom, many of us fall short. Such a goal is possible, however. It is through self-reflection that the will to change for the better is sharpened. The wise tend to be better at knowing themselves than the rest of us because they dare to look and to be honest about what they see.

Endnotes

[1] Aleida Assmann, "Wholesome Knowledge: Concepts of Wisdom in a Historical and Cross-Cultural Perspective," In *Life-span Development and Behavior, 12,* edited by D. L. Featherman, R. M. Lerner, and M. Perlmutter, (Hillsdale, NJ: Lawrence Erlbaum Associates, Inc., 1994); U. M. Staudinger, J. Smith, and Paul B. Baltes, 1992, "Wisdom-Related Knowledge in a Life Review Task: Age Differences and the Role of Professional Specialization," *Psychology and Aging 7:2,* (1992), 11271-281.

[2] Steven D. Brookfield, *The Skillful Teacher* (San Francisco: Jossey-Bass, 1990), 177.

[3] John Meacham, "The Loss of Wisdom," In *Wisdom: Its Nature, Origins, and Development*, edited by R. J. Sternberg, (New York: Cambridge University Press, 1990), 12.

[4] Jack Mezirow & Assoc., *Fostering Critical Reflection in Adulthood: A Guide to Transformative and Emancipatory Learning* (San Francisco: Jossey-Bass, 1998).

[5] John A. Meacham, "Wisdom and the Context of Knowledge: Knowing That One Doesn't Know," In *On the Development of Developmental Psychology*, edited by D. Kuhn and J. A. Meacham, (London: S. Karger, 1983), 30.

[6]   Mihalyi Csikszentmihalyi and Kevin Rathunde, "The Psychology of Wisdom: An Evolutionary Interpretation," In *Wisdom: It's Nature, Origins, and Development*, edited by R. J. Sternberg, (New York: Cambridge University Press, 1990), 42. The quote was taken from *Gargantua I*, 39.

[7]   James H. Austin, MD, *Zen and The Brain: Toward an Understanding of Meditation and Consciousness* (Cambridge, MA: MIT Press, 1999).

[8]   One of the reasons for choosing the name White Elk is because of another wise Native American medicine man, Black Elk, of the Sioux tribe. I saw similarities in the outlook and advice of these two men.

[9]   Religious Movements Homepage Project, University of Virginia. Religiousmovements.lib.virginia.edu (17 April 2006). The Native American Church is not traditionally Navajo. It is a rather recent phenomenon on the reservations. The Native American Church is not even a traditional indigenous religion. It has roots in tribal traditions, but is a Christian denomination, one that uses peyote as its sacrament. Peyote cactus (*Lophophoro williamsi*) had been used by indigenous peoples living along the Gulf of Mexico since pre-Columbian times, but during the stressful period in the 1880s, when Native Americans were being displaced and persecuted by the American Government, peyote became the basis of a new religion—the Native American Church. Because government had forbidden so many native rituals, many indigenous people were drawn to the ritual of this new religion. Officials of churches and the government alike protested this new religion. In 1918, the religion was incorporated in Oklahoma. It has gradually spread across the States. The Native American Church battles against poverty and alcoholism quite effectively. Ministers of the church are called "road men." They officiate in prayers and are assisted by others, called firemen, drummers. About 60 percent of the service is singing, usually in the native language. There are no professional or paid clergy. The Native American Church was opposed for a long time on the Navajo Nation but has been gaining membership steadily and is acknowledged more readily today.

[10]   Ibid

[11]   Robert Nozick, *The Examined Life: Philosophical Meditations* (New York: Simon and Schuster, 1989), 276.

[12]   John Kekes, *The Art of Life* (Ithaca, NY: Cornell University Press, 2002), 15.

[13]   Robert Nozick, *The Examined Life: Philosophical Meditations* (New York: Simon and Schuster, 1989), 275-276.

[14]   Lawrence W. Hinman, "Seeing Wisely—Learning to Become Wise," In *Understanding Wisdom: Sources, Science, and Society*, edited by Warren S. Brown, (Philadelphia, PA: Templeton Foundation Press, 2000), 415.

Chapter Nine

Self-Sufficiency

The final forming of a person's character lies in their own hands.
—Anne Frank

The name *Anne Frank* is familiar to most of us because she kept a diary. While many fifteen-year-old girls keep diaries, Anne's diary documented the conditions that forced many Jewish individuals to go into hiding during the dark days before and during World War II. Anne's diary, found and published after her death, recorded her fears, dreams, thoughts, and insights while she and her family and one other family spent a little more than two years hiding from the Nazi Gestapo in an Amsterdam warehouse attic. If caught, the eight people in these two families faced being sent to concentration camps where starvation, disease, and possible death awaited them.

By recording her thoughts and feelings in her diary, Anne brought the reality of that period of history in which she lived to our awareness. Wise beyond her years, Anne's words revealed that she had genuinely attempted to understand and know herself—and perhaps the rest of humanity as well. In the process, she realized many of life's important lessons. One of her insights is found in the third to the last entry of her diary.

Saturday, July 15, 1944

I have one outstanding trait in my character, which must strike anyone who knows me for any length of time, and that is my knowledge of myself. I can watch myself and my actions, just like an outsider. The Anne of everyday I can face entirely without prejudice, without making excuses for her, and watch what's good and what's bad about her. This "self-consciousness" haunts me, and every time I open my mouth, I know as soon as I've spoken whether "that ought to have been different" or "that was right as it was." There are so many things about myself that I condemn; I couldn't begin to name them all. I understand more and more how true Daddy's words were when he said: "All children must look after their own upbringing." Parents can only give good advice or put them on the right paths, but the final forming of a person's character lies in their own hands.[1]

Anne became aware of the importance of personal responsibility. Taking responsibility for one's self—thoughts as well as actions—is not easy. It determines the kind of person one is and the person one can become. Clearly Anne realized this. Three weeks after she wrote the above entry in her diary, Nazi gestapo raided the house where the two families had been hiding. They found and arrested Anne, her family, and the others, sending them to German and Dutch concentration camps. Anne died of typhus in the camp seven months later, but her thoughts and her insights—her words of wisdom—live on through her diary.

What Anne knew about personal responsibility at age fifteen is rarely mastered, even by people much older than she was. Perhaps living with the terror of being discovered and possibly killed helped Anne to grow up more quickly than the teenagers of today. Nonetheless, Anne knew that when it came to doing what was right, she was in charge. But also, when it came to doing wrong, she still was in charge.

Some blame God or others when bad things happen to them. Looking to others, government, religions, or secular organizations for solutions to one's troubles does not strengthen one's character. Assuming personal responsibility does. What our friends, relatives, politicians, employers, or even people in the media are doing and saying does not ipso facto mean that we too must do or say the same. Rather, what we choose to do should be a conscious decision; it is a reflection of our character.

Unfortunately, the realities of life can supersede good character. Under certain governments and in certain situations, people of good character lose their lives defending and refusing to abandon what they know to be right. Anne Frank did. Abraham Lincoln did. Martin Luther King Jr. did. Many others have. Living a life true to one's convictions requires courage. It requires trusting one's own intuition—being self-sufficient—and standing alone when necessary.

Such self-sufficiency is relatively rare. The self-reliance and self-sufficiency I am attributing to wise individuals refer mostly to their abilities to assume responsibility for what they do with their lives—physically, intellectually, emotionally, and even spiritually. Almost all of us know people who embody the age-old attitude of self-sufficiency. They are the "I can do it!" people.

According to his Kenyan peers, James Mbatia is such a man. He represents what many term a self-made man—one who has found considerable success in the business world of Nairobi. Many Kenyans know James's incredible life story since he had been the subject of several Nairobi newspaper articles. Jagi Gakunju made arrangements for me to meet with this African icon. I had no knowledge of James's adventuresome life before our meeting.

On a beautiful September afternoon in 1999, Robert and I walked out of the Nairobi Hilton Hotel where we were staying, planning to take a cab to James Mbatia's office, the meeting place that Jagi Gakunju had arranged. The shiny black English-style cabs were lined up and available in front of the hotel, as always. The hotel bell captain assisted us in hiring a cab whose driver knew his way around the crowded streets of Nairobi.

As we were driven to James Mbatia's office, we saw that the infrastructure of Nairobi was in shambles. Throughout the entire capital city of Kenya, only one traffic signal was working. That signal was located in front of the government buildings where, at that time, Kenyan president Arap Moi entered and exited. There were other traffic signals at intersections throughout the city—but none worked. Most of them, dark, merely swung by a few frayed wires from their mounting poles. The streets were crowded with people.

Upon arriving at James's office location, my husband Robert and I climbed up five steep flights of stairs to reach his office. I later learned that James owned the entire building and leased the office space on the four lower floors to other businesses. Unpretentious and utilitarian, the office buzzed with activity. We were ushered into a small sparsely furnished private office. James, a friendly, slightly gray, and balding fifty-five-year-old man greeted us with enthusiasm and an infectious smile. He was dressed in business attire—a well-tailored suit and tie. He immediately made me feel at ease.

Extremely polite, I noticed that James addressed the women in his office who were helping him with his various endeavors with great courtesy and respect. He answered his own telephone whenever it rang, explaining that he really didn't need a secretary to do the things that he could do himself. At the time of our conversation, he had recently retired as the president of one of the more important Kenyan banks. He was preparing to embark on a new phase of his life.

A member of the Kikuyu tribe, James was born in 1944. He lived an incredible life! The turbulent struggle for independence in Kenya, known as The Emergency, had significant repercussions on his early life. James was proud of his heritage as a Morana member of the Kikuyu tribe.

Explaining his heritage, James said, "We are Kikuyu to start with, which is probably the predominant tribe in this country in terms of number, in terms of location—because it is in central [Kenya] where the good lands are. I am not sure in terms of academic performance . . . . We are divided into three different main groups . . . . The original [group] was called *Morana*—that's where all the Kikuyu came from. And then they spread into two districts. One is called *Nyeri*, and the other is called *Kiembu*. So I and my grandfather [ancestors] still remained in Morana. It is this Kikuyu tribe [the Morana] that was the key prime mover in fighting for freedom. They are the primary members of the Mau Mau. So that is my background as far as the tribe is concerned. We are the most widespread tribe—almost anywhere you go, you will find a Kikuyu."

James asked if I had heard of the Mau Mau. The terrorism wrought by the Mau Mau movement in the early 1950s led to the Kikuyu people, who lived everywhere in East Africa, being brought back to Kenya and detained (or imprisoned) by the British. It was a significant uprising prior to Kenya acquiring independence from Britain.

Born before the Mau Mau Rebellion began, James was the first and only child born to his mother and father. His mother died when he was about four years old. Even so, he believes that she had an enormous influence on him.

James explained, "I would like to say that the death of my mother must have been a major contributor to the route I took [in life]. Because although my mother died quite early and I don't remember what she looked like, I remember what she used to say and do . . . . I do remember that before she died, she had tried to take me to school—very early. Very early, indeed! There weren't any classes for toddlers, and I hated it. But what surprises me is that many years after she departed, when I was on my own, I ended up liking education."[2]

Because his family was living in Nairobi, where his father was working, James was separated from his grandparents and other relatives. Sometime after his mother died, the British detained (arrested) his father, who was involved with the Kikuyu fight for independence. Eight-year-old James was left on his own on the streets of Nairobi.

James said, "As for my grandparents, there is not much I can say. Because my mother died when I was quite young—probably four—and then my father was detained for fighting for independence when I was eight. Thereafter, I never lived with anybody . . . . Since I was eight, I have lived on my own."

The British declared a state of emergency (a euphemism for war) in October 1952. Contrary to British expectations, the amount of violence then increased. The British claimed that the Kikuyu men who were rounded up and detained in Nairobi were not seeking independence—instead they labeled them as criminals. Many innocent people were ripped from their homes.

The treatment of the Kikuyu tribal members and others belonging to the Mau Mau was horrific. The British and Kenyan armies kept a running tally of how many Kikuyu they could randomly shoot. A reward of £5 for "kills" was given; proof of the "kill" was the cutoff hand of the victim.[3] Evidently, James's father was gathered up with the other Kikuyu men in Nairobi, like Muthoka and Mburu, and detained in one of the detention villages—places ringed with barbed wire, surrounded by deep trenches. James never saw his father again. Perhaps his father was one of the thousands of Kikuyu who were killed.

Obviously, James did not have the advantages of those African children whose families remained intact. He did not acquire a cultural background, a knowledge of how people are to live, or the important stories, proverbs, and beliefs of his people. Instead, he ended up alone on the streets of Nairobi—just a little boy of eight years. And he was not the only child who was orphaned. Hundreds of children had been left on their own when their parents were detained.

Without the advantages of any family to survive, James became a *chokola*, or "packing boy"—a person who steals or "pinches" wallets from people on the streets. Although some resources were available for the abandoned Kikuyu children living on the streets, James and many others survived by stealing. He was also *moska* (the Kiswahili word for *homeless*). At night, he and the other street urchins slept wherever they could find a spot on the streets of Nairobi. As we talked about this painful part of his life, he sighed and said, "That is exactly how I came about." He shook his head and then said, "Thankfully, I still had the ability to pull myself out of that mess."

James's life on the streets eventually came to an end. The British, after becoming aware of the problem they had created by arresting thousands of men, rounded up the women and the children and returned them to the central province—their original homelands. The young abandoned Kikuyu boys in James's age-group were gathered up from the streets of Nairobi and placed in "approved" schools. They were taken to the schools, in his words, "not necessarily to learn—but to be *tamed*."

In the "school," James discovered that he enjoyed learning—and that he had a talent for learning. So when he was released from the approved school in 1957, he went into business for himself to earn enough money to continue going to school. He became a "hawker" on the streets of Nairobi.

"Schools were cheaper then, anyway," he said. "But I had to support myself. In fact, I kept books most of the times—until the time I managed to go to a formal school for three years only. The rest I had to do on my own . . . . And so I went through that process until I managed to get myself not only out of the streets but to develop a successful career in accounting and banking."

There were people along the way who were kind and generous to James. He attributes that to the fact that he is highly principled, and he is not a troublemaker. He laughed as he confided, "I am not very controversial. I work extremely hard, and I can be very tough."

In 1972, at age twenty-eight, he married. He and his wife have a son. His family is the most important thing in his life—ahead of his career "or anything else."

An example of a self-sufficient person, James Mbatia is a self-taught man who, nevertheless, believed that his business skills are more of a talent than something that he learned on his own.

When I asked James about his academic skills, he humbly replied, "I cannot say I was brilliant. No! I wasn't stupid—but I was not one of the top. But I had one advantage—that was that I put in so many hours that at the end of the day I came out the best. So there I was—much like a donkey. I have always thought that that could have been a blessing in disguise—that I had nobody to cover me. I was on my own."

With an obvious aptitude for business, James modestly denied that he had accomplished anything unusual, saying, "I would like to think that as far as business is concerned, the bottom line is talent. You either have it or you don't have it. And if you have it, you can still improve it now through the process of learning. I'd like to say, first of all, that I cannot boast of being a big successful-in-business man. But I'm not a failure either."

In building his career, James rose through the ranks while working at the bank to became its president, but he also invested in properties and now owns and manages several Nairobi properties. At the time of our interview, he had recently officially retired from the bank. He immediately enrolled in law school.

As far as his plans for the future, he had a clear vision. He hoped to develop a business that he believed would provide badly needed jobs to some of his fellow Kenyans—people who desperately needed employment. He explained, "Now is the time that I am going to test my abilities to do business because I'm no longer employed and I can devote time to try my hand in new businesses. I want to develop my land—my properties. I would also like to start a business—a formal business. I am trying to go through some of my own thoughts on some other things to see what type of business am I going to be in because I would like to think that after fifty-five, I still have another fifteen very active years, and I want to make use of these fifteen years—not only for my own benefit but for the benefit of others."

James then stated, "What I believe is that people usually learn from others. Once you succeed, the examples you leave help others. The bank I was working for was started by somebody who had retired as a general manager of another organization. He started it at fifty-five, and it is now forty years old, and it is a name to reckon with in this country. It employs many people; it provides opportunities for many other people to develop. So I have always felt that I will be quite happy if I can start something that I can look forward to, or I can look backward—at seventy or seventy-two—and say, 'I started that.'"

When asked what he thought wisdom was, James replied that he felt it had to do with humankind's ability to differentiate between good and bad. He believed there is a perceptible difference—i.e., some things are good and other things are harmful to people. He was confident, however, that wisdom had nothing to do with money. Succeeding at what he attempted to do motivated him. "I want to succeed . . . but the only thing I know is that to be able to succeed, you must know what [it is] you are trying to achieve."

Being a contributor to his people and to society in general was James's ultimate goal. He said, "It is not an easy goal, but not all goals worth doing are easy."

At the time of the interview, besides attending law school and establishing a new business to give jobs to the people in Kenya where unemployment is a real problem, James was also working at establishing a business that would benefit the many South Africans who were living in Kenya. South Africans were having difficulty getting credit from Kenya's banks, and so James was helping them set up a credit rating service.

"It will be a bank with information—particularly data that can determine the credit ratings of people," he explained. "So we have been working on this for the last one year. Here in Kenya, I am the one who is helping them to get credit. The information will be sold to the companies and so on."

From the twinkle in his eye and his passion for his work, I sensed James would succeed in his new businesses—whatever they entailed. Here was a man energized by helping other people succeed. His responses to the interview questions were humble, honest, and direct. He was indeed an admirable self-made man—one who had assumed the responsibility for himself and his actions since he was a small boy. His sense of responsibility extended to those about him whom he believed he could help as well.

James could have placed blame for his circumstances as a child, could have allowed anger and frustration to block his progress, or he could easily have given up and not tried to make something of himself and could have decided to selfishly keep the fruits of his labors only for himself. Instead, he assumed the responsibility for what happened to him, for the path he followed in life, and he generously shared his talents for the good of others.

Another interviewed person who accepted responsibility for his situation, a trait of most wise ones, was Dr. Helaman Krause, a German chemist. After determining that he met the qualifications for inclusion in my research, I telephoned Helaman from the United States to ask for his participation. He speaks English but is more comfortable speaking German. Actually, at the time of my phone call, he was not sure if he wanted to be interviewed; however, when I arrived in Prenzlau, Germany, to interview his father Walter, Helaman generously agreed to an interview about his life.

Athletically fit and knowledgeable about many things, Helaman is gracious, humble, and kind. We met in the living room of the beautiful home he himself built. His lovely wife, Doris, joined us.

Prenzlau is northwest of Berlin, Germany, near the Polish border. Helaman was fifty-one years old at the time of the interview. The last of Walter Krause and his first wife's four children, Helaman was born in Prenzlau, in an old barrack previously occupied by soldiers in World War II that had temporarily converted into apartments. His three sisters are all much older. Eventually, the Krause family moved to an apartment in an older house, one with walls that were very thin. Helaman remembered that one morning, he woke to find his cherished aquarium frozen solid. "All the fish were dead. It was a very cold apartment, and one had difficulty getting any heat in there."

From the age of twelve, he lived behind the iron curtain under the Russian-led Communist regime of the Deutsche Democratic Republic (DDR). Prenzlau was 85 percent destroyed during the World War II; Helaman remembered the city being rebuilt from the destruction. He experienced the deprivations of living in East Germany during the cold war.

Helaman loved music and books. "Books have always been a part of my life. In my home, we have always read a lot. Books were always a great joy to me."

In addition, he loved to sail and, at least in 2004, still ran in marathons. Like his father, he is a member of the Church of Jesus Christ of Latter-day Saints. Because the church was so small in Prenzlau when he was growing up, he told me, "I had to learn quickly how to work and serve in the church."

Noting that he had many stories from his youth of the struggles that occurred after the war, Helaman told me some of them.

"It was the time after the war, and I believe it was on my fourth birthday. I received from one of my sisters a big roll of cookies. I remember holding it—thrilled that it was all for me. That was, for me, a very big present. In those days to have a roll of cookies so big and all for me—that was a feeling of happiness, a treasure one can't imagine today!"

As Helaman grew older, he began to accompany his father on trips to West Berlin, some fifty miles south of Prenzlau.

"The first time my father took me to West Berlin, he took me into KDW [the department store Kaufhaus des Westens], and there I saw for the first time chocolate bars heaped up like a tower. I still see it in my mind's eye—so much light and so much chocolate. My father said to me, 'Son, what do you want to have? Pick out what you want.' But I said, 'Dad, I want to get out of here!' I couldn't understand that there could be so much light and so many beautiful things that gladden the hearts of children. I wanted to get out of there. I couldn't decide which chocolate bar I wanted. It was too overwhelming!

"I accompanied my father frequently. He often went to West Berlin . . . . That was for me a totally different world. One went at that time to the west sector of Berlin. In the East, we still had brownouts, or blackouts, when the electricity was turned off. Then we had to light candles. Groceries were rationed, and we all had ration cards. One could not buy anything without the ration cards. It was different in West Berlin."

Helaman remembered well the day that the iron curtain was closed, leaving those living in East Germany cut off from the West. Until that time, he had been able to spend his summer vacations in West Berlin, living with his father at the church mission home where his father performed maintenance chores. Helaman played with the children of the mission presidents sent to Germany by the Church of Jesus Christ of Latter-day Saints from its headquarters in Salt Lake City, Utah. Suddenly, his world was turned upside down.

Describing the circumstances, he said, "I was in West Berlin during July of 1961. On Saturday, August 12, my father came and said, 'Son, we have to go home. There is a problem here in Berlin. There will be trouble.' So we traveled home, and the next morning we heard on the radio that the border to West Berlin had been closed. That was for me a sad and shocking happening—because I understood at once that I wouldn't see my friends again. I wouldn't be able to travel there again. It made me very sad, I must say. I could not go back to West Berlin and could not go there for twenty-five years—1961 until exactly 1986. Then in 1986 I went across the border, and after twenty-five years, I saw West Berlin again."

Even though the erection of the wall changed his life as he'd known it up until then, Helaman positively stated, "It didn't influence my life adversely. My life continued. My life was, after all, here in East Germany. Here I went to school. Here I had friends. Here I had my acquaintances in the church. So it didn't have such an influence on my future. It was for the moment a sad and cutting experience, but for the future, we knew that our life was here, and everyone tried to make the best of it."

During the twenty-five-year period that he and his family were sealed off in East Germany behind the wall, Helaman finished his schooling. For the most part, Helaman was able to go to school and live his religion without any problems. He couldn't leave East Germany, but other than that, "we didn't feel a disadvantage to life here." There were many youths in his church in other communities with whom he developed bonds of friendship. He met his future wife at a church event.

There were consequences for being a member of an organized religion in East Germany, however. Helaman had dreamed of being a high school teacher. That, however, was not possible. No person with a religious affiliation was allowed to teach the youth of East Germany. It was also difficult to be accepted to the university if you were a church member and if you didn't participate in certain political organizations, like the Communist Youth League. Nevertheless, in spite of the odds against him, Helaman was admitted to a university because of his high grades in school. He was such an exemplary and outstanding student that he couldn't really be denied.

Helaman entered the University of Greifswald in 1967. The problems came, but he faced them head-on. He was not a member of the Communist Youth League, and that was unusual for a German youth. "I should not have been able to make it to the university, but I had teachers who wrote me very good recommendations, and in this way, I got to the university."

One day, after a class discussion, his professor mentioned that the youth work was the most important thing happening at the university. He then asked those who were not members of a youth group to raise their hands. Although the teacher knew from the registration papers for the members of the class which students were not members of the Communist Youth, he asked the question anyway. Helaman, choosing to be honest, was the only student to raise his hand.

Helaman explained, "It was hard for me, and for a moment, I had to deliberate. I was only eighteen. Should I raise my hand or should I pretend not to have heard? It was a dangerous mood, but slowly and fearfully, I raised my hand. I still see how the teacher ripped his glasses off and jumped up and yelled, 'What do you want here? Where did you come from? What are you doing here?' I was shook up and pale, and after the meeting, he said that we had to have a talk about that. Afterward, my friends came to me and asked why I had admitted it, and that it was not necessary for me to have done so. I told them that that was something I had to do."

He continued, "That night, I had a very bad night, and I couldn't sleep. The next day, I decided that I needed to talk to the professor, and so I went to the building, asked the secretary where I could find this professor. I told her I needed to talk to him personally. So I asked him if we could talk about the previous day and if he thought that I would not fit in, if he wished for me to leave, to let me know soon so that I wouldn't waste too much of my time. After all, I could always become a street sweeper. He answered that we would talk about it later. But there was never another mention about it. I believe that he too wanted to meet his responsibility. After all, they [the professors] were all being watched. He never sought a conversation with me again during the five years I studied there."

As we sat in the Krause's comfortable living room, Helaman offered insight into his actions. "There is a time when one has to make the decision if one wants to be true to one's convictions or if one wants to make compromises, if one wants to take detours or if one wants to throw out any of one's principles. One has to have a bit of courage and stand up for one's beliefs. One could feel the respect others gave if they also were respected."

When I asked him where he obtained his courage, Helaman said that he found it hard to explain, but nonetheless, he did so eloquently. He said, "One has to live their life the best one can. If one has the strength, one shouldn't fear opposition, and one should seek another direction if one hasn't got the strength for it . . . . You can't force a person to do this or that. Each person has to decide for himself if he can carry a larger burden. One will then usually find more strength than one thought he had."

Helaman earned his Dr. rer.nat (*Doktor der Naturwissenschaften*), the equivalent of a PhD in Chemistry, from the University of Greifswald. After graduation, he married his lovely wife, Doris, a talented, gracious woman. Subsequently, the Krauses began their family, which included three children and a grandchild at the time of the interview.

Helaman found work at a hospital in Buchenwalde, a city south of Berlin, where he was a chemist and the laboratory supervisor. He also did postgraduate work in chemistry and medicine. He became a *labor arzt* (laboratory doctor). The couple then moved to Berlin where he was employed at the Institute for Pharmaceuticals Wesen. They chose to return to Prenzlau in 1977 where Helaman built the family's beautiful house by himself.

"Actually," he remarked to me, "the best times are those when one has a lot of work and is constantly involved with good things. I always say that the most beautiful time in my life was the time when I built this house. In those days, one really had to build a house by oneself. In this house, there is not a brick that I have not held at least three times in my hand."

Helaman continued explaining this difficult time of his life. "The day began at 5:30 a.m. One tried to get materials, bricks, cement, gravel, boards, nails—all the things we needed. This was not easy in the DDR. Then at 7:00 a.m., I went to work. At 4:30 p.m., I got home from work and worked until 10:00 p.m. on the house. That took two years, and it was a lot of fun. I always slept well—never was in a bad mood. I was always satisfied. I saw that things were happening. Everything grew upward. That was a hard, a very difficult time, but also a very nice time. I think that those times are the best when one has goals and is able to solve problems."

Helaman's work was in a hospital in Prenzlau—at least until the reunification of Germany occurred in 1989. At that point, he wanted to do something different than he had been doing. The people of Prenzlau were very anxious that he seek a position in the county government. Helaman, however, was a chemist and really had no desire to serve in leadership or political office. Nevertheless, when asked, he agreed to serve. When I met him in 1999, he had been the Prenzlau county administrator since 1989.

The position was an appointed one—second in responsibility for the county of Prenzlau.

Like most politicians, Helaman discovered that holding political office has its hazards. He had new and fresh ideas. For instance, he had the idea of turning an old abandoned church into a concert hall, which was done. However, politics has its downside as well.

There was a time when he was not at all popular with the townspeople in Prenzlau. Helaman had come to the realization that in order for things to work efficiently in the area, four small county governments would have to be combined. Therefore, he made efforts to combine the four governments into a central location. He even proposed an underground parking garage—quite a progressive idea for little Prenzlau.

At this point in the interview, Doris Krause, Helaman's wife, laughed and commented, "Well, such ideas infuriated many people. They were saying that Helaman Krause was turning Prenzlau into 'Krause Village.' We even stopped taking the local paper for a while because of the terrible and critical things being said about Helaman."

In 2004, elections were held in Prenzlau County, and in a three-way race for the *landrat* (land commissioner), Helaman garnered the most votes. However, the number of votes was not a majority, and a runoff election was held between Helaman and his opponent. Unfortunately, Helaman (espousing no political party) received one less vote than his opponent from Social Democrat Party (SPD). Thus, disappointments continue in his life; but for Helaman, they are viewed as leading to new opportunities.

During our interview, Helaman humbly neglected to mention many aspects about himself and his service to others. Those who know him, however, admire his character and the service he gives to others. I telephoned one of his nominators, Alberta Burroughs, to discover more about him. She informed me, "Helaman has friends all over Germany. They all delight in spending time with him. One of his best friends is a professor from Berlin—a titled man. Together they bought a small palace in a nearby town. They often meet there to rest, relax, and cook wonderful gourmet meals. Once a year they plan a musical or civic event, and they open the palace to the town's people. One year Helaman arranged a Pushkin concert. A Russian string quartet and soloist came to perform. First on the program was a talent show performed by the villagers and then the Pushkin concert. Helaman was asked to speak during an intermission. He is very good at extemporaneous speeches and is often asked to speak. It is always excellent—and is warm and genuine, no matter what the occasion."

Helaman spoke on this occasion about how Pushkin had influenced him in his youth. He personalized Pushkin for those in attendance at the concert. Alberta added, "He is an excellent teacher. He is very sincere and authentic, and he is very personable."

In our interview, I asked Helaman about his mentors. He mentioned that the people who impressed him have changed over the course of his life. Of course, his father, Walter (chapter 7), was an important mentor. "My father and I talked a lot. We were quite different. What I valued in him was that he could listen. He never stagnated. He had a totally different education than I have. He said that he had had only six years of schooling. No one knows this for sure. In spite of this, I am amazed how educated he was. He had read so much and had seen so much and had such logical thinking. He had so many life experiences. I had talks with my father over a wide spectrum of subjects . . . . I treasure these talks."

In a manner typical of the Western wise ones in my research, Helaman had difficulty identifying the wise people he has known in his life. He acknowledged receiving "wise advice" from people, however.

Helaman is a caring man who respects himself, his peers, and those whom he serves. It is no wonder the citizens of Prenzlau admire him. In addition, he is an excellent musician, appreciates art, is deeply religious, and is committed to serving others however and wherever he can.

As it was with Helaman Krause and James Mbatia, so it was with all the wise I interviewed. They maintained peaceful attitudes, in part because of their self-sufficiency. It also helped them to keep their lives in balance. Relying on and trusting themselves and taking responsibility for their own thoughts and actions is a hallmark of wisdom. The wise ones seemed to have a clear vision of their lives, believed in a definite direction in which they were headed, worked indefatigably to sustain themselves and their families, and lived lives of service to others. They did not count on the government or other organizations to solve the problems that they faced. In fact, engaging in meaningful endeavors and working hard to achieve their goals empowered them.

Endnotes

[1] Anne Frank, *The Diary of a Young Girl* (New York: Doubleday and Co., 1952), 274-275.

[2] Personal interview, September 8, 1999, Nairobi, Kenya.

[3] Thomas Pakenham, *The Scramble for Africa: White Man's Conquest of the Dark Continent* (New York: Random House, 1991).

Chapter Ten

Maintaining Balance

Wisdom never forgets that all things have two sides
—*C. G. Jung*

The word *balance* is used in many contexts—a balanced diet, a balanced curriculum, a balance of powers, balance of payments, balanced checkbooks, and a balanced life, to name only a few. Balance or integration appears to function as a mechanism for maintaining stability in situations, to "make life bearable and worthwhile."[1]

Wisdom is also about balance. The philosopher John Kekes noted that good lives, marked by moral worth and satisfaction, are identified with balanced lives. Living a balanced life in today's hectic and chaotic world is no easy task. It often means that we have to periodically regroup or to change our priorities and the directions our lives seem headed. Kekes wrote,

> The influences we encounter in normal living are heavily weighted toward keeping us locked into the ordinary perspective and point of view . . . . [T]here are a few people who seem to have been born wise and caring, or who developed wisdom at a young age as the result of special life circumstances. The rest of us need psychological/spiritual practices to ripen us, to shift the gestalt balance, to develop our mental adequateness . . . . We can change our personal situations in ways that alter the balance of influences to which we expose ourselves."[2]

Balance is similar to the psychological concept of *integration*. Balance involves selecting priorities. It involves the integration of life's experiences and the moderation of emotions and behaviors. Careful observation (self-reflection) is required to avoid getting out of balance.

Although all the people I interviewed inferred that balance is necessary for one to maintain a healthy perspective on life, the Navajo wise ones, perhaps because of their culture, stressed it emphatically. Balance and order are important concepts to the Navajo people. I learned about the impact of these concepts from conversations that I had with Philmer Bluehouse, a Navajo peacemaker (*nataanii*).

The late fictional writer, Tony Hillerman,[3] wrote mystery books situated in the Navajo Nation. [If you are a fan of his books, you'd recognize the similarities between one of his main characters (Navajo policeman Jim Chee) and Philmer Bluehouse.] I first met Philmer at the Navajo Peacemaker Division office in Window Rock, Arizona, where he was serving at that time as its director, supervising 243 peacemakers in communities throughout the Navajo Nation.

Navajo peacemakers are part of the Navajo justice system (*hozhooji naat'aanii*).[4] In 1982, the judges who adjudicated the Navajo Nation chose to revive the ancient indigenous process of restorative justice known as peacemaking. They did so because it was apparent that the prescribed court system of the United States government was not effective in solving many of the disputes on the Navajo Nation.

Because peacemaking incorporates old Native American ideas of justice, it reflects Navajo traditional values and experiences. It is different from most criminal justice systems that rely on adjudication between individuals to settle disputes. Rather, it "seeks to reconcile parties and repair the injury caused by a dispute through the active participation of victims, offenders, and communities to find solutions to conflict."[5]

Navajo peacemaking goes beyond mere retribution and punishment for crimes. It is a process of reconciling all the parties in a dispute. It restores the traditional concept (*nalyeeh*), which involves confronting someone who has hurt another person or persons and demands that they talk about what was done and the harm that it caused. Navajo spirituality plays an essential role in peacemaking. "The experiences of the ancient creator beings and spirit forces, taught in the creation scripture, create the context for Navajo dispute resolution."[6] It is the source for the *healing way* of the people.

The peacemaking process proceeds like this: Offenders and those who were harmed by them are brought to a session moderated by the peacemaker. The relatives of both parties are part of the session. The process begins with everyone introducing himself or herself in the Navajo way—"I am born to [mother's clan] and born for [father's clan]." A prayer[7] is said, and then "the action is put on the table. People talk about what happened and how they feel about it."[8] A lecture by the peacemaker follows—although it isn't really a lecture in the Western sense. It is more like using stories and examples to teach and give guidance for problem solving and an eventual healing. James Zion, writing in the *Journal of Contemporary Criminal Justice*, described it as follows:

> It is a process of communication whereby an offender learns the inaccuracy of the given excuse and begins to change attitudes toward others. It is also a process whereby others learn more about the offender's motivations and why the excuses are offered. The same holds true of the other participants who also hold false attributions [assumptions] about what motivated the offender. The process is guided by traditional teachings that tap the internal learned values of everyone in the group.[9]

A plan is then devised to deal with the problem. Ideally, consensus is reached. The plan may include what needs to be done to resolve the problem, to make restitution or reparations. Perhaps Navajo curing ceremonies may be agreed upon. At the end, *hozho* (a beautiful, healthful, and peaceful environment—balance) is reached. In a way, the peacemaking process is similar to family therapy,[10] but it uses traditional Navajo ceremonies and practices.

During my first meeting with Philmer Bluehouse, I asked him how Navajos viewed the concept of wisdom. He made a drawing with colored pencils as he explained that wisdom began with the creation. He explained the Navajo creation story to me, explaining its connection.

"In my mind," he said, "wisdom began in creation. It was formed at the time of creation, and then began the subsequent journey where those wisdom ideas were then implemented and placed into motion."

Philmer called the time of creation *La'i Naaghaii, T'sideezkeezgi* (at the thought of the Creator), but he explained that it had other names like God, the Trinity, Allah, or Jesus Christ. But for the Navajo, it was called the Singularity, or the Creator, which is neither male nor female, but rather a combination of both. The Singularity began with thought—it was the beginning of wisdom. The next sacred event was speech. Speech implemented the formation of wisdom.

He explained, "Out of that wisdom—out of that creator with the male and female concept being together—is the balance that we all possess. When we maintain balance within ourselves [in our minds, bodies, and spirits], wisdom is possible."

Philmer described the process of creation as a sort of metamorphosis—a process that involved balancing the oppositional elements of life. It began with a thought of the Creator, and that thought was followed by speech. "Words, like thoughts, are considered to have creative power."[11] Navajo ceremonies, involving speech, song, and prayer, review this creation process.

Philmer noted, "The descriptions are clear when you go back to creation and journey narratives, and the songs that are recited . . . . From the beginning there was a need for balancing the opposites as they came into being—such as chaos and order, or light and dark.

The Navajo researcher Gary Witherspoon explained the significance of the Navajo creation story from a Westerner's viewpoint.

> Thinking and singing the world into existence attributes a definite kind of power to thought and song to which most Westerners are not accustomed. It is rather obvious that the Navajo ontological conception of thought and speech is very different from our own.[12]

Navajo traditional teaching not only stresses the importance of thought and speech but of respect (kĕh) as well.

Philmer carefully explained this process, saying, "So now, in our language, in our way, our thought becomes reality through our speech (hazaad diyin). So be careful what you say. Be careful what you talk. You are making things into movement . . . your voice is very holy. Your thought (Ni T'sahaakees) is very holy. Be careful what you say. Be careful what you think. In other words, have respect (kĕh) and be responsible for your language, your words, and for your thoughts. This is wisdom."

The following day, I met Philmer at the Gallup Public Library to interview him about his life. He is of Navajo and Pueblo heritage and could trace his genealogy back generations. More importantly, he understood the spiritual qualities of his progenitors. He also had an understanding of himself and what his purpose seemed to be in life.

Extremely knowledgeable about Navajo customs and beliefs, Philmer patiently explained and described his life history, including the Navajo clan relationships and their meanings.

"We normally say that we are born for—so that makes us a matrilineal society. In that sense, I am born of my mother and I am born for my father.

My father is *Hoonaghaahnii* (the one who walks around you). His spirit—the spirit that was placed within [during the mist format of creation]—was the protector-warrior spirit. The other side of him, his gentle and peaceful side, is the philosopher spirit, *'ayoo da'aneeh*. So in that sense, my father's side is both the warrior and the peaceful one, the humble/ not humble one, the philosopher. This is very important—this duality, this balance in all creation."

Philmer spoke of his ancestors and described the spiritual significance they brought to his life. His maternal grandfather was *T'se Nee'ji' Kinni* (those who live on or below the cliff).

"My ancestors are the cliff dwellers in this region. History needs to be corrected. The people that they call Anasazi are still here. We have not gone anywhere. We've been here for a long time. I'm a living example. As my grandfather used to say, 'We came from Mesa Verde. We migrated to this area. We sought refuge among the people of this region.'"

Philmer's paternal grandfather was Hopi, Bamboo/Reed People (*Lokaa' Dine'e*). He was of the Red House *(Kinlichee'nii)* Many Goats Clan (*Clizzi Laani Dine'e*). The people of this clan migrated from the Pueblo Colorado (south of Santa Fe) to Jemez Pueblo and then sought refuge among the Navajo peoples.

"So in that sense, I am Pueblo first," smiled Philmer, adding, "However, I still call myself Navajo. I am a member of the Navajo tribe. Now my father's side is one of the four original clans. So in that sense, that part of me is Navajo—*Hoonaghaahnii*—the one who walks around you in the way of protector. The next clan is the Mesa Verde group, *T'se Nee'ji' Kinni Dine'e*—the ones who live on the cliff. The first clan group is the Bamboo/ Reed, out of the Hopi tribe. So you might say that I'm quarter Navajo, three-quarters Hopi or Pueblo. And in our tribe, it is that way. I think that is what makes us strong, because we are able to allow people to contribute and to share their knowledge to help one another." Balance.

The Navajo Nation has made itself unique and made itself self-sufficient to some extent. However, some reliance on government programs developed out of the war process that happened back in the 1800s.

Philmer Bluehouse was the last of six children in his family. When he was six years old, his mother had severe medical problems and was in the hospital for a very long time. He was looked after by an aunt from the time he entered first grade until he entered parochial school in seventh grade when his older sister took over. His sister was an important mentor to him. She and her husband operated a small store where he learned more than how to work.

Philmer explained, "My oldest sister taught me a lot about values. I was operating the cash register when I was about eight years old. I was helping in a little store and had a lot of responsibilities."

Even so, Philmer said that he felt very much alone as a child. He confided, "It was like I had to put my boots on and pull my boots back off all by myself." He did have some interaction with both parents, however.

Speaking of his mother and father, he said, "My mother is a Presbyterian. She taught me the way of the Bible. My father was very traditional. He did not speak one word of English . . . . He spoke only his language and could not write his name . . . . He used our traditional and cultural healing methods; he knew herbology—he knew those types of things. He taught me in that some. So for me, I cannot ever state that one is better than the other. I can't—because my mother's values complement my father's values. So they complement each other. In that sense, the whole idea that Christianity is better than what the heathens do is the fight I had to fight when I came out of here. I think that as a survivor of that situation that I can understand both ways."

Philmer grew up and was educated on the Navajo reservation. After going to school most of the year, he spent his summers learning traditional Navajo ways. Sometimes his father would take him from school in order to participate in traditional ceremonials. He attended public school until seventh grade, when he was admitted to the Otis School of the Presbyterian Ganado Mission in Ganado, Arizona.

In the late 1960s, Philmer had what he called a negative learning process, about which he said, "My free mind went out the door, and the inevitable came." He was expelled from the Ganado mission school and subsequently ended up in public schools again. However, he was eventually able to get back into the Ganado parochial school from which he subsequently graduated.

Because Philmer wanted to go into law; he went to college and majored in administration with an emphasis in pubic safety. While in college, he met his wife. It is important that a Navajo person not marry a fellow clan member; therefore, once the couple determined they were not members of the same clan, they married. His wife was raised as a strong Christian type person. To some extent, he explained, "She has kind of not exactly wavered from it but had to recover from it."

After their marriage, Philmer modified his plans to become a lawyer in order to support a family, which soon grew to include two sons. He said, "I have tried to modify my objectives, and I figured, 'Well, law enforcement is not a bad profession—as long as I was in the law.' So I figured that if I could I would try to be accepted into the police force of the Navajo Nation. I worked with them. I have also been a federal agent—working for the federal government in its counsel office here and providing cases to them."

As a police officer for the Navajo Nation for seventeen years, Philmer gained experience and knowledge. He perfected the "peaceful warrior" side of his spirit, explaining that balancing his law enforcement (warrior) side with his teaching (peaceful) side was a personal struggle.

When Philmer became a peacemaker, he had to figure out how it could be accomplished. The peacemaker program at that time was undefined. He described how he decided to proceed. "I was to go back and talk to medicine people, medicine women, and really bring that information forward. I love these kinds of challenges—to discover and then to share that with others. So in that sense, it's what I've been able to do with my life. And that's where I think the natural process of peacemaking then became a little bit clearer because I already understood the other side."

By taking the information of traditional peacemaking and coupling it with the Euro-Western philosophy of judicial process, Philmer was able to apply the information, where he could, to different situations and to different tribes.

"It's been very difficult," he said. "It is a very difficult journey because Euro-Western philosophy always wants to overbear. I am going through that right now. This one [Euro-Western] is trying to overbear this one [Navajo traditional ways]. It is trying to shut out the other . . . . I think my objective is to balance it. But at some point in time, I think that our people—if they finally realize that this balancing process is very important—will realize that by redoing the courts as we know them now, we would be going back to responsibility, proper relationships, and respect for each other, as opposed to having it be forced on us."

Philmer compared the Euro-Western court systems as those trying to treat the symptoms of a disease rather than its source—a specific crime and a specific punishment. Peacemakers, on the other hand, seek to find the "root causes" of problems.

Philmer believed, "Peacemaking does that because it includes the peacemaker, the perpetrator who caused a problem, and the person who was victimized. The extended clan members of the perpetrator and the victim are invited as well to come and discuss the issue. The idea is not to blame, not to label, but to recognize the need to talk about the issue realistically. To find out why the murder occurred. And how do we fix the spirit of that murder? How do I (a perpetrator) make amends? How do I (a victim) forgive?"

Philmer found it challenging to attempt to meld the two systems of justice together. "The rules were created to allow these two systems to function together. So in that sense, my challenge is to take this information, to make it applicable to everybody's situation and tribe. And then allow the court to do it together . . . . I think that my objective is to balance them," he said.

In Navajo peacemaking, the skills of reason (thought) and speech—used by medicine men—are utilized not to punish but to help everyone understand why events took place. The injured must be repatriated. "Because he's got relatives—or she's got relatives. So the peacemaking process is really a healing process."

Philmer noted that the balancing process is very important. It is related to the Navajo concept of k'ĕh. "I think when one understands that balance, then you understand self, you understand nature, you understand things around you. You establish what we call k'ĕh. K'ĕh, in my mind, is when we understand our self—the relationship within our self—that responsibility that the self has toward one another. In other words, the male/female side—how they interact and how they maintain the balance within your being. Now k'ĕh is respect, responsibility, and relationship."

Philmer had important mentors in his life. He especially felt that he was helped, nurtured, and mentored spiritually when first seeking for wisdom and answers on how to get the Navajo peacemaker program to work effectively. "I've had all kinds of mentors. The most important one was when I started with peacemaking. I came into the whole process with this idea that I can plan, [and] I can assemble information—from my law enforcement experience. And then that carried over to peacemaking. But I had to ask myself, 'Where do I find this information about peacemaking?'

"So for whatever the reason, I was compelled to go behind Window Rock—the actual rock itself. There is a little place back there where you can jog in a circle. Back there, I spent at least a month and a half every day at noontime—going back. And I would just select a spot—I called it my place. It's still there. It is just like a ten-foot-by-ten-foot area. I would sit. I would listen. I would look. I would smell—use all the senses. And I think, reaching back to nature, that those are the teachers that taught me in that little ten-by-ten-foot area . . . . I was able to see the relationship between the water and the earth. I was able to hear the earth. All these types of things. It's not like we can hear right now. It's a different level—the esoteric level. It's a holy level of understanding. So that journey—I think that was my greatest mentor."

When I met with Philmer Bluehouse, not only was he the coordinator of the judicial branch of the Navajo Nation's peacemaker division, he was also studying to become a Navajo medicine man—a long process and an important transition in his life. He told me that he was being mentored and guided by many wise men, his clan brothers, on the Navajo Nation. He has since begun practicing the "flint protection way" and the "crystal-gazing sacred diagnosis" ceremonies of the Dinĕh. He heads his own company, the Bluehouse Peacemaking Services, and is involved with writing Navajo common law (the Navajo Law Project) as well as furthering the peacemaking idea with other cultural entities.

During my interviews with Philmer in 1999, he spoke of his future plans, saying, "There's a lot of transition that happens in life. I want to get into the community more. I think that is an important thing for me. And maybe at that point, it will come full circle for me. I started with community, and then went into Western-style law enforcement, and then peacemaking, and then back to community."

He is now back to the community.

Philmer believed that people need to discover their own strengths. "I think we are all created with an impression, an imprint. And the challenge is to discover those imprints and weigh them out and balance them out. That's part of our growth. That's a part of our wisdom getting."

Asked why he believed he had been nominated for my study, Philmer attributed it to his innate ability to teach and to talk to people—Western people like myself. He does it well. I will long remember his instruction in Navajo ways—the importance of thought and speech, the importance of respect, the duality in ourselves and on the earth, the need for one to balance the positive and the negative, and the importance of k'ĕh—balancing the values of responsibility, respect, and harmony. The Navajo philosophy is one of beauty and balance.

Interestingly, many psychologists and other wisdom researchers have included balance as a significant factor in wisdom.[13] Robert Sternberg, perhaps the leading psychological researcher into the concept of wisdom, has put forth a well-respected theory, the balance theory of wisdom. The balance referred to in Sternberg's theory is a balance maintained between a person and the environmental or the psychological context that exists in each particular situation. Information, emotions, or impulses in themselves are neither wise nor unwise. "Because wisdom is in the interaction of person and situation, information processing in and of itself is not wise or unwise. Its degree of wisdom depends on the fit of a wise solution to its context."[14]

Sternberg suggests that tacit information, knowledge one knows without knowing one knows it, plays a large role in making wise decisions. He defined wisdom as "the application of tacit knowledge as mediated by values toward the goal of achieving a common good through a balance among multiple interests (intrapersonal, interpersonal, and extrapersonal) to achieve a balance among responses to environmental contexts (adaptation to existing environmental contexts, shaping of existing environmental contexts, and selection of new environmental contexts.)"[15] Sternberg's model stated that a person's values mediate how they use their tacit knowledge. He did not define what values these are or even, for that matter, the role played by the concept of the common good. The wise ones I met had clear ideas of both. They lived balanced lives—balanced in body, mind, and soul.

Endnotes

[1]   Aleida Assmann, "Wholesome Knowledge: Concepts of Wisdom in a Historical and Cross-Cultural Perspective." In *Life-Span Development and Behavior, 12*, edited by D. L. Featherman, R. M. Lerner, and M. Perlmutter (Hillsdale, NJ: Lawrence Erbaum Associates, Inc., 1994), 194.

[2]   John Kekes, *Moral Wisdom and Good Lives* (New York: Cornell University Press, 1995), 31.

[3]   Best-selling author Tony Hillerman wrote mystery novels set primarily in the Four Corners area of the Southwest. He passed away in 2009.

[4]   Eric K. Gross, *Evaluation/Assessment of Navajo Peacemaking*, NCJRS Document 187675 (U.S. Department of Justice Research Report, April 5, 2001). Navajo peacemakers are *naat'aanii* in Navajo tradition, a term sometimes inaccurately translated as "peace chief." Instead, a naat'aanii is a community leader whose leadership depends on respect and persuasion and not a position of power and authority . . . . Words are powerful in the Navajo language, and the dispute resolution procedure is "talking things out." The word *naat'aanii* has a word root that relates to speaking. A naat'aanii is someone who speaks wisely and well, with the content of the speech being based in Navajo tradition, often the creation of scripture and associated songs and stories. A *naat'aanii* has an opinion about the dispute, but it is not expressed as a command. A *naat'aanii* peacemaker is a teacher who participates in peacemaking respect because the community chooses the person based on his or her reputation. The Navajo process is also unique because of the

participants: they are not only the immediate disputants but their relatives as well. The relatives include persons who are related by clan affiliation as well as by blood. They participate in the process of "talking things out" and have significant input in the form of expressing an opinion about both the facts and the effects of the dispute, the parties' conformity to Navajo values, and the proper outcome of the dispute.

5   Eric K. Gross, *Evaluation/Assessment of Navajo Peacemaking*, NCJRS Document 187675 (U.S. Department of Justice Research Report, April 5, 2001).

6   James W. Zion, "The Dynamics of Navajo Peacemaking," *Journal of Contemporary Criminal Justice* 14:1 (February 1998), 58.

7   Ibid., 63.

8   Ibid. Prayer prepares the parties for the "talking out" to come, commits them to engage in that process sincerely and "in a good way," and starts them on the beginning of the process of reconciliation to achieve *hozho* through consensus.

9   Robert Yazzie (the Honorable). 2000. Navajo Justice. http://daga.dhs.org/justpeace/reflective/navajojustice.pdf (24 October 2006).

10   James W. Zion, "The Dynamics of Navajo Peacemaking," *Journal of Contemporary Criminal Justice* 14:1 (February 1998), 68.

11   Robert Yazzie (the Honorable). 2000. Navajo Justice. http://daga.dhs.org/justpeace/reflective/navajojustice.pdf (24 October 2006). The Honorable Robert Yazzie, chief justice of the Navajo Nation explains, "Traditional Navajo law requires families to take responsibility for their family members. It is not a coerced responsibility, but one that comes from the respect and love people should have for their relatives. In peacemaking, the relatives of those who hurt someone else come forward to help with restitution and to watch over their relative to be sure he or she does not offend again."

12   Gary Witherspoon, *Language and Art in the Navajo Universe* (Ann Arbor, MI: The University of Michigan Press, 1997/1995), 17.

13   Ibid., 22.

14   Labouvie-Vief, (balance in thinking); Kramer (balance in cognitive, affective, and conative self-systems); and Kitchener and Brenner (balance in points of view). In *Wisdom: Its Nature, Origins, and Development*, edited by R. J. Sternberg, (Cambridge, England: Cambridge University Press, 1990).

15   Robert J. Sternberg, "Intelligence and Wisdom." In *Handbook of Intelligence*, edited by R. J. Sternberg (New York: Cambridge University Press, 2000b), 637.

Chapter Eleven

Altruism and the Common Good

*Every man must decide whether he will walk in the creative light
of altruism or the darkness of destructive selfishness. This is the judgment.
Life's persistent and most urgent question is "What are you doing
for others?"*

—*Martin Luther King Jr.*[1]

The stories of personal sacrifice for what is often termed the common
good are innumerable. They are found in every culture throughout time,
resounding in fairy tales, great literature, historical accounts, biographies, the
world's great wisdom literatures, and individual family histories. Within the
past decade, the term *common good* has come to represent a social behavior
that is almost coercive to individual choices for self-determination,[2] but
coercion had no place in the lives of the wise people I interviewed. Altruism,
or acting for the common good, occurs when an individual acts selflessly
through his or her own free will and choice, not someone else's idea of what
constitutes the common good.

An ancient example of altruism is seen in the heroic actions of Queen
Esther as recorded in the Old Testament. She risked her own life to save her
people, the Jews, who were in captivity and spread throughout Babylon and
Persia in about 525 BC. An example of altruism from the last century can
be seen in the actions of Oskar Schindler, who single-handedly also saved
Jewish individuals from the death camps during World War II—more people
than any other individual.

Consider also the actions of two doctors charged with quelling the
outbreaks of yellow fever and malaria among the men working on the

construction of the Panama Canal in the early years of 1900. In an attempt
to understand the pathology of yellow fever, as well as to prove the theory
that the disease was born by a particular kind of mosquito (*Stegomyia
fasciata*), Dr. James Carroll and Dr. Jesse W. Lazear, working under Dr.
Walter Reed, allowed infected mosquitoes to bite them. As human guinea
pigs, both contracted yellow fever. Dr. Lazear passed away soon afterward.[3]
These individuals freely sacrificed and risked their own lives to eventually
preserve the lives of others.

What is it that drives a person to put his or her life on the line for another
or to sacrifice his or her own material and physical goods for another?

Often cited as a beacon for wisdom, the common good, or altruism, has
been associated with wisdom since the time of Socrates. Two thousand years
ago, Plato, Aristotle, and Cicero were discussing the connections between
wisdom and the common good. Recently, the common good has been the
topic of philosophers and others who write about ethics, especially political
rhetoric. A contemporary ethicist, John Rawls, defined *common good* as
"certain general conditions that are . . . equally to everyone's advantage."[4] It
is often evoked when people discuss the many economic and social problems
that plague our societies (including health care, education, terrorism, and
the environment, to name a few).

Human selfishness, we are constantly reminded, is the cause of most
of our society's problems. In a 1992 issue of *Newsweek*, Robert J.
Samuelson noted,

> We face a choice between a society where people accept modest
> sacrifices for a common good and a more contentious society
> where groups selfishly protect their own benefits.[5]

That selfishness exists is a human truth. But those who believe that people
will not contribute to the common good without being forced or coerced by
governments or civic leaders see the common good from a rather limited angle.

People dedicated to principles of individual freedom and choice believe
that the common good is served through the *freely given* generosity of
individuals. These are individuals who, without force or coercion, give of
their wealth, time, and talents to benefit *all* who live in a society. These
altruistic people are the servants of the common good.

Wealth is not a necessity in order for a person to serve the common good.
For example, when people pick up their own litter from the picnic in the park,
they serve the common good. When they volunteer for community service—be

it Meals on Wheels, rocking babies in hospital nurseries, or serving as unpaid aides in the grade schools—they serve not only specific individuals but also the general welfare of their communities. They improve conditions little by little.

One might ask the question, "Since everyone benefits from efforts for the common good, don't most of us act with that in mind?" Unfortunately, we don't. Observers, including psychologists, have published pessimistic sentiments that most people act selfishly in their own interests, not for the common good.

Some reasons for this perceived inaction of individuals toward the common good are

1. people will never be able to agree on what constitutes a *common* common good;
2. the common good infers that everyone is eligible for its benefits—including even those who work against the common good in what they do and say. It is argued that those who do not support the common good undermine the community; and
3. the burdens of society are not shared equally by all its citizens, and thus some groups sacrifice more than others for the common good. Many claim this is unfair.[6]

The above three reasons as to why the common good does not function well in modern societies are drawn from the overall perspective that *everyone* (especially government bureaucrats) *knows* what the common good entails, and the only way the common good will be achieved is when everyone complies with the idea of a common good imposed on society by civil authorities.

Yet in ordinary life, this view is problematic. It appears that legal institutions do not even always sustain the common good. In the United States and Great Britain at this time (2009), individual rights and freedoms seem to be in peril. Long before the world's current economic crisis, one group of researchers noted, "We seem to be hovering on the brink of disaster, not only from international conflict but also from the internal incoherence of our own society."[7]

This group also concluded,

In thinking about what has gone wrong, we need to see what we can learn from our traditions, as well as from the best currently available knowledge. What has failed at every level—from the society of nations, to the national society, to the local community, to the family—is integration. We have failed to remember "our community as members of the same body," as John Winthrop[8] put it. We have committed what to the republican founders of our nation was the cardinal sin: we have put our own good as individuals, as groups, as a nation, ahead of the common good."[9]

In contradiction to this pessimistic viewpoint, during the course of my research, I have observed the opposite. I have seen that those known to be wise do work and will work for the common good, even when others about them do not. The wise ones helped friends and foes alike with specific problems, and they tried to improve existing conditions any way they could. They regarded all people equally. They were aware of the problems that people in their own cultures (and even other cultures) faced.

The wise ones also exhibited a real sense of caring for others and the environment—a finding that was predicted from the past discourses on wisdom in the literature. Aleida Assmann, a German psychologist, for instance, wrote,

> The wise person abstains from the desire to change the world according to one's desires. For this reason, wisdom is rediscovered at the end of a century that has seen the most violent and most destructive schemes in the history of mankind. The impulse is no longer to change the world but to stabilize it and preserve the ecological balance.[10]

Bethwell Kiplagat, a distinguished Kenyan, is certainly a laudable example of a person working on his own for the common good. Even though he was an extremely busy man, he graciously consented to talk with me about his life and his views on wisdom.

After another cab ride through the crowded streets of Nairobi, my husband and I arrived at Bethwell's modest office, located upstairs in the back of an unpretentious architect's office building in Nairobi, Kenya. We were ushered into his modest but attractively furnished office by a secretary. She invited us to be seated. We met at noon on September 9, 1999, and I suspected that Bethwell was skipping his lunch hour to meet with me.

Bethwell soon entered the room and sat down behind a large desk. An impressive man, he was wearing a well-tailored dark suit, white shirt, and tie. Fit, well groomed, and articulate, he looked and acted the statesman he is. Humble and devoutly spiritual, he spoke persuasively and thoughtfully about his life and his guiding philosophy. In his calm, soft, and authoritative manner, Bethwell addressed often-difficult topics with reassuring words that were remarkably moral, respectful, and wise.

In fact, he taught me a great deal about wisdom. He told, and even created, entertaining stories to clarify his points. An eloquent speaker, he explained that he never used prepared notes or a script when he spoke, explaining that he responds "as the spirit directs." His great love and respect for the people of Kenya and Africa, and for people in general, was apparent.

Bethwell's ancestors, he explained, were Nandi tribe members, an egalitarian society. "I come from a group called the Nandi. These are the people who live on the plateau of western Kenya—west of the Rift Valley. Originally pastoralists, they settled fairly early over the last century and did mixed farming. Even though the majority of the people always had livestock, they did not depend entirely on cattle."

"So I come from that tradition—that group." Bethwell continued, "They are a Nilotic-speaking group that extends all the way to Sudan and up to the borders of Tanzania. It is one large ethnic group, with different languages. It was a very highly structured society. We had what are called age sets.[11] Everyone belonged to an age set. Within their specific age set, individuals underwent ceremonies of initiation—marking one's movement from childhood to manhood. This was the period that caused you to follow the wisdom [of the tribe]."

Bethwell learned the traditional ways of the Nandi from his grandmother. At one point, he stayed with her for several months. "My grandparents on both sides were very simple folks. I only knew my grandmother on my mother's side. The others died when I was young. I didn't know them. They had not gone to school—neither had my mother. They were, in many ways, very traditional. It was a good tradition."

Bethwell also spoke about his immediate family. His father, who died when he was 12, was a jack-of-all trades. He was polygamous (a custom of his Nandi tribe); he had two wives. Therefore, the family consisted of fourteen children. One of the wives had eight children; the other had six. At the time of our interview, all of his siblings were still living—quite a remarkable statistic for a Kenyan family of that size.

Speaking of his mother, he mentioned that she brought him up to be confident and positive. He said, "I actually had two mothers—both of them have died," he told me. "We lived together as one family. And again, through wisdom, we were able to live very humbly and very close together . . . . But within a very short time, there was a change."

That mentioned change was a move made by the family that placed them closer to a small city so that Bethwell and his brothers could go to school. The older members of the family remained somewhat traditional in their lifestyles, but the children learned of a different world. Bethwell soon learned to speak Swahili and English. He went to a primary school close to where the family lived. After that, he attended a Christian secondary school in Nairobi. Education became an important influence in his life. The Christian schools encouraged him, and his teachers and friends inspired him.

When I asked Bethwell about the individuals who had most influenced him in his life, he replied, "What motivated me were my teachers—some of my teachers were very good—and also some friends whom I met. My friends were much older than myself. They, in a very strange way, took me even though I was very young, and we used to have very deep conversations and discussions—about things, about life, about the world. They encouraged me to go on with my education . . . . I continued on until I finished."

"But also, my school was a great influence. It was a school with values—values about service, values about quality, values about justice, which I absorbed, as it were, in attitude. Blended with that was my own culture—unconsciously, of course, since one is never conscious or deliberate with one's own background. So there is that blend of the African wisdom, the Western wisdom, and the Christian wisdom—all mixed up. And I think I was produced from all that!"

Bethwell continued to explain, "Through that very process, I gained one of my own basic philosophies about life. Coming from the Christian background as well as my own tradition is the idea of a fundamental importance of life and people—all of us being members of one family. We are all children of God, having his image."

He added, "I'm using the Christian language. That's something I believe very, very strongly and something I work for."

Bethwell's firm conviction that all people are important has been evident as he has labored throughout his life to help others.

Following high school, Bethwell went to the Makerere University in Uganda, a small university that was a constituent college of the University of London. He studied the sciences and graduated in 1963. Following his graduation from college, Bethwell made the decision to take a year off so that he could volunteer with other young people to work in the rural areas of Africa.

This service was eye-opening for Bethwell. "I took a year off after graduating in 1963, and I went and did voluntary work for a year with other young people from all over the world. There were about fourteen or fifteen of us. We lived and worked together in the rural areas—building schools and helping people in the rural areas. That was a very good experience to have after my graduation."

Bethwell next found work with the World Council of Churches, and he moved to Geneva, Switzerland. After a period, he was transferred back to Kenya. His entire career has been involved with international politics, regional politics, and world globalization. In 1978, he was appointed the Kenyan ambassador to Paris, France. Following that assignment, he served as the Kenyan ambassador to London, England. Returning to Kenya, he then served as a cabinet secretary in the Kenyan Ministry of Foreign Affairs for nine years.

Having traveled extensively all over the world, Bethwell had technically retired when I met with him in 1999; he was still working full-time as a consultant, however. He was one of the directors of Africa Peace Forum, an organization working for peace throughout Africa. He told me, "I enjoy it. It is painful sometimes, but we can see little positive changes." Bethwell had served as chairman of the Nairobi Stock Exchange, and he is a member of Kenya's constitutional review committee.[12]

As for his immediate family, Bethwell was married. He and his wife had three grown children. His overall philosophy of life reflected his great respect for all people, regardless of educational and cultural background.

Bethwell spoke of how he viewed the people who worked with him over the years. "In the early days, there was a feeling that those of us who had gone to school had the wisdom, the 'white man's knowledge,' and that it was superior. 'It will develop you,' we thought. But as you begin to undertake development work, you realize the tremendous reservoir of knowledge and of wisdom that all people have. And so, translating that into the places where I worked—whether as an ambassador or as a parliament secretary—I recognized every single person in the organization, first of all as a member of my family. Secondly, they are of intrinsic value. And thirdly, they have knowledge and wisdom, which is important to enable them to express. So writing off people because they may not have been as highly educated or rich or something else—that is something that I don't do. You listen to people; you listen together."

Working tirelessly around the clock to resolve the serious problems that confront Kenya and all of Africa, Bethwell attempted to help individuals, and eventually nations, to understand how they could help themselves. He labored for what he considered the common good of all Africans. Describing a time when African countries in the United Nations were bemoaning the fact that their countries had not been given money or even attention from the World Bank—even though at that time (as now) most African countries were suffering with desperate financial burdens.

Bethwell explained his viewpoint on this matter. "For Africa to resolve its problems, two things have to happen. First, we need to own the problem—the ownership. I consider this great 'wisdom' that the spirit has given me. And it's very interesting—the reaction all over is very positive. I say, 'We Africans own *all* the problems. Don't look anywhere else. Don't blame anybody else. Take it on board. Whether it's underdevelopment, whether it's corruption, whether it's conflicts. Take it!' Because I believe once you own the problem and you say, 'It's our problem,' then you've faced the problem."

"The next immediate question after we own the problem," Bethwell continued, "becomes, 'Now how do we overcome this problem?' If you don't own it, it will be always outside your 'force,' and you will be looking for somebody to blame or to take the responsibility for the problem—which they can never take. It has to be you . . . . I'm not saying that we should never be concerned with the World Bank, but first we must say, 'This is our problem!'"

At the time of the interview, Bethwell was working out the direction for his future endeavors. He noted that he was going through "a change—a shift—in his life." As he reflected on his own life, he felt that he wanted to spend the rest of his life helping to rebuild and encourage others.

Bethwell encouraged people to be altruistic and to understand the common good. Showing individuals that they have a stake in their own problems, he often convinced them of their own responsibility to act. He did this not through lecture or scolding but through wise example—his own or those of a metaphor or a story. For instance, he talked of the problems in Kenya with plastic. I had witnessed that both the streets of Nairobi and the rural countryside were thickly littered with plastic bags, plastic bottles, plastic sheeting, and other items.

Bethwell deplored this condition. He noted that he took ownership of this problem by never personally accepting plastic bags when he went shopping. "Plastic is a big problem with us. So every shop I go to, if they give me plastic bags, I say, 'No no no. Please. I don't use plastic. Do you know the dangers of plastic?' And they say, 'Why?' And then I explain why plastic is a problem. Now when I go to those shops, I find shopping bags made from degradable material. So we talk. I leave the thought there, and then I go to another shop. Now there is an organization here that is trying to do a cleanup of plastics. We will go even further, and maybe one day, we will have rules about plastic."

Bethwell's hopes are coming close to fruition. In June 2007, the Kenyan finance minister banned the importation and use of the thinnest bags and imposed a 120 percent tax on thicker ones in his latest budget. Uganda, Rwanda, and Tanzania have also banned the use and import of thin plastic bags.[13]

Bethwell encouraged everyone to assume responsibility for their own problems and to resist the tendency to blame others. Even so, he opined that "the ultimate solution to Africa's problems is of a spiritual nature."

Explaining, he said, "What I am saying today is that Africa needs to take another look at its inner life—to put an emphasis on its spirit. I call it the spirit rather than just knowledge. We need to go back to the spirit . . . .

"And therefore, what I would like to do with the remaining part of my life is to put an emphasis on this area. To say what is important is not the money or the time that you give us [speaking of the World Bank], but first and foremost, it is to rebuild the broken spirit of our people. Because if your spirit is weak and broken, then it really doesn't matter what people do to you. You will not overcome whatever problems you have. But if that spirit is strengthened, then anything that comes, you'll face it . . . and then say, 'Now what can I do?'

"Some react, of course, and say, 'No, at the World Bank, the corruption is because of the president or because of the party.' And I say, 'Yes, but we take it on board.' We can say, 'This is our problem!' Now, once we have done that, we also need humility—not the humility of crawling on the ground. You will say, 'Now, I have brothers and sisters all over the world who have gone through this process. Where are they? What ideas do they have that can help me? But basically, it's still my problem.'"

Although denying that he was wise, Bethwell had a profound sense of what wisdom entailed. He spoke eloquently about it, noting that wisdom had at least seven aspects.

1. Wisdom is a guide for a wholesome life. Bethwell explained, "Wisdom represents the wholeness of life. It is a guidepost to help so that one doesn't get into difficulties in life. There are so many roads, as it were, in life, and wisdom . . . will lead you to a wholesome life.

A wholesome life would mean, for me, an inner life—a relationship with one's self that is integrated and wholesome."

2. Wisdom encompasses the rules that enable people to live harmoniously together. "Wisdom is the guidepost, if I may use that term, that enables one to relate to others in a way that brings harmony—in a way that enhances life rather than destroys life and in a way that helps one develop wholesome relationships . . . The manifestation of wisdom is sometimes [seen] in the rules that, through the ages, have distilled a sort of knowledge that enables communities to live harmoniously with one another."

3. Wisdom is equated with special types of knowledge. Bethwell said that it was sometimes difficult to distinguish what is specifically meant by the term *wisdom*. He believed that with wisdom "we are really looking to human behavior and what it is that guides human behavior." In this respect, he believed that indigenous knowledge contains much wisdom. It is a broad knowledge, relating to agriculture, health, and other topics that can guide people's actions.

4. Wisdom sayings and metaphoric stories are effective teaching tools. Proverbs are a common form of wisdom literature in Africa, as are stories about animals. Bethwell noted the importance of storytelling, saying, "Words of wisdom can be things that people say, like 'Don't do this.' But quite often, words of wisdom are in the form of a story. Stories are useful because they capture the imagination. Now in more primitive homogeneous societies, stories are the conveyors of a lot of wisdom. Stories about animals and stories about people are used to educate and to teach the community and even the younger generation how people live.[14]

"There are also sayings where I come from, for example, about mistakes. The idea is that everyone makes mistakes. So when somebody has made a mistake, the word [the saying] you use is 'Don't worry.' Even a cow that has but four legs will slip and fall, let alone you with only two legs. The chances of your falling are even greater. So 'Don't worry, we'll sort this out.' I would say that this response is also wisdom. It gives people inspiration. It gives people encouragement. So these are, I would say, words of wisdom15 that come in."

5. Religions and/or traditions and rituals transmit wisdom. Bethwell mentioned that religions "in a more sophisticated way" transmit

wisdom through "words that are spoken at the spur of the moment—words that can come out of old stories that are still told. But also wisdom is manifested in rituals that then convey a message to the community as a whole." Thus the wisdom of religion, through things that are said and done, helps a community survive.

Bethwell gave the example of the wisdom found in the African tradition that values children. "First and foremost, the wisdom is that the child belongs not to the father and mother but first to the extended family. But even more so, it belongs to the community. So that when one sees a child in difficulty, you do not ask the question, 'Whose child is this?' Instead, you say, 'He is my child,' or 'She is my child'—and you run and rescue. Secondly, if you see a child making a mistake that would undermine life and bring problems, either to himself, to herself, or to others, you intervene to correct that child. You say, 'This is not the way we do things.' That is the wisdom of the old tradition."

He continued to explain, saying, "The rituals and ceremonies of the group reinforce the value of respect. You respect people. Immaterial of their standing in the community and in life, people are respected. A great emphasis was also placed on respecting your mother and your father, but more mother than even father."

6. Wisdom is about equality. Bethwell espoused that all people deserve an equal voice. He gave an impressive description of how traditional tribal communities make decisions. "When people sit down to discuss issues of the community's problems that have arisen," he said, "one of the cardinal rules is that everyone has a choice whether to speak and has a chance to air his or her views. When the meeting is conducted well, you never interrupt a person until he is finished. Whoever is leading and facilitating the meeting may decide (this is now wisdom, intuitive wisdom, that comes in) to say, 'Now we have heard everybody. We will break, and we will go and sleep over it.' We use that saying 'You don't rush. You sleep.' So you go over and rest and let it, as it were, work its way through your mind, your system. Then you come on the next day and the facilitator will say, 'I think this is the way we should resolve the problem.' You know, it's all related to the wisdom, as it were, of keeping the community together."

7. Wisdom is discernment. In terms of the leadership of a family or a community or the nation, perhaps the most important function

of wisdom is discernment and knowing how to decide when to decide.

Bethwell explained, "Because it's not so much the technical knowledge that one needs—it's not so much the economics and so on—but the wisdom of discernment. Asking 'How do we manage this nation?' or 'We have this problem. What words can I use that will bring understanding and harmony among my people?'—that's also wisdom. It is also wisdom when you don't say anything. You decide, in this case, to say not a word. So discerning . . . knowing when to speak, what to say and what not to say . . . or knowing not to speak it all . . . is one of the tools that one uses in managing one's self and also managing the community. Without that, we are careless if we just depend on knowledge without wisdom."

Bethwell believed that it was crucial that wisdom be imparted to others. "Every century, every period, has its men and women of wisdom. The words these people speak and say all the time, their words of wisdom, are an enormous help to guide us."

He didn't have an absolute answer as to how wisdom could be transmitted or passed on, but he felt that religion was one way to impart it. Traditional stories were another. He lamented the fact that storytelling was no longer a strong tradition in Africa.

In January of 2003, I learned that Bethwell Kiplagat had been selected as the special envoy to the Somalia peace talks that were taking place in Kenya at that time. The intractable problems in Somalia require the wisdom of people like Bethwell. The goal of the Somalia peace talks was to end the fighting between warlords to unite the country of Somalia with Somaliland.[16] The problems in Somalia have been enormous. The talks had broken down completely in October of 2002, with the competing warlords complaining that the previous envoy, Elijah W. Mwangale, was not managing the talks well.

As the new special envoy, Bethwell hoped to bring all the interested parties together, utilizing his well-respected skills at bringing people to agree on a consensus. His would be the fourteenth attempt to try to resolve the Somali problem. Many Africans were of the opinion that if anyone could help unite the bickering warlords, it would be Bethwell. In an article on the Awdai News Network about Somaliland news, the talks were called the Kiplagat Mission.[17] Some called Bethwell Kenya's Nelson Mandela.[18]

The problems for Bethwell were legion in trying to keep the peace talks in Somalia on track. He faced many obstacles as he tried to get numerous people to agree on cease-fires and the constitution for a Somali government.

For instance, the location of the talks had to move from the Kenyan town of Eldoret to just outside Nairobi. Then the place of the talks had to be changed again because some Muslim delegates complained about the wild pigs running about the grounds at their hotels. The Somali warlords complained about the Ethiopian, one of the mediators, having too much influence; and in fact, many key warlords would not participate because of this.

One report from the talks stated, "Of those who signed a ceasefire accord in October, fewer than half were present at today's [February 25, 2003] session. But Kenyan mediator, Bethwell Kiplagat, remained upbeat. 'We are here to establish a united Somalia, a peaceful and prosperous nation through reconciliation,' he told the opening session of the conference."[19]

In 2007 he concluded, "The problem of Somalia can only be solved by the people and not by leaders alone. Let the people decide through free and fair elections which leaders and what government they want. After all, this is what the regions of Somaliland and Puntland have done, and they have enjoyed relative stability."[20]

On numerous occasions, Bethwell has been noted in the press as a peacemaker. He has helped to establish peace in Southern Sudan, and as of August 2007, hostilities cooled in Somalia. Unfortunately, in February 2009, the Somali Civil War erupted once more. In 2009, Bethwell continued to serve Kenya as the head of its constitutional review committee, another challenging appointment.

What is Bethwell Kiplagat's personal motivation? Why has he devoted his life to finding peaceful solutions for Kenya and Africa? First, he believes that all people are God's children—made in God's image. Second, he believes that God only wants the best for everyone. Third, he believes that all men and women have a divine spark within them that needs only to be kindled through kindness and understanding. "People need to be shown a better way—a wiser path." Bethwell attempts to lead the way for others.

Bethwell Kiplagat appears to possess sentiments similar to U.S. president Abraham Lincoln—a man whom many now believe was wise. Lincoln said, "I have an irrepressible desire to live 'till I can be assured that the world is a little better for my having lived in it."[21]

Even though there are many people who place their own selfish interests ahead of their neighbors, that was not true for the wise ones I interviewed. They were the kind of citizens that any country would be proud to claim. They projected their attention outward—to other people, to their surroundings, and to the problems in their communities—rather than inward on themselves. Remarkably unselfish individuals, they acted, without coercion, altruistically from their own value systems, of their own free will and choice, mindful of working for what they believed to be the *good* within their sphere of influence.

Endnotes

1   Martin Luther King Jr. was a Minister and Campaigner for Social Justice through Nonviolent Voluntary Action (1929-1968).

2   Manuel Velasquez, Claire Andre, and others, "The Common Good," *Issues in Ethics,* 5 (2) (Spring 1992).

3   David McCullough, *The Path Between the Seas: The Creation of the Panama Canal, 1870-1914* (New York: Simon and Schuster, 1977), 414. In August 1900, the Army Yellow Fever Commission thought that yellow fever was caused by "filth" or "fomites," soiled bedding and clothing of victims. The doctors' sacrifices convinced the authorities that action must be taken to eradicate the mosquitoes access to humans—especially all the foreign white people. Native Panamanians were often immune because they already had been exposed to some form of yellow fever in their youth. Once infected, if one survives, he or she becomes immune.

4   John Rawls, *A Theory of Justice* (Oxford: Clarendon Press, 1972).

5   Robert J. Samuelson, "We Face A Choice," *Newsweek Magazine* (1992).

6   Robert N. Bellah, Richard Madsen, William M. Sullivan, Ann Swindler, and Steven M. Tipton, eds., *Habits of the Heart: Individualism and Commitment in American Life* (Berkeley, CA: University of California Press, 1985/1986), xii.

7   Robert N. Bellah, Richard Madsen, William M. Sullivan, and others, eds., *Habits of the Heart: Individualism and Commitment in American Life* (Berkeley, CA: University of California Press, 1985/1986), 284.

8   John Winthrop was the Puritan leader who founded the Massachusetts Colony.

9   Robert N. Bellah, Richard Madsen, William M. Sullivan, and others, eds., op. cit. 284-285.

10 Aleida Assmann, "Wholesome Knowledge: Concepts of Wisdom in a Historical and Cross-Cultural Perspective, Ed. D. L. Featherman, R. M. Lerner, and M. Perlmutter, *Life-span Development and Behavior* (Hillsdale, NJ: Lawrence Erlbaum Associates, Inc., 1994), 195.

11 *Encyclopedia Britannica Online,* www.britannica.com/eb/topic-io42/age-set (24 April 2007). Age sets are traditional social groups to which every male belongs from birth. The Nandi age grade system is cyclical, with seven normal grades covering approximately 15 years each. A single full cycle being 105 years.

[12] Jerry Okunga, "Of the Killing Fields That Is The Constitution of Kenya," *Club Africa*. http://www.clubafrika.com/phpnuke/index.php (April 2, 2009).

[13] Suite 101.com. http://africatravel.suite101.com/blog.cfm/east_african_ban_on_plastic_bags (April 17, 2008).

[14] Bethwell Kiplagat told me an African tale similar to the Western tale of *Chicken Little*. It dealt with the need for everyone to work together:

> There is a story that in a way encapsulates what I was saying about the spirit—owning a problem and taking action. It is the story of a man who was riding on a horse along a path. Suddenly, the horse stopped.
>
> The man wondered, "What is this?" He saw a bird in front of him that was lying on its back with its two legs pointing upward. The bird was lying there, looking up.
>
> The man on the horse said, "What is this that you are doing?"
>
> The bird said, "Are you the only one who is walking through here who doesn't know what is happening?"
>
> The man said, "What is it that is happening?"
>
> "Haven't you learned that the sky is going to fall?"
>
> "So what?"
>
> The bird said, "Well, get down and put your arms and legs up and let the horse also do the same, and if you do what I'm doing and everybody else does, we'll be able to hold the sky from falling."

[15] Bethwell Kiplagat explained in a 1999 personal interview, "I put it in a story, which has been helpful to me, of the past and the future. Again, this arose out of people always looking back and complaining and saying, 'Things were better in the past.' 'Things were real in the past.' So, as I give lectures and talk to people, I give them the story of a person driving a car at night. There are no lights in our rural areas. It is very dark.

"A man was driving at night; another car came from behind with its full beam on, and at night, there was a reflection from the rearview mirror, and this reflection hit his eyes, blinding him. He could not see his way ahead. Even so, he tried to drive in this strong beam.

"But what he had to do in order to avoid an accident was to step aside and ask the person to dim the lights. And when the lights were dimmed, there was no reflection on his eyes, but the car driving from behind strengthened his own lights, and he was able to see the way forward even better.

"So as part of my own teaching, it is that the past is good, but if you put on full beam of your past, it will blind you from seeing the future. But you need the past to enlighten and strengthen the light that then you can use to see where you are going.

"So the wisdom of the past is important. You don't negate the past, but you allow it to light the future."

[16]   Arabic German Consulting www.arab.de/arabinfo/somaliihis.htm (Feb. 20, 2008). Somaliland is a very small area—about the size of England and Wales. Before 1960, it was British Somaliland. Somalia, a much larger area, lies to the south. Somalia is not a homogeneous country that speak one language; rather, Somalia consists of many people who are distinctive from each other in terms of their language, culture, and history. Somalia had been formed in 1960 from two former African colonial territories—British Somaliland in the north, a protectorate of England since 1886, and Italian Somaliland in the south, which has been a protectorate of Italy since 1889. On July 1, 1960, both protectorates were combined and the Independent Somali Republic came into being. But in 1991, rival clans began fierce fighting for territory within southern Somali. In the north, however, peace prevailed. Only the international community thought that the two Somalis were one country.

Mark Bowden, "Blackhawk Down: How a Relief Mission Ended in a Firefight," *The Inquirer* (Dec. 14, 1997). "How did Americans go from feeding Somalis to fighting them?" In an effort to find peace, in October of 1992, peace talks were initiated by the elders of the clans; and the conflict was quelled. However, people were starving and the situation was grave. America sent in troops on a humanitarian mission for peacekeeping and to help feed the people. The soldiers were not even protected by armored vehicles. One of the warlords, Mohamed Farrah Aidid, had gone to war against the Americans; and the elite American Delta Force had been sent to get him. However, when eighteen American soldiers were killed and seventy-three were wounded, President Clinton ended up withdrawing American support. Worse, Somalis mutilated the bodies of the U.S. soldiers, dragging their dead bodies through the streets.

[17]   Awdai News Network, "Veteran U.S. diplomat urges Washington to Recognize Somaliland," (August 11, 2004). http://www.awdainews.com (20 December 2004).

[18]   Jerry Okungu, in *Club Africa Portal* on August 17, 2007, wrote, "In my own judgement, Ambassador Bethwell Kiplagat is our own version of Nelson Mandela despite the fact that he has never been imprisoned or led a country like Mandela did. However, apart from his look-alike Mandela figure, in his own way he has achieved a lot for this hostile continent through his proven diplomatic and negotiating skills. Because of him and of course along with others, we now have peace in Southern Sudan and hostile tempers drastically cooled in neighbouring Somalia. As I write

this article I can state with authority that he is the current chair of eminent persons in the entire African continent dealing with governance reforms in Africa under the African Peer Review Mechanism." www.clubafrika.com/phpnuke/modules.p hp?name=News&file=article&sid=75 (24 August 2007).

[19] African Institute of South Africa (AISA) organized a one-day Somalia Peace Process Briefing last May 27, 2004, in Pretoria, South Africa.

[20] Bethwell Kiplagat, *Somalis Must Have the Last Word on Who Leads Them.* Somaliland Times, Issue 256, Kenya: *The Nation* (2007). Bethwell recognized that the key leaders of the UIC are on the United States' terrorists list, which motivates the UIC to avoid joining with the TFG. These men don't want to be deported and placed on trial. Bethwell wrote, "As unpalatable as it may seem, a way forward would be to remove them [the terrorists] from the list. The talks could be further enhanced and the people of Somalia given hope . . . Ethiopia is not going to just stand by and watch Somalia being used as a launching pad to destabilize it." Bethwell's insight was proved correct in January 2007 when Ethiopian troops took over Mogadishu and subdued the UIC Islamists.

[21] Abraham Lincoln's quote is from Gene Griessman, *The Words Lincoln Lived By: 52 Timeless Principles to Light Your Path* (New York: Simon and Schuster's Fireside Press, 1998).

Chapter Twelve

Concern For The Earth

The wise one sees himself in the Earth
The wise one sees himself in the Sky above
The wise one sees himself in the Air
The wise one sees himself in the River
The wise one sees himself in the Plant
The wise one sees himself in the Animal
He plays with his great great-grandchildren
The Fool sees himself in nothing, except himself
He goes to sleep early
—Traditional African Proverb/Song [1]

We in the West live in a time of heightened environmental consciousness—a time when many are beginning to be aware of the close connection and crucial interdependence between humans and the natural world. This is certainly not a new realization. Indigenous peoples have long considered the earth a sacred and beloved place; even though of necessity, they, like modern societies, exploit the resources of the planet just to survive. Humanity depends on the resources of the earth for survival.

Most native peoples understand the importance of what has been termed the web of life. "The 'web of life' is an ancient idea—one that has been used by poets, philosophers, and mystics throughout the ages to convey their sense of the interwovenness and interdependence of all phenomena."[2] The knowledge of the natural world possessed by some indigenous men and women is extensive and quite sophisticated. Among native societies, certain individuals (male and female), called elders, were, and still are in certain societies, thought to possess genuine wisdom. These characteristics that signaled their wisdom are the topic of this book.

There are people all over the world who address the earth in their ceremonial prayers and songs with awe, love, and respect. They intuitively sense the planet's nurturing role toward all life forms—toward "all my relations," as my Native American friends would say. To notice these unseen connections undoubtedly involves keen observational skills as well as an experience-honed awareness of one's world. George Eliot, a novelist, described such sensitivity when she wrote,

> If we had a keen vision and feeling of all ordinary human life, it would be like hearing the grass grow and the squirrel's heart beat, and we should die of that roar which lies on the other side of silence.[3]

Thus, being aware of humankind's relationship with the earth and her living creatures and plants is an undeniable aspect of wisdom. Even recent "scholarly" researchers mention the connection of wisdom to the natural world. Wisdom researchers Mihalyi Csikszentmihalyi and Kevin Rathunde expected that one obvious characteristic of wise individuals would be their interest in "the environment that sustains us."[4]

I was not surprised, therefore, when I found that the wise individuals I interviewed often mentioned the importance of responsibly caring for the earth's environment. No one spoke more eloquently of the earth's environment, however, than Wangari Muta Maathai, PhD, an incredible Kenyan woman whom I met in Nairobi, Kenya.

By Tuesday September 7, 1999, I had been in Nairobi for four days; and I had somewhat adjusted to conditions in the capital city of Kenya. The morning I was to interview Wangari Maathai, Robert and I left the hotel and found a waiting British cab. As we climbed into the back of the spacious vehicle, I gave the driver the address where my meeting with Wangari was to take place. It was the headquarters of the Green Belt Movement, located on Kilimani Lane, off Elgego, Marakwet Road, Adams Arcade. I sat back and enjoyed my ride through the streets of Nairobi. The cab driver, whose name was James, became a tour guide of sorts as he negotiated the crowded streets, which were in deplorable condition. The city had no money for maintaining its infrastructure. For instance, there were many problems with the phone system. The number dialed might not match the number reached, or calls that did get through would unexpectedly be disconnected.

As we drove along, I noticed that small patches of dirt on the sides of the roads were under cultivation—a few corn plants here and other greenery I did not recognize there. Individuals were selling anything and everything from the sides of the road—secondhand clothing being a favorite item. Secondhand clothing, generously donated by individuals in other countries, arrived in Kenya in such quantities that the Kenyan garment industry had been nearly driven to extinction.

Soon, James drove the cab into the expansive driveway of a lovely home. It was surrounded by green trees and lush plantings. We had arrived at the headquarters of the Green Belt Movement, established in 1977 by Wangari Maathai. I asked James to wait for us.

Before our meeting, I had no idea who Wangari Maathai was, nor what she represented to her fellow Kenyans. I knew only that she had been selected by many of her peers as being a wise woman. Jagi Gakunju, who served as my Kenyan cultural liaison, had arranged for our meeting but had not discussed her accomplishments with me.

I introduced myself to the receptionist inside the front door of the Green Belt Movement building, and soon after Wangari Maathai arrived. She led us outside to her *office*—the front garden. Robert set up the recording equipment as Wangari and I sat and talked in the ample shade of a beautiful African fig tree. I immediately felt at ease and even nurtured by the presence of this intelligent, warm, and passionate woman. Professor Maathai, as she is affectionately called by many people in Kenya, is an eloquent spokesperson and strong advocate for the environment as well as human rights.

In spite of her many exceptional accomplishments and the environmental leadership role she holds in Kenya and, indeed, the world, Wangari is an extremely humble woman. Elegant, dignified, articulate, and thoughtful, Wangari was most cordial and respectful to me. She told me of her life and her hopes for the people of Kenya with its forty-two separate tribal cultures.

Following the interview, I returned to the waiting cab. The driver, James, asked if I had met with Wangari Maathai. When I said "Indeed, I had," he proceeded to sing her praises as he drove back to the hotel. He told us that Wangari was a "strong and powerful woman" who was greatly admired and loved by the "common people" of Kenya. She was a friend to the poor, to the homeless, and to those who felt powerless in the world. She worked with the people on the farms and in the slums.

James also remarked, "Wangari is an honest woman. She speaks up—even to President Moi [then president of Kenya], who does not like her because she opposes his treatment of the environment and the people."

When I told James why I had been talking to Wangari, he agreed that she was an ideal participant for a study of the wise. James's glowing opinion of this incredible Kenyan woman was not the only one I heard; I learned much more about her from newspapers, and the same message was repeated by most of the Kenyans with whom I interacted. I learned from several of the cab drivers who drove me through the streets of Nairobi that Wangari had not let me know about all the times she had been brutally attacked by those who were threatened by her words and actions. She always spoke positively about her life, failing to mention most of the painful situations she faced—her own honing in the refiner's fire.

Wangari Muta Maathai was born on April 1, 1940, to a poor family of squatters in Ihithe, a small town nine miles from Nyeri. Her father was a mechanic who had the reputation of being an extremely strong man. Her mother was the second of his four wives (polygamy was common). When Wangari was three years old, the family moved to Nakuru in the Rift Valley north of Nairobi, where her father worked on a citrus farm in Tetu for a white settler. One of her earliest memories was picking pyrethrum[5] with other children.

When she was seven years old, her mother and siblings moved back to Ihithe, which, she told me with a wink and a smile, was "the most beautiful part of the country." Although she was not the oldest child born to her parents (she had two older brothers), following tradition, she took on the usual role for the firstborn girl in a Kikuyu family—collecting firewood, fetching water, and helping her mother with all the chores. She also helped watch over her two younger sisters.

Wangari's parents converted to Christianity (as had Muthoka [chapter 1]), and thus, Wangari and her siblings were the first generation of children to grow up as Christians. She noted that her family was "therefore introduced into a culture that was completely different—completely foreign."

Wangari recalled, "At that period in time, most of the Kikuyu people spent a great deal of time running away from their traditional culture, having decided or having been 'persuaded to decide' that it was inferior in some way."

Because her parents had been *persuaded* to be Christians, Wangari admitted that she didn't learn much about being Kikuyu from them. Her parents decided that their old beliefs were not good ones to follow. Both of her grandmothers had died; she knew only one of her grandfathers. His name was Kibicho Ngetha. But Wangari had an aunt whom she very much admired—"a wonderful woman who cannot read or write, but who is a wonderful, powerful woman in my life." Her aunt, Nyakweya, told good stories—traditional stories. She told the Kikuyu stories that were traditionally told to all children as they gathered around the family fireplace every evening.

Wangari explained, "In our culture, we women were very busy during the day. People didn't eat much during the day—they had snacks in the course of the day. The main meal was in the evening, and it was prepared after the day's work. So mother and children would gather around the fireplace, and as the food cooked, children were told stories. My aunt was a very good storyteller. In fact, I regret the fact that because we did not put much emphasis on that culture, today the culture of storytelling has died. The stories were very encouraging, and they managed to arouse a lot of curiosity and imagination in children. They were also very entertaining because my aunt was a very good singer, so she could sing along with the stories. I really enjoyed that."[6]

Actually, besides her aunt, Wangari credited several strong women in her life with helping her along her path. She especially gave great credit to her mother, saying, "Of course, in all of this, in the background was my mother. My mother too was virtually illiterate. But my mother was a soft, very soft, woman—very unassuming, just doing her job. She was forever encouraging me and making me feel like I was definitely on the right path . . . . I find that what I have come to value, even as I pursued education in a new culture, has now reinforced the very values that my people valued in their old culture."

Wangari credits her older brother N'deritu with making it possible for her to go to school. One day, he asked their mother why it was that Wangari did not go to school with him and his brother. He subsequently persuaded her that Wangari should attend too. This was at a time when education for girls was almost unheard of in Kenya. Wangari subsequently went to the Ihithe primary school run by the Presbyterians. Later, in 1951, N'deritu persuaded their parents that Wangari should continue on in school. He located a Catholic boarding school that she could attend, St. Cecilia's Intermediate Primary School.

Wangari said of his encouragement, "I'm very grateful that he thought that I too should go to school. He was very encouraging . . . . It turned out to be a very good thing because once I was in boarding school, the Mau

Mau movement started in this country. I probably never would have gone to school and would probably have been sucked into that conflict had I not been in the boarding school at that time—in a protective environment. Young as I was [she was eleven], I was able to go to school despite the conflict that was in the country."[7]

Wangari remembered her years in the boarding school and her association with the Italian nuns with gratitude. Her teachers obviously saw her talents and encouraged her to pursue her studies. From 1951 to 1956, she attended St. Cecilia's School, where she was encouraged to learn by a wonderful Italian nun named Sister Germana.

"She was a very lovely nun . . . . She was beautiful, and she looked just stunning in her white gown. She loved me, and she always coached me. She told me, 'You must continue doing well.' And I did well—partly because she was encouraging me, but also because she instilled in me a lot of desire to learn. So I could only see school ahead of me and nothing else—which was very helpful because at that time, girls married very young."

From 1956 to 1959, Wangari attended Loreto Girls High School in Limuru, outside Nairobi. It was the only high school in Kenya that African girls could attend. Wangari attributes her interest in science to one specific teacher—an older Irish nun, Mother Teresia.

"Mother Teresia Joseph was really the woman who put me on the scientific path because she too loved me, and we got along very well in high school. She was like the grandma I never had. She loved to take me to the laboratory to help her wash the dishes. She really put an interest in me of science and made me feel like 'Wow! I can do science!' So I became very interested in science."[8]

After graduating from high school in 1959, Wangari received a scholarship to continue her education in the United States. Because Kenya was then scheduled to become an independent country in 1963, many politicians of that day from various countries were anxious that local Kenyans would be prepared to participate in the postcolonial administration and the management of their country. John F. Kennedy, soon-to-be-elected president of the United States, was instrumental in arranging for six hundred Africans to receive the funds and support to continue their university training in the United States, where they could also learn about working in a democracy.[9] Wangari was one of those selected for this training. She and three hundred other Kenyan students [including U.S. president Barack Obama's father] were flown to the United States in September 1960.

Wangari Maathai attended Mt. Scholastica, a small Catholic college in Atchison, Kansas (now Benedictine College), where, she told me, "I spent four of the most wonderful years of my life." In 1963, she wrote a paper that foreshadowed the focus of her life's work. It was a paper on leadership—specifically on how to help and meet the needs of women in rural areas. She earned a BS degree in biology in 1964. She was accepted at the University of Pittsburgh in Pennsylvania, where she studied from 1964 to 1965, earning her master's degree in the biological sciences.

Returning to Kenya in January 1966, Wangari, who had accepted a position at the University of Nairobi, found that the job was no longer available to her—evidently at that time because she was a woman. She eventually became a research assistant in the Department of Anatomy of the Veterinary Medicine School at the University College of Nairobi—becoming the first woman to teach on the faculty—hence, her title "Professor" Maathai. She also pursued her PhD degree at Nairobi University and at the University of Munich in Germany.

Many firsts hallmark Wangari Muta Maathai's life. In 1971, she became the first Kenyan woman to receive a doctorate from the University of Nairobi. She was also the first woman in central or eastern Africa to earn the PhD degree. In 1976, she became the first woman to chair veterinary anatomy at the University of Nairobi and become an associate professor of veterinary science in 1977. She taught microanatomy and developmental veterinary anatomy at the university.

During this period, Wangari became alarmed about the cattle and livestock on Kenyan rangelands. In 1972, while conducting research into ticks as vectors for African east coast fever at the University of Nairobi's Veterinary School of Medicine, she became curious about the prevalence of these parasites among farm animals. In the interview with me and in an interview she gave to the *New Scientist* in 1999, she restated, "I wanted to know the prevalence of the parasite among animals, so I'd go to farms and collect ticks to find the rate of infection. I felt I was doing useful work, but when I spoke to farmers, their real problems were not the tick but the availability of water, the productivity of the soils, and the shortage of fuel wood."[10]

As Wangari soon discovered, the lack of water and fuel wood were widespread problems in Kenya. Soil erosion silted up the rivers with topsoil. She also noticed that the forests she remembered from her childhood were gone. They had been cut down to make room for the cash crops of tea and coffee. She knew that the environment was being challenged.

She explained, "The connection between the symptoms of environmental degradation and their causes—deforestation, devegetation, unsustainable agriculture, and soil loss—were self-evident. Something had to be done. We could not just deal with the manifestations of the problems. We had to get to the root causes of those problems."

In 1972, the United Nations was in the process of setting up the UN Environment Programme in Nairobi. Many environmental groups were also forming, including the Environmental Liaison Centre. This organization was formed, as its name infers, to facilitate communication between the United Nations Programme, Kenyan governmental environmental programs, and nongovernmental environmental groups. Wangari stated, "The Environmental Liaison Centre needed local people. I joined and got hooked."[11]

In their book on Wangari, Frances and Anne Lappé[12] quote Muta Mathai, one of Wangari's sons, as he described his mother's early attempts to grow trees in their home for Envirocare.

> Dad thought it [the growing trees seedlings] made the place look too messy, so my mother put the idea on hold. But she didn't give up. She saw what her husband could not see when he saw only a messy house.[13]

Wangari's transition to her life's mission began as she listened to rural women talk about their difficult lives. She told me, "Here [in Kenya] we were mainly considering, what are the problems that women face? Now, I was then teaching in the University of Nairobi. I considered myself a privileged woman in many ways—I didn't have the problems that many women in the rural areas were facing. Many of them were literally still living the life I had left as a child to go to boarding school . . . . The women in rural areas were still fetching water from the rivers. They were still collecting firewood. They were still struggling to get food. But here I was now. I had acquired a lifestyle that was quite successful and quite privileged."

Wangari joined the National Council of Women, an umbrella organization for women's organizations. "There, when I heard women talk about the need for firewood and the need for food, of diseases associated with malnutrition, when I heard women say that they couldn't produce enough food because they were very busy producing cash crops, like coffee and tea and such, it came home! Maybe the reason why I reacted to it is I am bred from that—I came from that. So I responded very quickly to the

[National Council of] women. I said, 'You know what I think? We should plant trees.'"

The chairwoman of the National Council of Women gave Wangari the authorization to go ahead with her idea, and appointed her as the council's chairman of the Committee for Environment and Habitat. Since then, Wangari has dedicated her life to humanitarian and environmental causes.

Wangari's description of her goals at the time of our interview was revealing of her character and motivations. "I try to teach adults about how to take care of their environment and how to take care of themselves, how to make decisions and be in charge of [their own lives]—because partly when you don't do that, then you destroy not only yourself but also the environment . . . . I try to say that in our environment today, we have a lot of problems. We are poor. We are overmining the environment. We are consuming pesticides and herbicides. We are killing the soil with all these chemicals. We are polluting our water, our air. And I say we are in the wrong bus, and we are walking toward the wrong destination. Because if you step in the wrong bus and if you walk toward the wrong destination, you will surely get into a lot of problems."

Wangari often uses the metaphor of walking on a journey or riding on a bus to a specific destination in order to help people understand her message. It is a powerful metaphor since walking or catching a crowded *matatu*[14] (a form of minibus) is the most common form of transportation in Kenya.

The idea to plant trees soon led to the establishment of the Green Belt Movement by the National Council of Women in Kenya (*Maendeleo Ya Wanawake*) under the direction of Wangari. Over 150 years, the deforestation of Kenya had wiped out three-fourths of the forests.[15] Alarmed at the increasing desertification of Kenya, Wangari realized that deforestation contributed to this phenomenon.

> [She] knew that when trees go, so do the roots that retain topsoil and capture what little water does fall. When trees go, so does the protection from the wind that keeps soil from blowing away. She knew that this meant villagers, mainly women, were walking farther and farther to get water and firewood. She saw the vicious cycle of forest loss, desertification, and communities' growing inability to feed themselves.[16]

To celebrate Earth Day in 1977, Wangari planted seven trees in her backyard, and thus began "a huge movement that has literally changed the face of Kenya."[17] Wangari told me, "It started me on the path that I'm still on."[18]

Seventy percent of the farmers of Kenya are women. In order to convince the women that planting green belts of trees on their land would be beneficial to them and to their land, Wangari personally went out to the poverty-stricken villages. She explained to the women living there that planting trees would produce several positive results for them: a sustainable supply of wood for fuel; an income of cash; and depending on the type of tree, a source of food. In addition, the root systems of the additional trees would help combat desertification of the land and would curb the erosion of the land's valuable topsoil.

Wangari's primary goal was to improve the livelihoods and nutrition of the women and children of Kenya, especially those living in the rural areas. She was aware of the lack of nutritious food available to them. Women had difficulty finding water that was not full of the insecticides and herbicides used in the cultivation of the cash crops of coffee and tea. They also were forced to walk longer and longer distances to find wood for their fireplaces. As a consequence of these factors, mothers were feeding their children a diet of white bread and tea.

Wangari offered desperate people hope. She taught them how to plant and grow trees—from sprouting seedlings to mature trees. She helped them introduce indigenous vegetables into their gardens. She even went into the school classrooms of Kenya, teaching the children the importance of preserving their environment by planting native plants and trees.

Wangari called her vast army of indigenous tree growers Foresters Without Diplomas. In the beginning, she had approached the governmental foresters, originally established under the British, with her proposal to have thousands of Kenyans (mainly women) planting trees to combat Kenya's environmental problems. These men laughed at her idea, telling her that only professionals could successfully plant trees.

The professional foresters of Kenya had indeed been planting trees, but the wrong kind of trees. They planted fast-growing soil-destroying exotic species, like eucalyptus, cedar, and pine trees. These exotic trees used enormous amounts of water. In spite of the skepticism of the foresters, Wangari asked for 15 million seedlings of native tree species. Originally, the foresters promised her as many seedlings as she needed, but that offer was soon withdrawn. Wangari's Foresters Without Diplomas needed so many seedlings that supplying them free of charge became financially impossible for the government.

Wangari Maathai was not discouraged; she persevered. The women could not afford to buy the seedlings, so she decided they could propagate their own. She taught the Foresters Without Diplomas how to find and propagate native tree seedlings. She cautioned them to keep the sprouting trees off the ground, where goats, chickens, and other animals might eat them. Small trees could be protected by surrounding them with prickly brush. The Green Belt Movement was on the move!

Today, although many men participate in the planting of trees, rural women still do much of the Green Belt Movement work. They manage the more than six thousand nurseries based in villages throughout Kenya. Originally, those individuals who planted trees were paid for every tree that survived. In the thirty-plus years since its organization, the Foresters Without Diplomas have planted more than 30 million trees. Trees have been planted on farms, in forests, on public lands, and on school grounds. In the process, individuals have found a source of income, food, fuel for fires, and material for fencing. In addition, people have become politically empowered, and the desertification of the land has been lessened. In 1988, the Green Belt Movement even expanded into the Pan-African Greenbelt Movement, bringing the principles of the Green Belt Movement to other countries.

Though her work has been extraordinary, Wangari has paid a high price for her vision. Wangari married Mwangi Mathai, a politician, in 1969. They had three children—two boys and one girl. Mwangi ran for parliament, and in the process of running for office, as politicians do, he promised jobs for the poor and improved living conditions. Upon his election, Wangari felt that her husband needed to make good on his promises. She organized a grassroots business, Envirocare—a business organized to support good environmental practices. The business involved growing and planting trees. Unfortunately, that business eventually failed.

After our interview, I learned that Mwangi, her husband, having become a member of parliament, was under pressure to control his outspoken wife. In the early 1980s, on manufactured grounds, Mwangi Mathai divorced Wangari. He claimed that she was too strong-willed and difficult to control. During the divorce proceedings, Wangari was jailed for speaking out against the judge. Her husband demanded that she stop using his surname; instead, she changed it by adding an extra *a*.[19]

During our interview, Wangari mentioned the divorce and, with a chuckle, added, "And we lived happily ever after—apart!" In another interview, she told Frances and Anna Lappé,

> I have paid a heavy price, which is sometimes what people fear. When you step forward, you get exposed. Sometimes you get criticized, sometimes you lose friends—I lost a friend called a husband.
>
> Sometimes people say, "Why do you take that kind of a risk that makes you lose certain things?" But for me it has never felt like a loss. I always feel like I'm walking. When I get to a point where I have to make a jump, then I make a jump. Sometimes I get burnt, sometimes I get crushed, but I cross over . . . . There's always another promise on the other side.[20]

Wangari has suffered loss and adversity throughout her life, and yet she maintains a positive outlook on life—one that inspires most people.

As we sat in the shade of the beautiful trees that graced the front yard of the Green Belt Movement building, Wangari spoke with passion about the wisdom of the indigenous peoples of Kenya. Her Kikuyu ancestors instinctively knew how valuable and essential the plants, trees, and animals were to sustaining life. Their oral traditions and stories reflect a great respect for the trees and the plants of the region. They believed that certain trees should not be cut down—the magnificent African fig tree in particular. Certain plants that grew along the banks of rivers were also never to be cut.

She explained to me that as Christian missionaries began to arrive in Kenya, they mistakenly believed that the indigenous Kikuyu were worshipping the trees. They labeled their traditional and respectful beliefs as idol worship. Of course, the missionaries discouraged such beliefs and called them sinful. What the missionaries did not know, however, was that the plants growing along the rivers helped to purify the water and to stabilize the soils of the riverbank.

In addition, the trees, especially the indigenous wild fig trees, considered holy by the tribe's wise leaders, had root systems that, given enough time, penetrated the bedrock and reached down into the water table. Thus, the roots of these trees were able to bring moisture up to the surface of the earth, allowing other trees and bushes access to this water. The bushes and the trees, in turn, nourished and protected the animals, helping to establish a balanced ecosystem.

When the British colonizers of Kenya found that cash crops of tea and coffee could be grown in the rich and fertile soil of the highlands, they established large plantations by clearing the native trees and bushes—including the "holy" wild figs—that stood in the way of making money. Kenya's environment began to change.

Speaking of the British, Wangari generously understood their motives. "They didn't mean badly—quite often they meant well—but they just lived in another century. If it were today, with the environmental awareness that we have, they would have protected this land much more. And they would have reinforced our culture toward the earth—so that we would have continued to take care of it, and we would have continued to respect it. There is nothing idol worshipping about respecting the earth."

When Wangari spoke of her ancestors, she noted that they might not have known all the reasons for why they did what they did. Nevertheless, there were beneficial consequences to their wise actions, as she explained, "At this time in my life, I have been trying to find a space for our culture because our culture was condemned and trivialized as soon as we become colonized. We had become persuaded to believe that our culture was not worth it. This is true of any people who are colonized. The colonizers and the conquerors know—from the Romans, to the Greeks, to everybody—that if you want to subdue a people, if you want to exploit people, you must convince them that they are not worth it. You must convince them that you have come to save them from themselves even—and their ignorance—and that you will be a great help to them, you'll be a source of light to them. So people tend to think that they are coming from darkness to light—to think that the colonizers are moving you from your state of ignorance to wisdom. But if you give yourself time to think and to reflect and to stop being persuaded, at least when that period is over, as it is for us, you will discover that every community in this world—no matter how large, no matter how small—has wisdom."

She also gave her interpretation of what wisdom entails. "Wisdom, to me, comprises the experiences that people go through as they experience life. If you go back as far back as you can go with our primordial parents, whatever experiences they underwent—whatever was profitable, whatever was useful, whatever made life easier or made life more productive, whatever proved successful—was passed on to the next generation. And if the experience was really very good—like, for example, if they learned how to cure a disease through a certain plant or certain food crops—this experience became coded into what we call culture. So people say, 'This is how we do things.' They don't have a reason because quite often, it was not written—especially in communities that did not have an art of writing. So their wisdom and their experiences, their successful experiences, were 'coded' in a culture that became a tradition—that became a way of life."

Wangari continued, "So I like to persuade all people—especially communities that are marginalized and have been subdued and oppressed and exploited (persuaded to believe that their culture is not worth it)—to appreciate that, whatever it is, however trivial it may appear, it is wisdom. It is an experience that your people went through at a certain time in the period of millions of years that we have been living on this planet. That experience has been useful to us. We have come to this time in the life of this planet, and we ought to be really grateful that those who experienced it passed it on to us. And we should not be persuaded by anybody to throw it away at this time."

Cautioning that all the cultures of humankind must be respected, Wangari explained, "I think it is very important for all mankind, and especially the more aggressive cultures (those that consider others trivial and consider others not so important) to appreciate that as a human race, as a people, we are so much better off with all these bits and pieces of culture. We will be the poorer if we adopt a monoculture—and consider that a monoculture is our solution. We need all that wisdom."[21]

Wangari's insights about the environment, people, and cultures amazed me. She has not had an easy road to walk to this point. Her mission has not been without risk. For instance, not everyone appreciated her no-nonsense approach to protecting the environment. Under the Moi regime, 1978 to 2003, she fearlessly stated her opinions and strived to only support the environment and the civil rights of Kenyans. She was insulted and harassed by government ministers and politicians. She was called a traitor and a subversive who had no moral right to speak because she was a divorcee.[22] She was threatened with female circumcision if she could not "behave as women should."[23] She was teargassed, whipped, clubbed by baton-wielding riot police into unconsciousness, dragged from her home by police, and jailed many times (three times in 2001 alone). She stated that at one point, she was beginning to feel like a jailbird.[24] She was hospitalized numerous times with injuries from beatings that occurred simply because she wanted to legally plant trees on public lands and to encourage democracy and liberty in Kenya.

In spite of blatant abuse and persecution, Wangari showed no signs of retreat from her campaign to protect the environment and to assist the women and men of Kenya to better their lives, saying, "I'm on a path, and I'm walking."[25] She explained further, "Of course, such threats and abuse don't do your psyche any good. If you attack a woman by attacking her womanhood, she'll feel embarrassed and violated. You're human; you don't want to be humiliated. They hope you will be so hurt you will not raise your voice again. The real objective is to stop you talking. 'Are you going to give in, or what?' And for me, never!"[26]

In addition to beatings and jail, defeats have occurred regularly in Wangari's life as well. She ran unsuccessfully for parliament in 1988, losing her job at the University of Nairobi in the process. She ran for the presidency of Kenya in 1997, but lost. Through it all, she has been able to, using her words, "keep walking."

Wangari has a keen sense of right and wrong and a genuine concern for people as well as the environment. When asked about her goals, Wangari stated, "I have tried to seek the good!"[27] Because of her education and her environmental expertise, she is able to distinguish between helpful and harmful public policies. She abhors the political graft and corruption as well as the tribal conflicts, so common in Africa, that are set in motion by politicians seeking power.

In December 2001, Wangari entered the parliamentary elections in Tetu electoral constituency, a district that includes the city of Nyeri. She won in a landslide. As Mwai Kibaki became the new president of Kenya, defeating President Daniel arap Moi's handpicked successor in the same election and ending twenty-four years of rule by his party, Kibaki selected Wangari as his deputy minister of the Environment, Natural Resources, and Wildlife Ministry. She was then inside the process of improving the environment in Kenya. There was much speculation in the press about why Dr. Maathai was not named the minister of environment as many felt she was the most qualified person for that position.

Since Wangari had the perspective of then being in the government, in a 2004 press interview, she was asked what she saw as the greatest challenge to the environment. She answered, "I've always found that the biggest problem is the balancing act between what we know we need—the minimum that we should have for our environment—and our demand for development, for example. The government knows we need clean drinking water, that they should not cut trees if they need water—but they need trees, they need the timber, they need the paper. So balancing that becomes a problem. We all know that we need to conserve our wildlife, but we also want to expand our agricultural farms, we want to make them bigger, more productive. Therefore we want to [use] commercial agrochemicals—yet we know that those are going to destroy the soil. We know we need to protect the air, we need to release less harmful gases into the atmosphere, but we also want to move around, we want to fly, we want to drive our cars. We need a lot of information, especially for decision makers, so that they can make the right decisions. Secondly, we need the citizens to be more active, not to be apathetic, and to put pressure on their government because quite often, governments have short-term agendas and they may make a decision in favor of their own personal agenda rather than that of the environment."[28]

Nevertheless, since that good beginning, President Kibaki reverted to some of the tactics of President Moi. He dissolved his cabinet, appointing only those who fully agreed with his methods. He asked Wangari to take up her position again, but she refused, stating that until all parties and all sides are given a voice and listened to, she could not serve. The struggle for democracy in Kenya goes on.

The people of the world have taken notice. Wangari has received innumerable national and international awards,[29] including one of the most prestigious awards given—the Nobel Peace Prize. She learned of this great honor on October 8, 2004, from a call to her cell phone from Ole Danbolt Mjos, chair of the Nobel Prize Committee. She was the first African woman to receive this prestigious honor.

The prize was awarded in Oslo on December 10, 2004, complete with Kenyan drummers at the ceremony. By bestowing the award to an environmentalist, the connection between the world's resources and the maintenance of peace throughout the world were tied together. The Nobel committee cited "her contribution to sustainable development, democracy, and peace."[30] Wangari humbly commented to Norwegian broadcaster for TV2, "I feel extremely elated. This is something I would never have dreamt of."[31] She also said, "This, indeed, is not a recognition of one person, but a recognition of all people who work for the environment, who work for peace, who work for democracy, and who work for a better quality of life."[32]

What motivates this incredible wise woman? I believe it is her good and noble heart, her humility, her sense of justice and fairness, her dedication to a life of service, and her ability to act from her sense of fairness to all. She reflected on her own motivation, saying, "When you start doing this work, you do it with a very pure heart, out of compassion . . . . The clarity of what you ought to do gives you courage, removes the fear, and gives you the courage to ask. There is so much you do not know. And you need to know. It helps you get your mind focused."[33]

In 2006, Wangari and five other Nobel Peace laureates (Jody Williams, Shirin Ebadi, Rigoberta Menchu Tum, Betty Williams, and Mairead Corrigan Maguire) founded the Nobel Women's Initiative. They represent Africa, Europe, North America and South America, Europe, and the Middle East. They hope to promote justice and equality, strengthening the position of women throughout the world.

My memory of Wangari is of a strong, beautiful woman—one full of hope for the future. Her passion for her work, her respect for the environment, and her focus on what is good for the earth and its inhabitants were obvious. She has spent the last thirty-five years trying to raise environmental consciousness and also trying to improve and protect Kenya's fragile environment. She firmly believed, and has dramatically proven, that one person can make a difference.

In November 2006, Wangari Maathai issued a challenge to the peoples of the earth—plant trees, a billion trees! In her biography, *Unbowed: A Memoir*, published in December 2006, she cautioned,

> As women and men continue this work of clothing this naked Earth, we are in the company of many others throughout the world who care deeply for this blue planet. We have nowhere else to go. Those of us who witness the degraded state of the environment and the suffering that comes with it cannot afford to be complacent. We continue to be restless. If we really carry the burden, we are driven to action. We cannot tire or give up. We owe it to the present and future generations of all species to rise up and walk![34]

The Nobel Peace Prize has brought new challenges to this remarkable woman. It catapulted her to fame within the powerful leaders of the world—presidents, kings, and Hollywood heroes and starlets—as well as financial rewards. She has expanded her concerns to include all of Africa. She speaks passionately against the corruption that exists in most African countries. She has written another book, *The Challenge for Africa*.[35]

Wangari's last bid for being elected a member of the Kenyan parliament was rejected by the people of her district in December 2007 because many of her constituents were angry that she had not shared her money with them. She was constantly asked by the Kenyan media about what she planned to do with the money that came with the Nobel Prize. She answered that it would be used for environmental causes, but her answer did not seem to satisfy the public. Will wealth and the acclaim of stars, politicians, and environmentalist groups affect Wangari as it did King Solomon in his later years? Will it affect her ability to be wise?

As stated at the beginning of this chapter, the earth's environment was important to all the wise individuals whose lives are outlined in this book. Cultural differences did not alter their sentiments. Most were concerned not only with how we humans are managing the oceans, the skies, and the land but, more importantly, with how we see and care for all the creatures that share with us this spinning blue orb—especially each other.

Endnotes

[1] A traditional African proverb/song. Clemente K. Abrokwaa, Indigenous Music Education in Africa, In Ladislaus M. Semali and Joe L. Kincheloe, eds. *What is Indigenous Knowledge? Voices from the Academy.* New York: Farmer Press., 1999), 203.

[2] Fritjof Capra, *The Web of Life* (New York: Anchor Books, 1996), 34.

[3] George Eliot, *Middlemarch* (1871-1872).

[4] Mihalyi Csikszentmihalyi and Kevin Rathunde, "The Psychology of Wisdom: An Evolutionary Interpretation," In *Wisdom: It's Nature, Origins, and Development,* edited by R. J. Sternberg, (New York: Cambridge University Press, 1990), 44.

[5] Pyrethrum is an Old World plant belonging to the genus Chrysanthemum (*C. cinerarifolium*). Called the Persian chrysanthemum, the flower head looks much like a daisy, and its dried flower heads are an economically important natural insecticide. Kenya produces close to ninety percent of the world's pyrethrum. The plant grows at a height that made it easy for children to reach its flowers.

[6] Personal interview, September 7, 1999, Nairobi Kenya.

[7] Personal interview, Sept. 7, 1999, Nairobi, Kenya; Wangari Maathai, *Unbowed* (New York: Adolf F. Knopf, 1999), 64-65.

[8] Personal Communication, September 7, 1999, Nairobi, Kenya.

[9] The U.S. State Department made it possible for about six hundred Kenyans to study at various universities throughout the United States. This program was called the Kennedy airlift.

[10] Opinion: Interview. *New Scientist Magazine,* July 22, 2000.

[11] Ibid.

[12]   Frances Moore Lappé and Anna Lappé, *Hope's Edge: The Next Diet for a Small Planet* (New York: Putnam, 2002).

[13]   Ibid., 170.

[14]   http://www.apu.ac.jp/-jstuch1/matatu.htm (October 10, 2008). A *matatu* is a common form of minibus in Kenya. Built to transport a maximum of fourteen people, the driver of the matatu can squeeze in up to twenty. According to travel guides, riding in a matatu is "a thrill which is best experienced by the tourist on the sidewalk."

[15]   Frances Lappé and Anna Lappé, "Guerrilla of the Week: Wangari Maathai," *Guerrilla News Network*. http://www.guerillanews.com/environment/doc949.html (10 Nov. 2006).

[16]   Frances Moore Lappé and Anna Lappé, *Hope's Edge: The Next Diet for a Small Planet* (New York: Putnam, 2002), 170.

[17]   The World Wide Fund for Nature, Sustainability: A Matter of Choice (1996). http://www.panda.org/resources/publications/sustainability/choice/page12.htm (12 April 2004).

[18]   Personal Communication, September 7, 1999, Nairobi, Kenya.

[19]   Conservation and Feminism: Africa's Greenheart." *The Economist*, 21 Sept. 2006; Wangari Muta Maathai, *Click Africa.com*. Nov. 20, 2006; www.clickafrique.com/Magazine/ST019/CP0000001582.aspx (April 3, 2009)

[20]   Frances Moore Lappé and Anna Lappé, *Hope's Edge: The Next Diet for a Small Planet* (New York: Putnam, 2002), 190-191.

[21]   Ibid.

[22]   Katy Salmon, "Forest profile: Wangari Maathai Mobilizing the Mothers," *People and the Planet*, 8:4 (2000). http://www.peopleandplanet.net/doc.php?id=39 (December 2001).

[23]   Kerry Kennedy Cuomo and Eddie Adams, *Speak Truth to Power: Human Rights Defenders Who Are Changing Our World* (New York: Crown Publishers, 1999), 40.

[24]   Wangari Maathai, *Unbowed: A Memoir* (New York: Alfred Knopf, 2006), 295.

[25]   Personal interview, Sept. 7, 1999, Nairobi, Kenya.

[26]   Katy Salmon, "Forest profile: Wangari Maathai Mobilizing the Mothers," *People and the Planet*, 8:4, http://www.peopleandplanet.net/doc.php?id=39 (Feb. 13, 2002).

[27]   Priscilla Sears, "Wangari Maathai: 'You Strike The Woman . . . '" *In Context: A Quarterly of Humane Sustainable Culture* (Spring 1991), 57.

[28]   *Satya Magazine*, "The Tree Ambassador." (June/July 2004). http://www.satyamag.com/Jul04/maathai.html (April 24, 2007).

[29]   Other prizes Wangari has garnered include the Sophie Prize from Norway (2004), the United Nation's Environment Programme's (UNDP) Global 500 Award, *Time* magazine's Hero of the Planet Award (1998), the Woman of Hope Award (1999),

the Golden Ark Award (1994), Jane Addams International Women's Leadership Award (1993), the Edinburgh Medal (1993), the Africa Prize for Leadership for the Sustainable End to Hunger (1991), the Goldman Environmental Prize (1991), the UN's Africa Prize for Leadership (1991), the Woman of the World Award (1989), the Windstar Award for the Environment (1988), the Better World Society Award (1986), the Right Livelihood Award (1984), Woman of the Year Award (1983), the Indira Gandhi Award (2006), the Jawaharlal Nehru Award for International Understanding for 2005 and 2006, the Nelson Mandela Award for 2007, and many others.

[30]   Who2. Finding People Fast. http://www.who2.com/wangarimaathai.html (April 2007).

[31]   Bloomberg.com. www.bloomberg.com/index.html (23 April 2006).

[32]   *Democracy Now!* "Daughter of 2004 Nobel Peace Prize Winner Wangari Maathai Discusses Her Mother, Kenya, and the Environment," (Thursday, October 21, 2004). http://www.democracynow.org/article_pl?sid=04/10/21/1440249 (25 Nov 2004).

[33]   Priscilla Sears, "Wangari Maathai: 'You Strike The Woman . . . ' " *In Context: A Quarterly of Humane Sustainable Culture.* (Spring 1991).

[34]   Wangari Maathai, *Unbowed: A Memoir* (New York: Alfred Knopf, 2006), 295.

[35]   Wangari Maathai, *The Challenge for Africa* (New York: Random House, 2009).

Chapter Thirteen

Humility

All streams flow to the ocean because it is lower than they are.
Humility gives it its power.

—*Lao-tzu*

Humility is another virtue that has historically been linked to wisdom. Saint Augustine is credited with saying, "Humility is the foundation of all the other virtues; hence, in the soul in which this virtue does not exist, there cannot be any other virtue except in mere appearance."[1] Like wisdom, humility is a universally admired human quality. Like wisdom, humility is relatively easy to spot but difficult to describe in words.[2]

What then is *humility*? Humility stems from knowing that one may not know everything about a situation. It is the genuine denial of being the best or the most talented or, in this case, the wisest. When the oracle proclaimed Socrates to be the only wise man in all of Athens, Socrates explained that it was true only because unlike those who claimed to be wise, he assuredly knew that he was not wise. Humility stems from a lack of arrogance. It appears to come from a deep respect for all creation—including one's self and one's neighbors. It is often a companion of gratitude.[3]

The first time I met Yuichi Takenaka (hereafter called Takenaka-san) was when Hatanaka-san, Steven, and I arrived at his residence to conduct an interview with him. Takanaka-san and his wife live in a lovely new-style Japanese home in Osaka, Japan. The Takenakas are an attractive and cordial couple. They began their married life in traditional Japanese fashion; they had an arranged marriage. They have two sons; one is a doctor in

Kobe, Japan, and the other is an airline pilot. Takenaka-san's wife is a talented wood carver. To be invited to their family home was an honor.

Following introductions, Takenaka-san ushered us into the beautifully decorated tatami room of his home. We sat down on comfortable floor cushions at a low traditional Japanese wood table. The focal point in the room was the *tokonoma,* an alcove in the room that housed an intricate Japanese scroll (*suiboku-ga*) that hung above a striking vase containing an elegant arrangement of flowers (*ikebana*). Takenaka-san prepared green tea for us—skillfully combining green powdered tea and warm water, whisking them together in the traditional manner. Takenaka-san's wife served us *wagashi*, a delicious sweet transparent delicacy made from soybeans.

Sixty-four-year-old Takenaka-san had recently stepped down as the president of KIO Industries, a company that he founded and managed for thirty years. A Japanese intellectual, he understood some English; but throughout our conversations, he spoke Japanese. Typical of the individuals discussed in this book, when I told Takenaka-san that he had been suggested to me as being a wise man, he laughed and politely yet simply replied, "I am not wise." I could see that like the other wise ones I had met, he approached life humbly.

Takenaka-san—kind, polite, and knowledgeable—seemed acutely aware of the cultural differences between Americans and the Japanese people. He tried to make sure that, if possible, I would correctly understand how Japanese people viewed life. He also attempted to bridge the cultural gulf of understanding between us—especially as it related to the important concept of *wabi sabi*, the Japanese concept of beauty. To illustrate this concept for me, he referred to two bowls sitting on the table in front of us. One dark brown bowl had an irregular shape with a rough surface. The other was an intricate porcelain bowl, delicately painted on its outside surface with colorful flowers and greenery.

Takenaka-san explained that Japanese people consider the dark irregular bowl the more beautiful of the two bowls. He thought that Westerners would prefer the floral one, saying, "This example is symbolic of how the Japanese think about beauty. Our way of thinking about beauty is different from the Western thinking. The origins of wabi sabi are at the core of the representation of material things. In order to understand the way the Japanese think, it is important to understand wabi sabi. An example of the difference in the representation of things is evident in how Americans and Westerners view cherry blossoms. Westerners feel that the blossoms on blooming cherry trees are beautiful. But Japanese people believe that the cherry tree is the most beautiful when its blossoms *fall off.*"

Takanaka-san continued to explain the concept. "Another example of the differences in the views of material things comes from the World War II. The Japanese forces had the kamikaze fighter squads.[4] In the end, these pilots died, and that way of dying was beautified—viewed as dying in the same way as the cherry blossoms falling from the tree. It is the same principle. That is the origin of Japanese thinking with regards to beauty."

Born in Osaka on June 5, 1935, Takenaka-san was the middle child of five. He had an older brother and sister and two younger brothers. The events of World War II were influential in his life and the lives of his family members. When bombs began to be dropped on Japan during World War II, Takenaka-san was a young boy living in Osaka with his family. He said, "I remember seeing the B-29 bombers flying over the field of the school I was going to when I was in first grade. I remember that vividly."

When the Americans began escalating their bombing of Japanese cities, Takenaka-san's father, a company man,[5] seeking safety, moved his family from the large industrial city of Osaka to the small town of Shingu in Wakayama Prefecture. It was a logical move, since Takanaka-san's mother was originally from Shingu. In order to support the family, Takenaka-san's father became a teacher at a school in the Japanese countryside in order to support his family.

I asked Takanaka-san, "What was it like to be bombed and to survive?"

He replied, "The bombing wasn't just in Osaka. The Americans were bombing in Shingu too. The U.S. base used to be in Saipan during the war. The American planes would fly into Japan over Shionomisaki (Wakayama Prefecture). Then they would split off and go to Tokyo, Osaka, Hiroshima, and other cities. Therefore, Shingu was right on the way. They wouldn't drop bombs on their way into Japan because they had a target they were headed for. But if they had bombs left over on the way back to their base, then they would bomb us."

Takanaka-san believed that the hardship imposed on Japan by World War II helped him to learn to work hard and to build his physical strength. He was ten years old at the end of the war. Conditions were difficult not only during but also after the war.

"It was extremely difficult to find food, even when the war ended. Because of this, I spent a lot of time out in the forests searching for food and on the ocean fishing. I came to respect nature—animals and other living things. I learned from nature—it wasn't that someone taught me."

Takanaka-san then commented, "After the war, I learned that working diligently is connected with need—and food is one of the basic needs of life. There are many ways of getting food—working a plot of land or fishing or going to the mountains and picking berries. I did them all in order to find something to eat. I still remember the lessons such hard experiences taught me."

Explaining what he learned, he said, "Because I had those experiences of not having any food and of dodging the bombs, I learned and I have developed a way of looking at the bad things and the bad times so as not to become discouraged by them. I can always compare the difficult things that happen to those early experiences in my life."

After finishing high school in Shingu, where his father was one of his teachers, Takenaka-san eventually attended his father's alma mater, Doisha University in Kyoto. He studied law. At the university, he lived in a dormitory with many individuals of different ages and philosophies. The dormitory was self-governed. Through his association with some of the unique people with whom he lived, Takenaka-san learned another valuable lesson: each individual has a different way of thinking about the world.

Takenaka-san said of his dorm mates, "We discussed and debated many different topics; for instance, What is love? . . . What is peace?" He believed that these discussions were a positive influence on his life later on. Because of them, he became aware that people have different perspectives on life. Takenaka-san called himself a liberal person, by which he was not referring to particular political persuasion, but he meant that he assumed sole responsibility for his actions.

After graduating from the university, Takenaka-san became a company employee with the Japan Gas Company for ten years. He greatly admired Takeo Sugai, the naval commander who originally started Japan Gas Company. He learned a great deal about management from him but, more importantly, a lot more about how influential one's attitude can be.

Speaking about Sugai, Takenaka-san explained, "He had experience in war and had come close to death. Because he had experienced coming close to death, he believed that he had been given a second chance at life. And so he didn't pay attention to his self-desires. (Takenaka-san used the Japanese word *mushi,* which translates to English as a "lack of self.") So whatever was happening around him, because he had no desires for himself, he was not moved. He was always thinking about his subordinates. He gave freedom to his subordinates. In fact, he would take responsibility for all of their mistakes. I think that he was a wise person—a good person."

Using some of the skills gained at Japan Gas Company and risking his life savings and some family monies, Takenaka-san started his own company, KIO Industries. He said his business philosophy was navy "practicalism," which involved having a limited number of diligent workers.

"The strategy worked," he said. "I relate it to a submarine. In the submarine, the more electricity and water and air you have, the longer you can stay submerged. The best way to conserve a lot of the electricity and air is to reduce the number of people on board. When you man a submarine with a limited number of people, each person has to do many different tasks. Even a person who is not very noble [diligent] will become better by doing many different tasks. The idea of a small number of skilled workers applies to the submarine and also to the management of a company. You get rid of inefficiencies."

Takenaka-san's navy *practicalism* succeeded. KIO Industries received ISO 9001 status (an award reflecting a company's global standard of manufacturing and process quality). He retired as company president in 1998 and became its representative director (CEO).

Takenaka-san spoke of how important it is to respect other people. He explained, "It is an important thing that you connect with other people in your life. Of the five billion people who live on the earth, there are only a limited number that you can sit down and actually talk with, so it is important to make the best of those conversations. Because you have the opportunity to meet these people, you need to take care of or nourish those relationships. I developed this knowledge through many different experiences in my life."

I met Takenaka-san again a week later at an apartment he kept in Tanabe, Japan. There he spent time golfing, fishing, relaxing, and engaging in discussions with friends and acquaintances. At this final meeting, we talked about the concept of wisdom as it is understood in Japan. At my request, he had prepared a concept map, a diagram depicting the components he believed should be included in wisdom.

He explained his concept of wisdom, saying, "I could not answer your question of what a wise man is at our last meeting, but I can give you this now as my answer: wisdom is represented by the Japanese concept of *hannya*. Hannya means the ability to distinguish the correctness of things. This is a broad concept in Buddhism that is also related to universal knowledge.

Within hannya are knowledge, intelligence, and aggressive action. In addition, there is justice. Justice includes courage. Courage is necessary as one must act for just causes. And calm judgment is necessary to distinguish good and bad, which is the basis of justice."

Continuing his explanation of wisdom, he said, "As I stated before, love is also important. There are many types of love. Friendly love, love for family, love for mankind, and romantic love. Peace is another characteristic. A sense of balance is necessary for peace. Also, the ability to cooperate is important. Humility is essential. And then there is *rinri* [ethics, morals, code of conduct]. A person who has these characteristics is wise."

This noble and honorable man, Takanaka-san, taught me about Japanese culture, philosophy, and life. As we talked, I became aware of his depth of intellect and character. Successful in life, he strived to be better than what was ordinarily expected, to do what he knew to be right, and to respect others. His demeanor was devoid of pride. He expressed gratitude for the experiences of his life and for his family. He successfully practiced the art of life.[6] He sought truth.

Reflecting upon the men and women I interviewed, I recognize that all of them had similar characteristics. They had various talents and gifts. Some were musicians, some were painters, some were healers, some were counselors, some appreciated art and music, some were writers. When I expressed appreciation for a participant's talent, he or she politely acknowledged my compliment but made light of it.

Three of the wise ones discussed in this book chose to remain anonymous—mainly because they did not want to call attention to themselves. One of them, a beautiful and sensitive Navajo woman whom I call Nizhoni (a Navajo word meaning "beautiful"), was extremely talented. As we talked, she reflected a warmth and an acceptance that indicated to me that she knew how to "hold her heart" (in Itani-san's words) and that she appreciated people of all races and circumstances. More importantly, Nizhoni was sincerely humble. She did not consider herself a good candidate for a study on wisdom. She agreed to participate only because I asked; she wanted to assist me with my project, even though she felt her life story was not particularly significant.

Nizhoni and I first met on a warm July day at a restaurant in a city within the Four Corners region. At our first meeting, I was surprised by the number of people who stopped by our table to greet and speak to her. Obviously, she is respected and popular with people all across the vast Navajo Nation.

Nizhoni's story is one of difficulty and triumph. Born in a remote area on the Navajo Nation in the 1950s, she faced more than her share of adversity in life. Her father died before she was a year old. She had two older brothers, but both died of illnesses as babies. Nizhoni lived with her mother, but she became quite attached to her grandparents, who lived nearby. They raised her in traditional Navajo ways.

"I grew up without really knowing a father, and so, I guess, that's how I became a little closer to my grandmother and my grandfather than I did with my mom. We all lived in the same area—right next to each other. My mother sometimes would spank me, and I'd go run away to my grandmother's house and she comforted me. So that's why I wanted to be there."

When Nizhoni's mother remarried, her maternal grandparents remained her refuge and foundation in life. Her mother and stepfather subsequently had several children, for whom Nizhoni became the big sister.

A Western education was not a priority in their home. "My mother did not push us toward education. The way she was raised was to be, in the traditional sense, a keeper of the livestock, a keeper of the home life. And that involved a lot of work—moving the sheep from here to there. So she always wanted to keep her children home so they could help her."

Nevertheless, Nizhoni, like many of the wise ones, was forced by governmental edict to attend boarding school from the time she was six years old. Placing Navajo children into boarding schools at that time was thought to help them adjust to and succeed in the dominant (meaning Euro-Western American) culture, but it was a traumatic experience for the children. The American government believed that assimilation of the native population into the larger community could be facilitated through this practice.

Nizhoni related her experience. "I was only six years old, and I did not want to go to boarding school. I remember I did not want to go. I cried, and I cried. Every time I saw somebody from our home area, I would cry and ask them to take me home. So my introduction was so awful that by the sixth grade, I did not enjoy school that much . . . . For a stretch there, they told us not to speak Navajo. Of course, you know, a lot of people couldn't do that because that wasn't the way their life experience was. Most spoke Navajo at home. I made a personal choice in my heart to maintain the language. I felt I had no other choice. I couldn't desert my own language."

Each fall, Navajo children arrived at the boarding schools and were immediately assigned to an "acceptable" religion. Nizhoni's assignment was Presbyterian. "What I learned in school, and what I believe in myself, is that God loves us all. That's what they taught us in boarding school, and in Sunday school. I was a Presbyterian—not by choice, but because my name began with *X* [the alphabetic letter of her last name]. When we arrived at the boarding school, we were separated into groups and sent here or there to go to church. So the *A*s through *L*s went to the Catholics, and the *M*s through *Z*s went to the Presbyterians. Every Sunday, they would march us down the street from the boarding school, and we went to the Presbyterian church. It was not by choice."

Nizhoni mentioned that many children ran away from the boarding schools. This could be a dangerous thing to do, especially in the winter. Many runaway children died from exposure if they weren't found in time.

Although Nizhoni disliked school, she stayed there. She mused, "But you know, it's amazing! As much as I hated school, I didn't run away from school. I hung in there."

By the time Nizhoni was to begin sixth grade, however, she announced that she was not going to return to school. An uncle somehow heard of Nizhoni's pronouncement, and although Nizhoni had never met this uncle or his wife, they invited her to live with their family and attend school in another city. Nizhoni agreed to go, and she attended the public junior high school in the uncle's community for three years. She then attended one year of high school in another community.

"I guess I had somewhere in my soul the desire to try something different—you know, after three years in my uncle's house—I wanted to try something different. So I went to high school in a boarding situation for a year as a freshman. I noticed that it was kind of lonely and it was remote—it was too far away from my family. I never saw my family for that whole year. At the holidays, like Thanksgiving and Christmas, we had to find our own way home—so that was a harsh experience for me. I also noticed that being that we were so close to Gallup, every weekend students would 'go to town' by busloads; and when they came back to the dormitory, half of them had been drinking. My roommates used to be drunk all the time. And it was a problem. I didn't feel any sense of closeness to the school. I wasn't raised that way!"

Nizhoni never had the desire to drink with her classmates. She had seen her stepfather and her uncle drinking, but the women of her family never drank alcohol.

The following year, Nizhoni transferred to a large Indian school in another state. That opened up a new world to her. Because her parents could not support her, Nizhoni worked cleaning people's homes to earn a few dollars on the weekends. While at the school, she met Native Americans from all over the country.

"It kind of opened my eyes," she said. Following graduation, she stayed on in that city, thinking she'd like to work in the health fields. She was accepted to a professional school, but she soon found she didn't like it.

Nizhoni explained, "You know, I was raised in a way that I never thought about the future. I never considered things like, What will I be doing someday? What would I like to do? My mother never taught me those kinds of things. My family never taught me to think ahead. Navajo people don't think in the future. They live right now and go day by day almost. So when I was in high school I could never choose a career—I didn't know what I wanted to do. When I was selected to go to . . . school, I lasted not even the whole semester . . . . I discovered there were a lot of things I was uncomfortable doing."

Nizhoni stayed on to attend another specialized school, and she gained useful skills in several fields. She really enjoyed living close to shopping and other opportunities. Although she was always on her own financially, she never failed to send some money home to her mother. She never expected her family to support her although her beloved grandmother would slip her a few dollars whenever she left home to go back to school.

Nizhoni met a young man while she was attending school. She became pregnant and gave birth a month after graduation. She chose to raise her child by herself because the baby's father had drug and alcohol problems. When Nizhoni had difficulty finding a job, she returned home and lived with her mother until the baby was old enough to walk. She worked at a restaurant as a waitress and at a hotel as a maid. When the baby was old enough to walk, she went to college.

This strong young woman faced the difficulties of raising a child, going to school, and working full-time with courage. Nizhoni found a night job in a business office. Each night, she walked, carrying her child, three miles to and from work. "Sometimes it would rain. And sometimes it was cold at night. The baby slept on an office couch while Nizhoni worked. We did that to survive . . . . We struggled quite a bit."

Her day job as a waitress helped launch her into her next career. She learned the technical end of a very difficult business. Since then, she has been very successful in several related fields.

A decade later, Nizhoni's old boyfriend, her child's father, came back into her life. They eventually married, much to the delight of their child. Marriage brought another change in occupation for her. Nizhoni was dedicated to raising her child, who was and is still the light of her life—the motivating force in most of her decisions. Several times she told me, "You know, when you are a parent, you have a lot of responsibilities toward your child."

Part of Nizhoni's dedication to her child may stem from the fact that her relationship with her own mother was difficult. Nizhoni longed for more interaction with her mother; therefore, she made certain that she was there for her own child. She has also made sure that she taught her child to be responsible and to have a sense of respect.

As far as religion is concerned, Nizhoni is accepting of every faith. She mentioned that her mother's generation was caught in a transition from the traditional religion to the Judeo-Christian religions, and that created some problems for many Navajo.

She explained, "My mother's life got caught up in this religion thing—the Anglo way of religion. They led her away from her traditional beliefs. So she's right there in the middle. I try to help her see that it's not all bad. The Christians taught her that the traditional Navajo way is an evil thing—that it's not the way to live."

Nizhoni tried to help her mother understand that being Navajo is not the bad thing that certain individuals had preached to her. "I saw how distressed Momma was about this religion thing. I told her, 'You know, being Navajo isn't bad. If God didn't want us to be Navajo, he wouldn't have made us Navajo, and he wouldn't have given us an identity, which is our culture. Our way of life is good. We should do it and practice it and not feel bad about it. It's the way God made us. And God loves everyone—no matter who they are.'"

Nizhoni was keenly aware of the various church ministers and how they manipulated the Navajo people by preaching hell and damnation. She contrasted that with her own spiritual experiences where she noted, "I came away feeling really good, you know, and a sense of calm when I come home from church. The difference is in the respect shown by the clergy toward their congregation."

Many events happened in Nizhoni's life—life-shattering adversities. She has experienced prejudice and jealousy, and even abuse in her life. I asked her if she didn't find it hard to keep going on.

She replied, "Those are things that I had to come through throughout most of my life—realizing certain things and just accepting them. Moving forward. Because if you dwell on it, it can drive you nuts! I really think that when you dwell on things you can't do anything about, you'll be in counseling for the rest of your life. I wouldn't be there! There is too much going on in the world to be feeling sorry for yourself. Everything that's happened in my life has taught me—has contributed to molding my character, I guess. I'm still in the process of growing. I don't think anybody ever comes to a point in life where they are complete in their makeup. You grow. You grow every day . . . . But you must have standards."

The ability to communicate with others, to help other people who are struggling, and to understand another person's problems appear to be strengths that Nizhoni has in abundance. She has bounced back after many defeats in her career—changing directions and doing what it takes to survive honorably.

I asked Nizhoni how she was able to keep her balance. She said, "I guess having a positive purpose in my life and gaining a better understanding that as I went along, any of the things that have happened to me could have led me astray. But they didn't."

She recognized the importance of discipline, saying, "I think sometimes a little discipline does something to a person so that they can make the proper judgment as to how they should be with their lives. Sometimes people I know that have no self-discipline don't know what to do with themselves. They don't have guidance."

Nizhoni also mentioned that it was important to her to be productive. "You know, in our traditional way of living, it wasn't just the sheep. It was also the carding of the wool, the spinning of the wool, the weaving . . . . Many responsibilities and much work."

Nizhoni and I met many times over the course of the year—always in public places like the library or restaurants. Thus, I was able to observe her attitudes and actions toward other people. Keenly aware of the people around her, she treated everyone with respect, directness, and fairness. Her humanity and care for others, regardless of race, was evident in the details of her life. I could see it shining in her eyes and through her kind face as she spoke to me and to others. She saw the divine potential in everyone. Her softness and vulnerability, combined with her genuine humbleness, made her someone to whom one is immediately drawn. She was without guile and brimming with gratitude—even though her life had been exceedingly hard.

Wise individuals, like Nizhoni and Takenaka-san, on the surface looked like ordinary folks—like most of us. But in their company, one quickly becomes aware of their extraordinary presence. Although they would have been content to live their lives in the world unnoticed, their motivations were to be helpful to those around them while living lives of productivity and love.

Humility seems to emanate from some place deep within the individual who possesses it. The wise ones described in this book subdued their own egos. They were often silent, unless asked to comment. They did not talk or give speeches just to hear themselves talk. They certainly didn't expect or ask for credit or accolades from others. When asked why they thought they had been selected by their peers as being wise, all of them suggested reasons other than that they were wise. In fact, they all denied that they were wise. They acted from their own conscience, even if their actions were unpopular with those around them. They resisted the temptation to gain the praise of others. They did not acknowledge their gifts in a prideful way—indeed, like Nizhoni, they were a thankful group. If they were spiritual, they gave credit to a higher power for all they were and all they possessed. These qualities reflect true humility, imparting to the wise ones the greatness that is unique to those who are wise.

Endnotes

1   St. Augustine, *Summa Theologica*: Humility (*Secunda Secundae Partis*, Q. 161). De Virginit. Xxxi.

2   Copthorne MacDonald, *Toward Wisdom: Finding Our Way to Inner Peace, Love, and Happiness* (Willowdale, ON: Hounslow Press, 1996).

3   Gordon B. Hinckley, *Standing for Something: Ten Neglected Virtues That Will Heal Our Hearts and Homes* (New York: Times Books/Random House, 2000).

4   The World Trade Center and Pentagon attackers on September 11, 2001, demonstrated an eerie resemblance to kamikaze. Robert C. Christopher, *The Japanese Mind* (New York: Ballentine Books, 1983),47. Japanese kamikaze pilots in World War II were a secret weapon against American ships. They perfected the art of flying an airplane directly into the enemy, usually a ship, committing suicide in the process. The history of kamikaze originates in the eighth century when the fearsome Kublai Khan was poised to invade Japan. Miraculously, Khan's invading fleet was turned away from Japan by a typhoon sent from God. *Kamikaze* means "divine wind." In World War II, Japan sensed in 1944 that they were losing to the Americans. They assumed that pilots deliberately crashing into ships would unnerve the U.S. forces. In October 1944, off the coast of the Philippines, twenty-six Japanese planes were sent against the U.S. carrier *Saint Louis*. Thirteen of the planes were designated kamikaze, and the other thirteen would take advantage of the chaos that was expected to follow the kamikaze

attacks. The carrier was successfully sunk. The strategy was highly effective. Kamikaze pilots sank nearly sixty Allied ships. The Shinto pilots who died were to receive their reward in heaven.

5   Venture Japan Group, 2004. The company plays a unique role in Japanese culture and society. "To a great extent a Japanese man and his family are socially ranked by the reputation of the company he works for and the position and prospects he has there." In Japan, another name for "company man" is "salary man." Visitors to Japan find that the exchange of business cards is prevalent among the Japanese. One of the reasons is the pride men take in the companies for which they work. The company man is the norm, and the company he works for shapes his and his family's social expectations. The Japanese company man often works his entire lifetime for the same company (although this is now changing), and thus very strong bonds are created between the worker and the company. The terms used in the office are often familial in nature. Ibid.

6   John Kekes, *The Art of Life* (Ithaca, NY: Cornell University Press, 2002).

Chapter Fourteen

A West Devoid Of Wisdom

It is as if man, overburdened by the weight of technics,
knows less and less where he stands in regard to
what matters to him and what doesn't,
to what is precious and what is worthless.
                                        —*Gabriel Marcel*[1]

Although I had originally planned to only find wise Westerners in Germany—as Western a country as I could imagine—no one in Germany, or anywhere else in Europe for that matter, was initially willing to suggest nominators or people who could identify anyone wise in their communities. I was well into the interviewing process within four other cultures before I decided to expand my search for Western wise ones to any place in Europe. I had eliminated the idea of looking for wise Americans not because I believed that none existed but because I hoped to keep my searches within populations that historically were somewhat homogenous. Americans, living in the cultural melting pot of the world, generally are not that—or at least they had not traditionally been such.

I began to be fearful that I would not find *any* wise Western individuals. Finally, I resorted to networking with friends who had lived in Europe, and I eventually received the names of people who, when contacted, nominated two individuals living in Germany who satisfied many of the criteria that I had originally set out as being characteristics of wise individuals. No one claimed definitively that these individuals were wise, however. The Krauses were two of the Westerners selected (see chapters 7 and 9) who agreed, reluctantly, to be included in my research. The only Western woman I interviewed, Fleur Ng'weno, lives in Nairobi, Kenya. She was nominated as wise by Kenyans, not by Westerners.

Jagi Gakunju arranged for me to interview Fleur at the East Africa Natural History Society office housed in the National Museums of Kenya in Nairobi. As Robert and I arrived at the Museum, Fleur, an attractive blond-haired blue-eyed woman in her sixties, met us. Her unique delightful accent seemed British but might best be called international. We held the interview in a large conference room of the Natural History office. Fleur sat down on one side of a long wooden conference table, and I sat opposite her. Robert performed his usual task of recording our conversation.

Fleur laughed as she began to tell her story. "My story is quite complicated—quite different. My family is French. My father's family is from the coastal town of Nantes, in France. But my grandfather was an artist and cartoonist—and quite a famous French cartoonist. My grandmother was a schoolteacher. This is on my father's side. Then they were separated, and my grandmother really raised her family—my father's family in Paris. My mother's family was French and Swiss. My grandfather there died before I was born, and so I didn't know him, and my mother's mother lived in Switzerland."

Fleur's parents met in France while both were working with the Boy Scout movement. After their marriage, they chose to travel to other parts of the world, going to North Africa and then to Lebanon, where Fleur was born.

After World War II broke out, the family moved from place to place, so Fleur did not stay in Lebanon long. Her parents took her to Guadeloupe in the Caribbean and then to Martinique. While living in Martinique, her father was called back to war-torn France (World War II), and his whereabouts were unknown by the family for several years.

Fleur explained, "My father had to go back, and we didn't know if he was dead or alive really. We were living in Martinique. My mother did some work, and friends helped my mother, sister, and me survive."

Fleur's father was eventually reunited with the family, and they all moved to North Africa. After Southern France was liberated during World War II, they tried to return to France, but conditions there were chaotic. Fleur and her sister, formally declared refugees, were accepted by Switzerland, where their maternal grandmother lived. During the last phases of the war, this grandmother cared for seven-year-old Fleur and her sister. "Our parents," she explained, "remained in France caught up in the end of the war, but they survived."

After the war, Fleur's mother decided that the United States was the place where she'd like to raise her family. Her father subsequently found work as a linguist at the newly built United Nations in New York. Because her parents were both educators, they confidently home-schooled their girls, encouraging them to seek knowledge in many places. Fleur spent a lot of time in the American Museum of Natural History in New York and at the National Audubon Society camp in Maine. She did, however, attend a public school in New York for her last two years of high school.

With her parents encouraging her to follow her interests, Fleur went to Connecticut College for Women and the University of Michigan in the United States. Majoring in conservation, she was especially interested in birds. The books of James Oliver Kirkwood and mentors in the National Audubon Society (including Allan Cruickshank, Roger Tory Peterson, and Farida Wiley) inspired her. "My association with these outstanding naturalists was the turning point because I was going in the right direction." Fleur added, "It was a leap forward because suddenly, I found all these people who shared the same interest as I did, and it was like a revelation." She eventually became employed as a teacher for several years with the National Audubon Society in Greenwich, Connecticut.

After Fleur's father retired, he worked for the French government in Kenya, promoting French culture in the schools. On a visit to see her parents in Kenya, Fleur met and subsequently married her husband. She ended up staying on in Kenya, working as the honorary secretary of the East Africa Natural History Society. Her husband became the editor of the local newspaper. They have raised two daughters.

Fleur spoke of her heritage in a way consistent with her training as a naturalist—in terms of genetic inheritance. "When I was visiting my cousins in France fairly recently, one of my cousins said, 'It's funny. You look just like somebody I know.' I had long hair then and a bit of a lump on my cheek [an expression signifying that she weighed more then]. She hadn't seen me for some years. And then we realized that I looked exactly like the painting of my great-grandmother, whom I had never met as far as I know . . . . But that picture! Even now you look at the picture on the wall and you'd think it's a picture of me, with my hair long. So ancestry is very interesting from the physical point at least."

During the interview with Fleur, I soon came to view her as an excellent wise representative of Western culture. She was, so to speak, a citizen of the Western world. She loved and understood science and the natural world.

When asked, she reluctantly spoke of her accomplishments, "Well, I wanted to work in conservation, and I have ever since—in one way or another. I also wanted to work abroad if possible, and that's exactly what happened. When the children were very small, I worked part-time through my association with the East Africa Natural History Society. In 1976, my husband and I founded a children's magazine, and for nineteen years I managed and was the editor of this children's magazine. That took up all my time."

Rainbow, the magazine, was a popular general interest children's magazine that contained a lot of information about nature and science. Fleur noted that she often relied on the wisdom of children. Unfortunately when printing costs rose, the magazine was forced to close for financial reasons. That was a difficult time in her life.

Earlier, in 1971, Fleur, in affiliation with the East Africa Natural History Society, founded the Bird Watching Walk. Almost every Wednesday morning for twenty-nine years, she has met with anyone who was interested at the Natural History Museum. She leads the groups to a variety of birding sites in Nairobi—"which is," as she told me, "a lot of bird watching walks." It is her passion.

"Even when I was working quite hard, Wednesday morning I was not in the office—I was out bird watching. So this has been my main activity with the society—and I'm still working as a volunteer. Being older and having been with the society for more than thirty years, I'm able to say, 'Oh, yes! We used to do it that way. We used to keep it there [pointing to her temples].'"

Her expertise concerning the birds of Kenya has made her a valuable resource to all Kenyans. She noted that she was fortunate to have found her niche or passion in life very early. "I think I knew always that I was interested in nature and wanted to do something for conservation. I remember when I was very, very small (seven years old or so) deciding that I wanted to be a forester. Well, of course, I have never been a forester. I've been an editor—but being an editor, I've been able to promote conservation in my own way."

When asked if she knew any wise individuals, Fleur, without hesitation, mentioned her husband. When asked what qualities he exemplified, she replied, "Part of it is experience. He can weigh what is happening now with what's happened in the past. But also, I think he has the *right* values."

At this point Fleur smiled, anticipating my next question, asked it herself.

"What are those values? Well, again, values are judging things on what is *right* rather than what you exclude or what makes money, or things like that . . . . So the question of what is right is a hard one. But in public life, what is right is really what is for the common good rather than for private gain. I think these are some of the principles that would be wise. Looking for the common good rather than private gain."

Fleur admitted that doing this is difficult. She is an intelligent and sensitive woman who is able to analyze the pros and cons in various situations, examining problems from all points of view.

Why were the Kenyans who nominated Fleur Ng'weno and six other wise individuals able to identify those possessing wisdom living in their culture? For that matter, how were the Japanese, Saami, and Navajo nominators so readily able to identify many wise individuals living among them? Only in the West (and this included the United States) did it seem that individuals find it difficult to identify someone who was wise.

In a typical Western response, Helaman Krause, described in chapter 9, told me that *wisdom* is an archaic word in German. He said, "You asked what is wisdom? *Weisheit*? What does wisdom mean in Germany? For a German, this is a very difficult question. Even though we do have the word *wisdom* in our language, it is rarely used in everyday conversation. The word *wisdom* is often used in connection to stories we tell with the intent to teach a principle, mostly in connection with something from the past."

Following my interviews with the wise ones, I was left with perplexing questions: Why is wisdom considered obsolete in the West, or at the least relegated to obscurity? Why are wise individuals so difficult to identify in modern Western societies? These are complicated questions. When I ask average Americans to name a living person they know to be wise, they usually have to think about it for quite a while. If they think of anyone, it is often a grandparent—less often, a parent.[2] I am not alone in this observation. Other wisdom researchers have also noted that identifying wise individuals in the West is difficult.[3]

Most who have commented about the lack of wisdom in Western societies note that wealth and power are highly valued in these cultures—not wisdom. Some say the West's dependence on their gods of technology and science are responsible. As technological prowess has increased almost exponentially in Western cultures, there has been little increase in wisdom—in fact, some say there has been an overall decrease.[4] A few wisdom researchers have asked why this could be. S. G. Holliday and M. J. Chandler, early researchers of wisdom, attempted to answer that question, stating that presently in technological societies, productivity and directed problem solving are valued more than wisdom's broad "cognitively-based expertise in living."[5] Copthorne MacDonald, a researcher focusing on the development of wisdom, added,

> Many of us are knowledgeable, but few of us are wise. During this century, industrial society helped us become the most knowledgeable populace in history. Some of us applied our knowledge to the creation of powerful technologies. All of us have used those technologies to create comfortable lives for ourselves. Our intentions were usually honourable in all this, but our actions much of the time were not guided by that holistic, value-connected kind of understanding called wisdom."[6]

Tibetan lama and teacher, Sogyal Rinpoche, explained it in another way, saying, "Our society promotes cleverness instead of wisdom and celebrates the most superficial, harsh, and least useful aspects of our intelligence."[7]

The lack of appreciation of wisdom in the West is not a new phenomenon. Over half a century ago, the philosopher Gabriel Marcel warned of the impending doom facing wisdom in Western cultures. In 1955, Marcel, looking at a world of political unrest, noted that, "for every reason in the world, there is no longer anything in the least like wisdom."[8] Marcel blamed the decline in the influence of the modern family for the lessening of wisdom in the Western world, saying, "The family has been the nursery of a kind of secular wisdom and . . . this wisdom is today falling to pieces."[9]

> Marcel believed that even common sense was being lost in the West. That popular wisdom to which philosophers worthy of the name have always paid tribute cannot really be separated from common sense; and the disappearance of common sense is a phenomenon of immeasurable gravity and one which must inevitably bring about a real change in the climate of the mind . . . . With the disappearance of common sense, it is likely that wisdom also is doomed to vanish, or at best to become the prerogative of the very few.[10]

To Marcel's (1955) way of thinking, reliance on the increasing technologies of the day and the growth of larger and larger corporations presented inherent dangers to wisdom—thinking that appears to have been well-founded.

In addition to Marcel, others have also raised their concerns about this decline in wisdom phenomenon.[11] With early modernity, the concept of wisdom became viewed as the opposite of science. The reason for this is that science did not recognize anything outside the "logical realm."[12] The philosopher Friedrich Nietzsche termed wisdom an *unlogisches verallgemeinern*—nonlogical generalization.[13] He assumed that if something lay outside the normal perceptual boundaries, it could not be experimented upon and therefore was not really worthy of being considered. He believed that wisdom could not be examined as rocks could or even as could the physical and chemical processes going on in the world, like photosynthesis, weather, or electrical energy. Thus wisdom became, and often still is for some, a place for myths, folklore, religion, spirituality, mystical visions, proverbs, and all things subjective.

There are many reasons why it is hard for Westerners to embrace and understand wisdom. Based on my research and interviews with wise individuals, some of these reasons are generalized as follows:

1. The past is devalued.

Western individuals, in general, do not consider past historical events and past ideas as pertinent to their lives. Religious, patriotic, and genealogical traditions are considered unimportant. Take, for instance, the tradition of storytelling. We appear as humans to thrive on monomyths[14] and stories. They help us with a sense of direction, hopefully toward healthy growth. Stories help us integrate the present situations in our lives.

Stories bring understanding. Wisdom researchers William Randall and Gary Kenyan noted that understanding is found by "employing the appropriate lens to see what it is we want to understand. In the case of wisdom, we will not see it without stories."[15] But today, as mentioned many times throughout this book, there are few individuals who tell the old stories to the young in the traditional narrative style that has historically been associated with wisdom.[16]

Stories are often linked to traditions. But even the traditions of the past are ignored or dismissed by many as irrelevant to our modern lives, even though the wisdom traditions of various cultures reflect common human insights.[17] Time-tested traditions appear to help humans find wisdom; they help bring understanding to those who participate in them.

2. The elderly are devalued.

At one time in Western society, the aged were revered for their knowledge—as they are today in traditional cultures. In the West today, however, there is a general sense or belief that the knowledge found in written or graphic form is more reliable than that possessed by any individual.[18] One is more likely to read a book, go to a movie, or find information over the Internet through a computer search engine than to consult a wise elder in the community. The elders, men and women who may actually be wise, are often viewed as burdens on society, a drain on valuable health and economic resources, and not able to contribute positively (read: financially) to the community in general. Very few individuals in Western societies sit at the feet of older and wiser individuals to learn wisdom anymore.

3. Technology and change are considered the all-important keys to humanity's survival.

Western societies appear to solely look to evolutionary change and innovative inventions as being the source for progress and success in life. Scientific prowess and technology are seen as the means to man's immortality—they represent the never-ending progress of humanity into the future. The human genome project and human stem cell research are current examples.

There is no doubt that such prowess and technology are important to humankind. On the other hand, wisdom does not look for new problems and new progress. It solves the problems within a relatively stable world. Because the Western world places such great value on change above all else, wisdom is often lost to it.

Factual and procedural knowledge are not the hallmarks of wisdom. The factual and procedural knowledge gained by an individual in his or her lifetime is often out-of-date by the time he or she is old—or before. It is difficult to keep current with the new technologies. For example, owners of computers realize that their equipment is out-of-date within weeks of its purchase. Jon Franklin, a noted professor of journalism, brilliantly described the dilemma of rapid technological change as follows:

> [After the new technologies of automatic dishwashers, penicillin, condoms, and the pill,] change had become the new constant. Things were changing so fast that we could no longer define

what was happening to us. By the time we figured out the side effects of a new drug, it was outmoded and we were already well into another one. Before we had figured out television, Johnny had a computer. Divorce rates were up, and so were crime rates, and there had been so many changes that we didn't know what the causes were. Valium was rapidly becoming the most frequently prescribed drug in history. A phrase, "Future Shock," became the title of a book. There arose the perception that things were getting out of control . . . . Progress, once a magic carpet, had somehow become a juggernaut. We began to have some doubts.

. . . Each year 50,000 Americans were dying on the highways and another 250,000 were being maimed. Divorce rates were up some more, and the curve that described them was growing steeper. Alcoholism was a bigger problem than we had thought, and addiction to other drugs was growing. My God! There were drugs in grade school!

. . . a collective chill ran through us. With our technology we had created the tools necessary to convert life from hell on earth to heaven. But those tools, to be used safely, had to be used with wisdom. And wisdom, founded on self-knowledge, was the one thing we lacked.[19]

4. Individual achievement is heralded.

In Western thought, the individual is the most important consideration. (It is the opposite in Eastern thought and in many indigenous communities, where the community or the tribe often has preeminence.) An egocentric attitude pervades those living in the West. Perhaps more importantly, individuals are focused on achieving wealth and knowledge, status and position, or power and influence. People believe that if they have money, they'll be happy. If they have technology, they'll be happy. Or if they have weapons, they'll be safe. Individuals in society are admired for what they can do or for what "stuff" they have accumulated, for their wealth, for what they look like—and especially for their political or social power. Wealth, fame, or knowledge (expertise) is lauded in the media and elsewhere.

In addition, the pursuit of personal pleasure—regardless of its cost—is thought to be the most important factor in personal happiness for Westerners—thus the popular saying, "If it feels good, do it!" Copthorne

MacDonald noted that Western "cultural institutions prompt us to see the world from having, desiring, possessing, and consuming perspective."[20]

Contrast this view with the fact that, historically and conceptually, wise individuals do not view money and property as being important to living a good life. They attempt to live virtuously. They believe there are important things in the immaterial world. They act for others as themselves.

5. Experience is devalued.

Aleida Assmann, a German psychologist who has studied the problem of wisdom, wrote that "experience lost its value in the Twentieth Century. The knowledge most Westerners seek has little to do with experience. It could no longer be applied in a world that had changed beyond recognition."[21] For many, learning new and different things from books or the media is more important than having meaningful relationships with other people or with nature. Fantasy and virtual reality situations have taken the place of reality—real experiences in a natural world. Reality television programming crowds the airways—even though these experiences are not genuine; they are contrived.

6. Wisdom is not considered a topic worthy of study.

This attitude is perplexing because wisdom represents a rich and complex topic. As noted, all humans share a universal respect for wisdom. Worldwide, it is one of the oldest topics in literature and philosophy; however, only within the past thirty years has it become a subject for serious investigation within modern academia—and that mostly by gerontological psychologists.[22] University courses on wisdom, even in philosophy departments, are almost nonexistent.[23] It appears that because researchers and other inquirers after truth lack the understanding, faculties, or methodologies to truly study it, wisdom, like spirituality, has been deemed to be unimportant by academia.

Paradoxically, some individuals in the West, like Marcel, have realized that wisdom is important and believe that Westerners ignore it at their own peril. Certainly, poets have expressed the concern that technology does not bring us wisdom. T. S. Eliot wrote,

> The endless cycle of idea and action,
> Endless invention, endless experiment,

Brings knowledge of motion, but not of stillness;
Knowledge of speech, but not of silence;
Knowledge of words, and ignorance of the Word.
All our knowledge brings us nearer to our ignorance,
All our ignorance brings us nearer to death,
But nearness to death no nearer to GOD.[24]

At the present time, if wisdom is ever discussed as a human trait in Western cultures, it is often in connection with so-called New Age philosophies.

For some in the West, the advanced technological world does not satisfy nor answer their basic, deep human needs. Some people choose to explore and experience shamanism and other indigenous native rituals. This dabbling into beliefs other than of Western culture exerts a strong, even a romantic, pull for many. One of my Navajo friends described this phenomenon as, "Some people like to *play* at being Indian!" It may be that individuals are not turning their backs on Western cultural heritage as much as that they simply question whether the ways that we in the West usually construct reality are sufficient to provide real meaning in their lives. Thus, there appears to be an innate urge on the part of many Westerners to return to simpler human roots.

7. Science, aided by technology, is the only way to know truth.

Most Westerners seem to intrinsically believe that given enough time and the right equipment, there is nothing that men and women utilizing science and technology cannot conquer. This is undoubtedly correct. Science and technology have brought absolutely incredible lifestyles to most modern Westerners. These are positive things. We would be reluctant to give up these conveniences. However, could we be missing something?

One of the first Western scientists to raise the specter was David Bohn (1917-1991), a fearless challenger of scientific orthodoxy. He was a distinguished theoretical physicist and a colleague of Albert Einstein at Princeton University during the 1950s.[25] A quantum physicist, Bohn decided that the world at the quantum level is different from what humans are able to perceive. He raised the possibility that perhaps there are other areas that we, in our scientific quests, fail to see—realms that others with a different worldview are able, in fact, to comprehend.

Karl Popper, one of the leading philosophers of science, in his book with John Eccles, *The Self and Its Brain*, recognized three worlds or spheres of reality.

MERRIAM FIELDS BLEYL, PHD

1. the physical world observed by the senses and scientific instruments,
2. the mental world of human reason, which analyzes the physical world, and
3. the world of mental objects—that is scientific theories, which must have reality, because they are seen to act upon and transform the material world.

Popper remained in the Western world of reason and never could conceive of a knowledge that ultimately could not be discovered through conjecture and hypothesis, but he also recognized that the Western mind has difficulty comprehending things that cannot be observed by the senses. He said, "It [the Western world] has lost the art of meditation."[26]

Science itself is often blamed for the decline of trust in wisdom in the West. "The triumph of empiricism has had an unintended consequence. Although for many people it has driven away any hope of taking comfort in venerable creeds [religions], it has by no means led us to abandon the quest for meaning in our lives."[27]

Certainly, our technology-based cultures tend to indoctrinate our way of looking at knowledge to support our values and our interests. It is often difficult for those of us who presently live in Western cultures to recognize that there are other ways of knowing besides reason and logic. Few admit that Western knowledge has limits beyond which we do not go. Certain areas are off-limits or considered the realm of kooks.

Yet there are still many men and women who believe that the human senses do not record *all* that is real in the world. Maintaining their beliefs has become more difficult as Western values and ideas now encroach on every society in the world. Many in non-Western cultures must struggle to hold on to their unique forms of tribal and societal wisdom.

Suzuki and Knudtson, researchers of indigenous cultures, think that wise Western scientists should be judged according to the same standards placed on the wise in native societies, where wise individuals have "the capacity to *feel*, to exhibit *compassion* and *generosity* toward others, and to develop intimate, insightful, and empathetic *relationships* not just with fellow human beings but, in some sense, with the entire membership of the natural world."[28]

Of course, many in the halls of science are laughing at such qualities—qualities that seem to be the antithesis of a scientist. For sound reasons, feelings have been eliminated from the scientific process. And although scientists can be compassionate and generous, it is usually not in their experimentation or research that such qualities are found.

In a world where the educational systems adopted by a majority of cultures are based on the Western model, it seems unlikely that wisdom will increase in the world in the future. There are elders in many non-Western groups, like the Native American tribes, who issue warnings to the youth of their communities to be cautious about adopting Western ways in their entirety. Over and over, as I interviewed the wise ones, it was reported to me that the young people are mostly ignoring the warnings.[29] Perhaps this has always been the case, and only the wise are able to pay attention to what the Cibeque Apache elders call the trail of wisdom.

Because of the ubiquitous spread of Western philosophy and technology, people from non-Western cultures are coming to understand Western culture, to utilize its strengths, and to adopt its weaknesses as well. Our varied and wisdom-laden cultures are becoming one giant monoculture. It is becoming more and more difficult to compare cultures in any meaningful way.

Perhaps wisdom will eventually become an obsolete human trait. I hope not!

Endnotes

[1]   Gabriel Marcel, *The Decline of Wisdom* (London: Harvill Press, 1955), 49.

[2]   Informal research that I have conducted in classrooms and in conversations with people has led to this conclusion.

[3]   Aleida Assmann, "Wholesome Knowledge: Concepts of Wisdom in a Historical and Cross-Cultural Perspective," In *Life-span Development and Behavior, 12,* edited by D. L. Featherman, R. M. Lerner, and M. Perlmutter (Hillsdale, NJ: Lawrence Erlbaum Associates, Inc. 1994).

[4]   Gabriel Marcel, *The Decline of Wisdom* (London: Harvill Press, 1955).

[5]   Stephen G. Holliday and Michael J. Chandler, "Wisdom: Explorations in Adult Competence," In *Contributions to Human Development, 17,* edited by J. A. Meacham, (New York: Karger, 1986), 91.

[6]   Copthorne MacDonald, *Toward Wisdom: Finding Our Way to Inner Peace, Love, and Happiness* (Willowdale, ON: Hounslow Press, 1996), xiv-xv.

[7]   Sogyal Rinpoche, *The Tibetan Book of Living and Dying* (San Francisco: Harper-San Francisco, 1994), 123.

[8]   Gabriel Marcel, *The Decline of Wisdom* (London: Harvill Press, 1955), 41.

9   Ibid., 41.

10   Ibid., 46.

11   Aleida Assmann, "Wholesome Knowledge: Concepts of Wisdom in a Historical and Cross-Cultural Perspective," In *Life-Span Development and Behavior, 12,* edited by D. L. Featherman, R. M. Lerner, and M. Perlmutter, (Hillsdale, NJ: Lawrence Erlbaum Associates, Inc., 1994); John A. Meacham, "The Loss of Wisdom," In *Wisdom: Its Nature, Origins, and Development,* edited by R. J. Sternberg, (New York: Cambridge University Press, 1990).

12   Aleida Assmann, "Wholesome Knowledge: Concepts of Wisdom in a Historical and Cross-Cultural Perspective," In *Life-Span Development and Behavior, 12,* edited by D. L. Featherman, R. M. Lerner, and M. Perlmutter (Hillsdale, NJ: Lawrence Erlbaum Associates, Inc., 1994).

13   Walter K. Kaufmann, "The Literature of Possibility: A Study in Humanistic Existentialism," In *Ethics,* 70:4, edited by Hazel E. Barnes (July 1960), 333.

14   Joseph Campbell, *The Hero with a Thousand Faces* (New York: Pantheon, 1949).

15   William L. Randall and Gary M. Kenyan, *Ordinary Wisdom: Biographical Aging and the Journey of Life* (Westport, CT: Praeger, 2001), 5.

16   Aleida Assmann, "Wholesome Knowledge: Concepts of Wisdom in a Historical and Cross-Cultural Perspective," In *Life-span Development and Behavior,* 12, edited by D. L. Featherman, R. M. Lerner, and M. Perlmutter (Hillsdale, NJ: Lawrence Erlbaum Associates, 1994).

17   George Fowler, *Dance of a Fallen Monk* (New York: Addison-Wesley, 1995), 273.

18   Aleida Assmann, "Wholesome Knowledge: Concepts of Wisdom in a Historical and Cross-Cultural Perspective," In *Life-Span Development and Behavior, 12,* edited by D. L. Featherman, R. M. Lerner, and M. Perlmutter, (Hillsdale, NJ: Lawrence Erlbaum Associates, Inc., 1994).

19   Jon Franklin, *Molecules of the Mind: The Brave New Science of Molecular Psychology* (New York: Dell Publishing Co., 1987), 256-257.

20   Copthorne MacDonald, *Toward Wisdom: Finding Our Way to Inner Peace, Love, and Happiness* (Willowdale, ON: Hounslow Press, 1996), 3.

21   Aleida Assmann, "Wholesome Knowledge: Concepts of Wisdom in a Historical and Cross-Cultural Perspective," In *Life-Span Development and Behavior, 12,* edited by D. L. Featherman, R. M. Lerner, and M. Perlmutter, (Hillsdale, NJ: Lawrence Erlbaum Associates, Inc., 1994), 217.

22   Vivian P. Clayton and James E. Birren, "The Development of Wisdom Across the Life-Span: A Reexamination of an Ancient Topic," In *Life-Span Development and Behavior, 3,* edited by P. B. Baltes and O. G. Brim, (New York: Academic Press, 1980); Keith Lehrer et al., *Knowledge, Teaching and Wisdom* (Dordrecht, Netherlands:

Kluwer Press, 1996); John A. Meacham, "Wisdom and the Context of Knowledge: Knowing That One Doesn't Know," In *On the Development of Developmental Psychology*, edited by D. Kuhn and J. A. Meacham, (Basel, Switzerland: Karger, 1983), 111-134; Robert J. Sternberg, editor, *Wisdom: Its Nature, Origins, and Development* (New York: Cambridge University Press, 1990c).

23   One exception is the University of New Mexico, which periodically offers a course taught by Dr. Bleyl. It is entitled "The Role of Wisdom in Adult Learning." A few courses are offered by institutions other than universities.

24   T. S. Eliot, *Collected Poems 1909-1962* (NY: Harcourt Brace and Co., 1963), 147.

25   David Pratt, "David Bohm and the Implicate Order," *Sunrise Magazine* (Theosophical University, Feb/March 1993). "In what was to become his landmark work on plasmas (a plasma is a gas containing a high density of electrons and positive ions), Bohm was surprised to find that once electrons were in a plasma, they stopped behaving like individuals and started behaving as if they were part of a larger and interconnected whole. He later remarked that he frequently had the impression that the sea of electrons was in some sense alive."

26   Karl R. Popper and John C. Eccles, *The Self and Its Brain* (NY: Cambridge University Press, 1985).

27   Richard Smoley and Jay Kinney, *Hidden Wisdom: A Guide to the Western Inner Traditions* (New York: Penguin/Arkana, 1999), xii.

28   David Suzuki and Peter Knudtson, *Wisdom of the Elders: Honoring Sacred Native Visions of Nature* (New York: Bantam Books, 1992), 225.

29   If native or other cultural learning does take place, it is usually in an after-school or summer school environment—or, more probably, in the homes of individuals whose parents or caretakers are concerned that their unique cultural beliefs, their wisdom, not be lost.

Chapter Fifteen

Wisdom: A Gift From God Or In The Genes?

It is probably true quite generally that in the history of human thinking the most fruitful developments frequently take place at those points where two different lines of thought meet. These lines may have their roots in quite different parts of human culture, in different times or different cultural environments or different religious traditions; hence, if they actually meet, that is, if they are at least so much related to each other that a real interaction can take place, then one may hope that new and interesting developments may follow.

—*Werner Heisenberg*[1]

Many believe that wisdom is an irrelevant topic. Of all the individuals I interviewed, Odd Mathis Hætta was the most amused when I told him that I was investigating wisdom. He viewed wisdom as a useless topic, and he was certain that wisdom could not be researched scientifically. Odd Mathis, an athletic, unique, and brilliant Saami man, is a scientist who relies on well-established hard quantitative evidence. He explained to me, more than once, that he was "a materialist" and relied on physical evidence and provable facts.

Odd Mathis has a university degree in ethnography. In America, he would be called a physical anthropologist. He has an interest in and has studied prehistoric human development, especially as it related to the Stone Age people who left so much evidence of their culture engraved on the rocks bordering the seashore in Finnmark.[2] Nevertheless, he had been nominated as a wise person because he exhibited many *wise* characteristics—even though he, of course, denied such. In spite of his skepticism, he graciously answered my many questions and told me about his life.

I first met Odd Mathis when Kristian Kristensen (chapter 6) took me to his home in Alta, Norway. Kristian led me to the back door of the Hætta home, knocked on the door; and when Odd Mathis answered, the two of them spent several minutes conversing in Norwegian. When their conversation ended, Odd Mathis went into his house and returned with two of his publications, both written in English, which he generously gave to me. As he had been suggested by two other Norwegians as being a wise man, I asked if he would consent to being interviewed about his life. We agreed to meet again a week later at the Kristensen home for the interview.

Odd Mathis Hætta is strong and fit—he is a former ski jumper. He runs ten kilometers (about six miles) two or three times a week. Also, like most Norwegians, he is well-read. He also has a marvelous sense of humor. He noted that because of his experiences, he lives two lives: the first as a typical Saami individual and the second as a Norwegian. He has gained much from both cultures. From his Saami life, he learned to be dependent upon and respectful toward nature. From his Norwegian side, he learned about the Western world of science and inquiry. He believed that wise principles exist in both cultures. Both Saami and Western viewpoints have been helpful to him.

Odd Mathis was born in the Saami town of Guovdageaidnu (Kautokeino), Norway, in 1940. He was only two weeks old when the Germans invaded Norway in World War II. His father was serving as a soldier in the Norwegian armed forces and was out of the country at the time of Odd Mathis's birth and the Wehrmacht invasion.

Odd Mathis's parents and all his forebearers were Saami. He told me, "Their life was on the tundra." Although Saami was his first language, he learned to speak Finnish when he was only five or six years old. He did not learn Norwegian until much later. He explained, "I was fifteen or sixteen years old before I could speak Norwegian. My mother tongue is Saami, and the first foreign language that I spoke was Finnish. I was five, six, or seven years old when I learned Finnish—I spoke it every day. You see, after the war, all the buildings in Kautokeino were burned [as the Wermacht armies evacuated Norway], and the town was built back by Finnish carpenters who came to Kautokeino. That is why I learned Finnish as my first foreign language. My mother and father, and my grandfather (my mother's father) also learned Finnish because the contracts to rebuild the town were given to Finland and not to Norway."

Growing up in Kautokeino, Odd Mathis attended boarding school from the time that he was seven years old—the law for Saami children at that time. In the schools, children were not allowed to speak Saami. Odd Mathis described the difficulty he had at school. "I began in school when I was seven years old. The school was very short—only twice a year for six weeks: in autumn six weeks and in spring six weeks. It was an *internat* (boarding school). The teachers couldn't speak Saami, so they spoke Norwegian. I couldn't learn! When I was there the last year, there was finally a teacher who spoke Saami, Alfred Larsen. All the books were written in Norwegian, but Alfred Larsen taught us in Saami, and I finally understood."

At age nineteen, Odd Mathis went to the Norwegian city of Tromsø, to a teacher's training school, where he learned more about Saami customs and language and how to work with reindeer and sheep. He conducted research for a year, asking women and men to tell him the stories about their lives as traditional Saami. Even today, the older Saami residents of Kautokeino come to him, wishing to tell him of the old days.

Because of his understanding of both traditional Saami ways and Norwegian culture, Odd Mathis is often sought out to lecture and interpret both cultures. What he learned during this time in Tromsø made him keenly aware of the vast differences between the Western world and the traditional Saami world. One of those differences is in their economics.

Odd Mathis explained that the Western world's economy is entirely different from the old Saami's. "In the West, everything is based on the accumulation of 'capital'—goods, money, things (the more the better)—and is founded on a profit incentive. Living a traditional Saami life, it was not possible to accumulate capital. You had to live simply. In a family, the best situation was to have one room and a few kroner. But you couldn't base your life on it! You had to base your life on the seasons—a long program and a short program—weekly and shorter—day by day." [3]

Odd Mathis married when he graduated from college. He was twenty-four years old. His wife is Norwegian. In their home, they speak Norwegian; however, his wife, of necessity, also has learned Saami and Finnish. Saying this, Odd Mathis chuckled and explained, "Sometimes when we've been in Kautokeino at my parents' home—not often, but sometimes—there would be a Finlander, some Saami, and Norwegians, so we would speak three languages. Because my wife understands Saami, my parents understand Norwegian, and I understand Finnish, we could understand each other and have communication in three languages simultaneously."

The Hættas spent two years in Tromsø, where both taught in a grammar school and where Odd Mathis began a radiobroadcasting career. He then became a Saami language teacher for three years in Karasjok, the Saami capital city. Then, moving to Vadsø, Odd Mathis spent five years as an advisor during the times when school was in session in Finnmark. The Hættas had two daughters while living in Vadsø.

A man of broad experience, Odd Mathis edited a Saami newspaper for seven years as a job on the side. He led Saami radio, producing and broadcasting programs, for a total of ten years of experience in broadcasting. He has written several books[4] in English and many in Norwegian about the Saami. He lectures frequently.

After telling me of his many accomplishments, Odd Mathis sighed and said, "Which means at times I feel pressured. It is difficult to say no to giving a lecture to people . . . That's why I think it is so important that I run. During that time, I only have to think about getting up that hill—and of nothing else. No interviews, no lectures, no writing. It is important to me . . . . I don't always look forward to going running. It is even stressful to think about going running. But once I'm out there, it's relaxing. I don't define myself as a typical Saami, but more like the exception that proves the rule, with running as my way to relax."

Odd Mathis and his family moved to Alta, Norway, more than twenty-five years ago. He taught Norwegian students at the college in Alta at the Finnmark Teacher Training College. He initially taught courses in Saami literature and history, but in recent years, he also taught environment and sociology. He also taught Saami history, religion, and language at the University of Tromsø.

Odd Mathis's remarks to me about the concept of wisdom were interesting. "I have a degree in ethnography. My research is in material culture. Archaeology is my second subject. My research is more material. Wisdom is an abstract concept."

As mentioned at the beginning of this chapter, the topic of wisdom represented an entirely different epistemological realm than that in which Odd Mathis believed. When I asked him to create a drawing or to tell a story about wisdom, he chuckled, saying, "I have a different point of view when it comes to wisdom. I am a *realist*!"

When asked if he knew any wise people, he replied, "I don't really use that word—*wise*. It is not part of my vocabulary. But I think that there are many intelligent people. If you want to analyze something, you cannot just look *at the whole* scientifically. You have to put them into different categories.

And then you put the categories together. I am basically against the kind of analytic attitude that is called the holistic approach. It doesn't help the human race to have this holistic approach. *It is impossible for me to answer your question about what wisdom is.*"

My research, of course, looks at wisdom from a holistic point of view.

As far as having a mentor was concerned, Odd Mathis noted that there are not just one or two individuals who become what he termed ideals in one's life. "You will always have different 'ideals.' I think it is a myth that you only have one ideal throughout your whole life. If that is the case, it is not a good thing . . . . You learn by observing, and the closest people to you are your parents. You see how they do things, and you take after them. Also, if you read a good book and that author inspires you, you could say that he becomes an 'ideal' [a mentor or positive influence in your life], and you wish that you could write like that. So you will always have different *ideals.*"

Odd Mathis noted that the context of a situation makes a difference as to how things are perceived. He remarked that in America, he would be considered a Saami man from Norway; but in Alta, Norway, he certainly is not seen as a typical Saami person.

Asked why he felt he was nominated as a person who should be interviewed for my study of wisdom, Odd Mathis said it was because he is known by a lot of people, and he is asked to speak about the Saami often. He is a popular public speaker in Norway, especially on the topic of prehistoric men and women. "One period in human history is the Stone Age, and you asked me about my 'ideal.' If I were to say something about my 'ideal,' I would want to say it would be Stone Age man. He was quick, in good condition, had good musculature and development—and he was strong. He is my ideal. He lived a hard life and didn't live long. Why is this man so important in the Stone Age? There was not the possibility to accumulate capital and profit. The old Saami life was like the Stone Age man's life. I often think, "Why must all of us be like the modern, profit-hunting people?""

Many of the wise ones shared his point about living more simply.

Even though Odd Mathis admitted that he admired the Stone Age people, he also indicated that he was not willing to give up all the technological conveniences of modern society. He explained, "When I talked about the Stone Age man as an ideal, I don't think they had a good life. I wouldn't want to live a thousand years ago because they only lived to be twenty-five. They had no soap, no medicine. And it was dangerous. I wouldn't want to go back to that time and live then. But in our time, we can afford to, and we should, simplify our lives."

Odd Mathis's books are intriguing to read and informative about the lifestyle and culture of the Saami. According to him, the Saami are really a mixture of peoples, with a diverse ancestry. As such, they are much like the rest of humanity.

I asked Odd Mathis about spirituality among the Saami. He replied, "I haven't done any research myself on the Saami religion. But I think that people in general always seek simple solutions. It doesn't matter whether you are a Saami or a Norwegian or a Mexican—you seek those simple solutions."

He again emphasized that even though he realized that I was interested in Saami spirituality and religion, he wasn't.

Odd Mathis enjoys telling Saami stories, however. As in most cultures, storytelling used to be an important tradition among the Saami. He believes that traditional stories give continuity to people's lives and help them to know what to expect in the future. "One of the best ways to understand a culture is to examine the way people think. Nowhere is this more evident than in a country's proverbs—wisdom distilled over centuries into epigrammatic sayings, ways of conducting one's life.[5]

Odd Mathis's father was a storyteller. "My father told me stories, and if I were to tell them to you, something would be different—the story would have changed. Stories have to be adjusted to the environment you are in and the people you tell it to. That's true for every culture."

Even though the context of a story matters and often changes the story, the timing of the story is equally important. Stories change with time. Because of his experience and expertise in radio, Odd Mathis used the analogy of broadcasting the news to make his point.

"If you hear news on the radio and you want to tell it to another person, there has already been a change. It changes because the newscaster can stress some one thing but you want to stress something else to the person you are telling it to. The same incident that occurs in two different cities—Mexico City and Oslo—will be told differently."

Like his father, Odd Mathis Hætta is a storyteller. Even though he tells many stories, he doesn't have a favorite. A skilled teacher, he realizes the importance of the art of storytelling. "I tell them in the way I see them. Mostly I like to tell ghost stories."

The Saami people are famous for their ghost stories, so it is not surprising that Odd Mathis likes to tell them. However, he told me, referring to context again, that the time of our interview (in the bright daylight of a Sunday afternoon) was not the "right" time to tell such stories. With a smile, he said that ghost stories needed to be told in the dark. He was a practical, prudent, and pragmatic man.

Assuming that Odd Mathis Hætta and the other individuals described in this text are indeed truly wise, how did they become so? It certainly does not appear that wisdom was a quality that they set out in their lives to find or to develop. In fact, all of them dismissed the idea that they were wise people—with some, like Odd Mathis Hætta, even dismissing the idea that wisdom is a specific attribute that can be identified in anyone.

I conclude that the possibility to gain wisdom (to become wise) is inherent in all human beings, regardless of culture. The wise individuals described in this book represent at least five various cultures. Wisdom must be a human, not a cultural, characteristic. Nevertheless, there are endless questions about it. For instance, how is wisdom acquired? Is wisdom developmental? Can wisdom be taught?

The question as to how people develop their unique personalities and characteristics has been written about and studied for millennia. In the past, philosophers and spiritualists advanced their own theories about the development of human beings. Eventually, in modern times, physiologists, biologists, psychotherapists, and psychologists have made significant discoveries about life's developmental processes—most of which are applicable to human beings. Certainly, in light of modern discoveries about the role of DNA and RNA in determining human physical and mental characteristics, it seems legitimate to ask if genetic inheritance has a role in a person's becoming wise. Could there be a *wisdom* gene?

Today, physiologists and medical researchers offer explanations on how humans and other living organisms grow and develop physically. Researchers into human cognitive development[6] have made impressive progress in the past decade. Knowledge that can explain a person's personality and mental traits, such as courage or wisdom, has yet to be offered. Of all the information needed to deal with our technologically driven cultures, self-knowledge still seems to be the most important and the one that has been pitifully lacking.

For the past thirty years, psychologists and psychoanalysts have been the prime researchers of the knowledge of our uniquely human characteristics[7]—although computer programmers and artificial intelligence (AI) developers have lately waded into the fray. Molecular psychologists are now on the scene, stating that chemistry is the most important new connection in understanding human behaviors. The questions still abound.

How is it that the wise possess similar characteristics regardless of their culture? Since we humans are more alike than we are different, shouldn't all reach wisdom? Richard Dawkins,[8] a Darwinian biologist, described the neurological mechanisms that could explain how creative—and, I would add, wise—minds, perhaps spurred on by their innovative and efficient cultures, are able to prevail and be passed on generation after generation. Dawkins posited in reductionist fashion that the body and the mind, and consequently human behavior, are indirectly controlled by the genes in our cells—directed initially by their inherited DNA and later by the brain.[9]

> Genes are the primary policy-makers; brains are the executives. But, as brains became more highly developed, they took over more and more of the actual policy decisions, using tricks like learning and simulation in doing so.[10]

Even Robert Sternberg,[11] who has studied wisdom extensively, postulates that wisdom may be genetic—at least in part. Although no studies on the inheritability of wisdom have been found, other human potentials and cognitive abilities do seem to be linked to genetic makeup. [12] For instance, with regards to intelligence at least, it is known that genetic makeup appears to be a substantial factor, as found in twin studies, kinship, and adoption studies.[13] Can the same be said of wisdom? Perhaps it is a coincidence, but recall that the wise ones described in this text included a father and son, Walter and Helaman Krause. But before one accepts the inheritability of wisdom thesis, consider that another researcher, E. Hunt, concluded that the environment (or culture) is influential in varying degrees on a gene's expression.[14]

It is well-known that physical attributes are controlled by DNA and cell biology. But what about the cultural and social phenomenon that seem to underlie so much of the wisdom in the world? Dawkins believed in the biological principle that "all life evolves by the differential survival of replicating entities. The gene, the DNA molecule, happens to be the replicating entity that prevails on our own planet. There may be others."[15]

Dawkins proposed such a replicating entity—"a new kind [that] has recently emerged on this very planet"—which he believed could be affecting evolutionary changes in human social norms and culture. He chose to term the replicator of culture a *meme*—sounding like gene but coming from the Greek word *mimeme*, which meant "imitation" or "memory."

> Examples of memes are tunes, ideas, catch phrases, clothes, fashions, and ways of making pots or of building arches. Just as genes propagate themselves in the gene pool by leaping from body to body via sperms or eggs, so memes propagate themselves in the meme pool by leaping from brain to brain via a process that, in the broad sense, can be called *imitation*.[16]

Dawkins theorized that memes evolve in the same way as genes—through a selection process favoring memes that exploit the environment advantageously.[17] Eventually, a rather stable meme pool forms, and memes outside the pool have difficulty being incorporated. When a person dies, his or her genes are passed on to the next generation—if there is one. After about three generations the person's genes are diluted and do not have much of an effect on successive generations. However, when a person contributes his or her memes to the world—with ideas, music, poetry, and inventions—the memes of that person can live on indefinitely.

It seems possible that wisdom could be transmitted as a meme. Neurophysiologically and bioevolutionarily, it is plausible that the cognitive-social-active nature (virtue) of wisdom may be the product of evolutionarily selected memes. Dawkins noted that "the meme-complexes of Socrates, Leonardo, Copernicus and Marconi are still going strong."[18] Mihalyi Csikszentmihalyi and Kevin Rathunde have actually written about the "meme of wisdom."

> The meme of "wisdom," for instance, contains a nucleus of meaning that has been transmitted relatively unchanged for at least 80 generations, providing directions for human thought and behavior.[19]

In my opinion, however, genetics and memes do not fully explain the phenomenon of wisdom. I agree with Joe Franklin, the science writer, who noted,

> Philosophers, of course, object to the materialism inherent in the new science [of molecular psychology]. They point out, accurately enough, that the connection between chemical reactions and thoughts is unproved.[20]

Actually, psychologists, psychotherapists, and others seem to feel that the environment that surrounds the human child as he or she grows and develops is at least as important as genetic inheritance—and is, in their estimation, even more important. This decades-long struggle between humankind's *nature* versus the *nurture* given each person exists in any story of man's development. Most conclude that both nature and nurture play a role in human growth.

But again, what about wisdom? Is it acquired through nature or nurture or both? Some of the life stories of the wise ones in this book cast doubt on the nurture approach as a strong influence. Perhaps wisdom is the result of the buffeting process involved in normal human development.

More is known about human development, learning, perception, memory, and the like than ever before. Even so, human attributes such as courage, love, kindness, and wisdom are yet to be understood. In fact, in the field of psychology, until recently the only researcher to include wisdom as a piece of or connected to human development was Erik Erikson.[21] More than fifty years ago, Erikson proposed a model of human psychosocial development. Called the psycho-social stages of life, this model included wisdom as a desired positive end result as humans grew and changed throughout their lifetimes—although Erikson acknowledged that men and women rarely became wise.

Erikson's most famous work was in expanding Sigmund Freud's theory of stages of human mental development. Erikson believed that human development proceeds through an *epigenetic* principle. That is, he proposed that human beings develop according to a predetermined unfolding of personality as they progress through a series of eight stages. If something goes wrong at one stage, then the other stages may be at risk. The stages are identified by specific psychosocial tasks. In the Freudian tradition, Erikson called these tasks *crises,* but they are not specific crises. Each stage was built upon the preceding one.

An individual's psychosocial strength was built through the stages, and with each stage, Erikson theorized, a *virtue* is mastered. By virtue, Erikson meant a basic strength of human personality. The virtues included hope, self-control, positive accomplishments, competence, fidelity, love, care, and, finally, wisdom. With favorable developmental progress, the virtue from one stage helps a person to master the virtue of the next stage. If unfavorable circumstances occur at any stage of development, the resulting outcome is an undesirable aspect of personality.

The eighth and last stage of life emerged either with the virtue of wisdom or the unfavorable outcome of despair. This stage represented people from the ages of fifty and beyond. For Erikson, reaching this stage led either to despair or to the epitome of human development—wisdom. It marked the period when one came to terms with his or her life—and specifically with the end of that life. Erikson said that those who had no fear of their own death possessed wisdom. He declared that these rare eighth-stage individuals were psychologically well-adjusted, expressing a satisfaction with themselves and with their lives. A life well lived is the *good* result of this stage. Erikson said that a person had to be gifted to be truly wise, and he concluded that not many ever reach this stage.

Looking at Erikson's eight stages of human development, as the human being ages, the focus of his or her attention grows wider and wider, progressing from self-absorption to unselfishness, as follows:

Stage 1	Self-Mother-Father
Stage 2	Siblings
Stage 3	Playmates
Stage 4	Schoolmates
Stage 5	Significant role models
Stage 6	Intimate friends and partners
Stage 7	Community
Stage 8	Nation/World

Thus, in the eighth stage, one's focus could be said to be almost universal.

Erikson considered the virtue of wisdom to be the culmination of human social-emotional development. The strength of his approach to wisdom was in his recognition of "the importance of social change and its relation to the developing individual."[22] Erikson described the mature faith of wisdom that he claimed can develop at the end of life as a reconciliation of "opposing old-age tendencies toward trust and assurance, on the one hand, and toward wariness and uncertainty, on the other."[23] Erikson also saw wisdom as a balance between knowing and doubting. This balance remains one of wisdom's hallmarks.

The lives of the wise individuals presented in this text seem to fit well with Erikson's model. As for Erik Erikson, he lived a full and productive life and died in 1992 at age ninety-two. A friend said of him, "He walked into old age with a great deal of nobility and beauty."[24] Did he find wisdom?[25]

Today it is recognized by most investigators that human development is accomplished not in definite stages but through a spiral-like *process*—one achievement blending into the next. L. S. Vygotsky,[26] a Russian psychologist, was an early pioneer in this viewpoint; but he was followed by other psychologists, namely K. F. Riegel,[27] H. E. Gruber,[28] Mihalyi Csikszentmihalyi,[29] and more important, I believe, by Robert Kegan, a psychotherapist and researcher at Harvard University.[30]

Robert Kegan proposed that the process of development reflects five orders, or levels, of consciousness, which are developmental and cultural. The process of moving from one order of consciousness to another appears to be transformational. Most adults, he claimed, are at a third order of consciousness—out of a total of five possible levels.[31] The person who achieves what Kegan terms a fifth order of consciousness, like the person who is wise, is rare. In fact when Kegan associates conducted interviews with various people, not one "fifth order" individual was identified.[32]

Although Kegan has not directly addressed wisdom in his research or writings, his ideas on human development seem to address wisdom in much the same manner as Erikson. However, instead of stages of development, Erikson's and Piaget's framework, Kegan proposed the concept of orders of consciousness, reached through a lifelong developmental process, with the highest level representing an ability to think and act globally (and, I think, wisely). Kegan termed his theory neo-Piagetian. It combined various theories of stage developmentalists (Piaget, Kohlberg, Loevinger, Maslow, Erikson), including stage-object psychologists and psychoanalytic theorists. It provided a framework for what he termed the evolution of meaning.

While I am not making claims for wisdom being the same thing as Kegan's fifth order of consciousness, the concept of levels of consciousness fits well, I believe, in describing how wisdom develops—that is, in being aware of oneself at first and then expanding to awareness of others and eventually to one's place in the world. The similarities between the wise individuals described earlier in this text and those who fit into Kegan's fifth order of consciousness are obvious and convincing. Both have the ability to

1. question assumptions,
2. exhibit transformational processes,
3. reflect critically,
4. self-author (assuming responsibility for himself or herself, allowing for the differences in others),
5. self-regulate (control of emotions and impulses),
6. self-formation (dealing with paradox, contradiction, and oppositeness), and
7. value the common good (not just the good that benefits him or her personally).

Kegan's theory also recognizes that mere knowledge is not the stuff of human decision making. Knowledge is not even necessary for wisdom (as a level of consciousness) to function. As a person matures, however, it does not seem likely that all changes, processes, developments, or transformations lead to wisdom. Development implies growth and progress, not merely change.

But to what goal do adults grow? One obvious answer might be toward maturity and healthy well-rounded personalities within their own cultures.[33] Another fruitful possibility for wisdom's expression in a population lies in *epigenesis,* the process advocated by Erik Erikson in 1950 and more recently by Mihalyi Czikszentmihalyi.[34] The epigenetic approach to behavioral development in humans consists of three assumptions: (a) a person's behavior stems from both social (interpersonal, culture, and technology) and biological (genetic) origins; (b) the mixture of social and biological factors produces complex behaviors; and (c) the interactions of social and biological factors are transformational on behavior.[35]

Perhaps wisdom is at least partially genetically determined.[36] But genetics and development don't cover all aspects of wisdom. Epigenesis might.[37] One thing is clear. Even if people are not born to be wise, a scanty number of human beings through their life experiences, especially difficult and adverse experiences, do develop or acquire wisdom. Some of this wisdom must be because of their inborn characteristics (genetic inheritance), but perhaps even more of it may come through the experiences they have and the memes they contact while living on this earth. They are able to not only cope with the situations they meet on earth but also to maintain a view that sees all humanity and life as important. And then, again, perhaps wisdom is a gift given to some and not to others, much like musical aptitude and artistic aptitude are considered gifts.

I see the source of wisdom emanating from many directions—some of which are paradoxical. The scientist in me enjoys looking at the universe as adhering to God-ordained principles and laws. For instance, I see the divinity of a higher power in the beauty of the cell, with its DNA, RNA, and organelles. Others call the forces and organizing principles of life simply Mother Nature and view wisdom, if they consider it at all, as the end result of human evolution by chance.

Are the keys to wisdom yet to be found within the human genome—lying in wait somewhere within the strings of genes on a strand of DNA to one day be expressed? Is wisdom truly the epitome of human development, triggered by environment or by social and cultural interactions? Why don't universities foster wisdom? Why is it that only a relative few of us are wise? Could it be that Mburu's and Itani-san's idea—"Wisdom is a gift from God"—is just as likely an explanation? Many questions remain.

It could be that wisdom is a function of all of these possibilities—after all, they need not be mutually exclusive. Wisdom still remains in uncharted territory. Theories, questions, and speculations abound. Because we live in a world desperately in need of wisdom, we need the answers as to how can more of us acquire it and use it to benefit humankind and our planet.

Endnotes

[1]   Werner Heisenberg, *Physics and Philosophy* (New York: Harper Torchbooks, 1958).

[2]   Knut Helskog, *The Rock Carvings in Hjemmeluft/Jiepmaluokta* (Alta, Norway: Bjørkmanns, 1996). Finnmark is discussed more extensively in chapters 5 and 6. The rock carvings that are found there, especially in Alta, Norway, are prehistoric treasures. The first were discovered in 1973. More than three thousand rock carvings have since been identified, with the largest amount located in Hjemmeluft/Jiepmaluokta in Alta. UNESCO has designated the area a World Heritage Site. The carvings were made by Stone Age individuals living in the Altafjord. They represent people, animals, boats, etc.

[3]   The Saami followed the eight seasons of the reindeer. In fact, their lives depended upon it. The seasons are early spring (March-April), spring (May-June), early summer (June), summer (July-August), late summer (August), autumn (September-October), late autumn (November), and winter (December-March).

[4]   Odd Mathis Hætta, *The Ancient Religions and Folk Beliefs of the Sámi*, Alta Museum Pamphlets, #1 (Alta, Norway: Fagtrkk Alta as, 1994a); Odd Mathis Hætta, *Samene: Historie, Kulture, Samfun* (Oslo, Norway: Grøndahl, Dreyer, 1994b); Odd Mathis Hætta, *Die Sámit: Ureinwohner der Arktic* (Vaasa, Finland: Ykkös Offset, 1995).

[5]   David Galef, *"Even Monkeys Fall from Trees" and other Japanese Proverbs* (N. Clarendon, VT: Charles E. Tuttle Company, 1987) 11.

[6]   Steven Rose, *The Making of Memory: From Molecules to Mind* (New York: Anchor Books, 1992). Researchers into how the brain works abound. Steven Rose, an experimental and theoretical neuroscientist, has investigated memory and offers insights between mind and brain. Nick Herbert, *Elemental Mind:*

Human Consciousness and the New Physics (New York: Penguin Books, 1993). Even quantum physicists show an interest in consciousness:

7   Jon Franklin, *Molecules of the Mind: The Brave New Science of Molecular Psychology* (New York: Dell Publishing Co., 1987). A relatively new field, molecular psychology, offers insight into the workings of the mind. Jon Franklin won a Pulitzer Prize for his six-part series of articles on the molecules of the mind.

8   Richard Dawkins, *The Selfish Gene* (New York: Oxford University Press, 1976/1989); Richard Dawkins, *The Extended Phenotype: The Gene as a Unit of Selection* (Oxford, England: 1982): Richard Dawkins, *River Out of Eden: A Darwinian View of Life* (New York: Basic Books, 1995).

9   Daniel C. Dennett, *Kinds of Minds: Toward an Understanding of Consciousness* (New York: Basic Books, 1996); Steven Pinker, *How the Mind Works* (New York: W. W. Norton and Company, 1997).

10   Richard Dawkins, *The Extended Phenotype: The Gene as a Unit of Selection* (Oxford, England: W. H. Freeman, 1982), 142.

11   Robert Sternberg, "Intelligence and Wisdom," In *Handbook of Intelligence*, edited by R. J. Sternberg, (New York: Cambridge University Press, 2000b), 631-649.

12   Robert J. Sternberg and E. Grigorenko, *Intelligence, Heredity, and Environment* (New York: Cambridge University Press, 1997).

13   S. S. Cherny, D. W. Fulker and J. K. Hewitt "Cognitive Development from Infancy to Middle Childhood," In *Intelligence, Heredity, and Environment*, edited by R. J. Sternberg and E. Grigorenko, (New York: The Cambridge Press, 1997); E. Hunt. "Nature vs. Nurture: The Feeling of *viya de*, In *Intelligence, Heredity, and Environment*, edited by R. J. Sternberg and E. Grigorenko (New York: Cambridge University Press, 1997).

14   E. Hunt. "Nature vs. Nurture: The Feeling of *Viya De*," In *Intelligence, Heredity, and Environment*, edited by R. J. Sternberg and E. Grigorenko (New York: Cambridge University Press, 1997). The nature/nurture debate at present is over how much influence each aspect—nature or nurture—exhibits, and behavioral geneticists are not sure about what constitutes the environment. Hunt called those who are more for nurture in the debate the culturists.

15   Richard Dawkins, *The Extended Phenotype: The Gene as a Unit of Selection* (Oxford, England: W. H. Freeman, 1982), 142.

16   Ibid., 143.

17   Richard Dawkins, *River Out of Eden: A Darwinian View of Life* (New York: Basic Books, 1995).

18   Richard Dawkins, *The Extended Phenotype: The Gene as a Unit of Selection* (Oxford, England: W. H. Freeman, 1982), 144.

19   Mihalyi Csikszentmihalyi and Kevin Rathunde, "The Psychology of Wisdom: An Evolutionary Interpretation," In *Wisdom: It's Nature, Origins, and Development*, edited by R. J. Sternberg (New York: Cambridge University Press, 1990), 26.

20   Jon Franklin, *Molecules of the Mind: The Brave New Science of Molecular Psychology* (New York: Dell Publishing Co., 1987), 295.

21   Robert Coles, *Erik H. Erikson: The Growth of His Work* (Boston: Little Brown Co., 1970). Erik Erikson was born more than a century ago—in 1902—in Frankfurt, Germany. Originally starting out in life as an artist and a teacher at a Montessori school run primarily for American students in Austria, Erikson fortuitously met Anna Freud, the daughter of Sigmund Freud, in the late 1920s. She introduced him to the new field of psychoanalysis, and subsequently, Erikson studied psychoanalysis at the Vienna Psychoanalytic Institute with Freud. Erikson married, and with the Nazis coming to power in Austria, the Eriksons moved to the United States in 1933. In America, Erikson taught at Yale University and at Harvard. Because of his interest in the effects of society and culture on child development, he studied groups of American Indian children (Lakota and Yurok) to devise his theories about child development. In 1950, he wrote *Childhood and Society*, a summary of his theories and his own version of Freudian theory. Erikson rejected some of Freud's ideas about sexual needs, preferring to place the effects of society and culture as important in satisfying the primary needs of humans.

22   Vivian P. Clayton and James E. Birrin, "The Development of Wisdom Across the Life-Span: A Reexamination of an Ancient Topic," In *Life-Span Development and Behavior, 3,* edited by Baltes, P. B., and Brim, O. G. Jr. (New York: Academic Press, 1980), 120.

23   Erik Erikson, *Identity: Youth and Crisis* (New York: Norton and Company, 1968), 219.

24   Ibid., 58.

25   Erikson described wisdom as a detached concern for life itself, assurance of the meaning of life and of the dignity of one's own life, a sense of fulfillment and satisfaction with one's life, willingness to face death.

26   L. S. Vygotsky, *Thought and Language*, translated by Ed. Kozulin (Cambridge, MA: Harvard University Press, 1962/1986).

27   K. F. Riegel, 1973. "Dialectical Operations: The Final Period of Cognitive Development," *Human Development, 16* (1973), 346-370; K. F. Riegel, "The Dialectics of Human Development," *American Psychologist* (1976), 689-699.

28   H. E. Gruber, "Cognitive Psychology, Scientific Creativity, and the Case Study Method," In *On Scientific Discovery*, edited by M. D. Gemek, R. S. Cohen, and G. Cimino, (Dordrecht: Reidel, 1980).

[29]   Mihalyi Csikszentmihalyi, *The Evolving Self: A Psychology for the Third Millennium* (New York: Harper Perennial, 1988).

[30]   Robert Kegan, *In Over Our Heads: The Mental Demands of Modern Life* (Cambridge, MA: Harvard University Press, 1994). Although Kegan has not directly address wisdom in his research or writings, his ideas on human development seem to address wisdom in much the same manner as Erikson. However, instead of stages of development, like Erikson's and Piaget's frameworks, Kegan wisely proposed the concept of "orders of consciousness," reached through a lifelong developmental process, with the highest level representing an ability to think and act globally. Robert Kegan, *The Evolving Self: Problem and Process in Human Development* (Cambridge, MA: Harvard University Press, 1982. Kegan termed his theory *neo-Piagetian*. It combined various theories of stage developmentalists such as those of Piaget, Kohlberg, Loevinger, Maslow, and Erikson, including stage-object psychologists and psychoanalytic theorists. It provided a framework for what he termed, "the evolution of meaning." It does not seem likely, however, that all change, process, development, or transformation lead to wisdom. Development implies growth and progress, not merely change.

[31]   L. Lahey, E. Souvaine, R. G. Kegan and S. Felix. *A Guide to the Subject Object Research Group: Its Administration and Analysis* (Cambridge, MA: Subject-Object Research Group, 1986). The subject-object interview is an instrument that has been developed that, so Kegan claims, reliably indicates at which order of consciousness a given person is in their development.

[32]   Ibid.

[33]   M. Tennant and P. Pogson, *Learning and Change in the Adult Years: A Developmental Perspective* (San Francisco: Jossey-Bass Publishers, 1995). According to Tennant and Pogson, this growth is highly dependent on the culture as well as the individual. "The point is that what constitutes psychological development is legitimately contested, and makes little sense without reference to social and historical circumstances and processes" (113).

[34]   Mihalyi Csikszentmihalyi, "Toward an Evolutionary Hermeneutics: The Case of Wisdom," In *Rethinking Knowledge: Reflections Across the Disciplines,* edited by R. F. Goodman and W. R. Fisher (Albany, NY: State University of New York Press, 1995).

[35]   E. W. Gordon and M. P. Lemons, "An Interactionist Perspective on the Genesis of Intelligence," In *Intelligence, Heredity, and Environment,* edited by R. J. Sternberg and E. Grigorenko (New York: Cambridge University Press, 1997). While wisdom is not included in the biological genetic factors studied, it does not seem unreasonable to consider the possibility that it, as well as the other

cognitive abilities, may be genetically linked. Robert Sternberg, "Intelligence and Wisdom," In *Handbook of Intelligence*, edited by R. J. Sternberg (New York: Cambridge University Press, 2000b). Now and then an unexplained genetically influenced behavior occurs—one that cannot be explained by the usual rules of genetic transfer. This phenomenon is called emergenesis. A. R. Jensen, "The Puzzle of Nongenetic Variance," In *Intelligence, Heredity, and Environment*, edited by R. J. Sternberg and E. Grigorenko (New York: Cambridge University Press, 1997). Something combined, perhaps a new combination of genes, to produce the genotype and subsequent recognizable behavior—for instance, a genius in a family where no one exhibits other than normal characteristics, a musical prodigy in an unmusical family.

36   Mihalyi Csikszentmihalyi and Kevin Rathunde, "The Psychology of Wisdom: An Evolutionary Interpretation," In *Wisdom: It's Nature, Origins, and Development,* edited by R. J. Sternberg (New York: Cambridge University Press, 1990), 26; E. Hunt, "Nature vs. Nurture: The Feeling of *viya de*," In *Intelligence, Heredity, and Environment,* edited by R. J. Sternberg and E. Grigorenko (New York: Cambridge University Press, 1997); Robert Sternberg, "Intelligence and Wisdom," In *Handbook of Intelligence*, edited by R. J. Sternberg (New York: Cambridge University Press, 2000b).

37   Jeffrey P. Schloss, "Wisdom Traditions As Mechanisms For Organismal Integration: Evolutionary Perspectives On Homeostatic "Laws of Life," In *Understanding Wisdom: Sources, Science and Society*, edited by Warren S. Brown (Philadelphia, PA: Templeton Foundation Press, 2000), 156.

Chapter Sixteen

Conclusions

Wise people have a lot in common.
—Aeschylus[1]

A single conversation with a wise man
is better than ten years of study.
—Chinese Proverb

Throughout human history, wise individuals have served as beacons of light in their communities. *Finding Wisdom* is a book not only about contemporary wise people but is also about those qualities, behaviors, and innate human characteristics that are associated with wisdom. It examines the life stories of nineteen wise people from five different cultures and how wisdom manifested itself in their lives. These men and women are unique in and of themselves, and yet, they are similar to many of us. However, looking at their life histories and thoughts reveals important insights about people and wisdom in general.

It may seem foolish to focus on only nineteen individuals, especially when there are six-billion-plus people on earth living in multitudinous cultures—considerably more than the five cultures I investigated. Even so, these individuals were thought to be wise by their peers—the people who knew them best. They were humble, respectful, principled, and generous individuals; they were uncommonly aware of the world about them. They valued their cultural heritage and appreciated their ancestry. They possessed optimistic attitudes toward life; they reacted positively to events in their lives, especially the unpleasant ones. They strongly adhered to their own uplifting moral values, and they had a sense of balance and fairness. Yet they were empathetic and respectful toward others—even those with whom they disagreed. Like Solomon and the current Dalai Lama, they were capable of, and skilled at, seeing and understanding all sides of a particular situation. They seemed to see more deeply and more clearly the burdens others carried. They understood the ultimate consequences in human interactions. They exhibited an uncommon common sense, having the ability to exercise good judgment. They were able to rise above their cultural and learned ways of thinking and knowing—the so-called memes of their societies.

I found that the beliefs and expressions of wisdom of nineteen wise individuals were universally the same, regardless of their backgrounds. The common characteristics of the wise ones selected here include the following:

1. **They are grateful.** The wise express gratitude for family, for culture, and for life. Wise individuals valued their relationships with other people far more than they valued money and physical things. Each expressed the importance of their own family in their lives. They seemed to instinctively know that strong families are the bedrock of society. Even Mburu (chapter 2), who essentially raised himself as a homeless child on the streets of Nairobi, understood this principle. His pride in his own family and in his Kikuyu heritage was evident, yet he also valued people from other tribes and cultures.

2. **They live disciplined and principled lives.** Values are an important part of wisdom. The wise exhibited self-discipline and held to values (virtues) and goals that were helpful to them. They behaved in ways that supported their values, and conversely, they learned to avoid behaviors that would cause them problems. More importantly, they recognized the difference between the two. It was evident to me that each wise one had firm moral codes or beliefs guiding his or her unselfish thoughts and actions. The predominant value noted was that of respect—respect for other people and for the earth's environment. Individuals from every culture mentioned other traditional values, such as brotherly love, courage, honesty, justice, compassion, truthfulness, beauty, and simplicity—the principles lived by decent human beings. Brotherly love (defined here as an unselfish loyal and benevolent concern for the good of another) sustained the wise ones in their work with others. They showed a humanitarian concern toward everyone.

3. **They are honed by adversities in their lives.** The most striking similarity in the lives of the nineteen wise ones was the amount of adversity (my term) and loss they suffered in their lives. Their lives were filled with hard work, pain, sorrow, discrimination, and even discouragement at times. Yet none of them dwelt on the hardships in their lives; in fact, I learned of some of their negative experiences not from them but from other people or independent sources. The wise ones declared that difficulties and catastrophes are a normal part of life—events to be overcome, events that lead to broader perspectives, insights, and understandings. *Adverse experiences* are undoubtedly a catalytic key to becoming wise.

4. **The wise have a thirst for knowledge and understanding.** Constantly searching and pondering new situations, the wise ones seemed to be on a quest for wisdom without being consciously aware of it. They were curious and interested in many things. All the wise ones were lifelong learners; some chose to enroll in officially sanctioned academic courses of study, but most learned what they needed to know on their own. Many loved to read, and books often became important mentors. Some enjoyed discussion with their peers. Others gained skills and information by observation. All learned to listen carefully. They continued to hone their skills throughout their lives.

5. **They exhibit discernment and good judgment.** One of wisdom's definitions has to do with "judging rightly in matters relating to life and conduct."[2] Knowledge has been linked to wisdom, but through discernment, evaluation, and judgment. The reactions of the wise ones to events in their lives reflected their discernment and good judgment. Certainly, knowledge about things—"the knowledge of that and how"—helped them in forming good judgments. Even though, in all probability, one must have some knowledge to be considered *wise,* a more important criterion seems to be an ability to *judge* or *evaluate* well.[3] The wise evaluated each problem or dilemma in context to determine what the best solution or answer might be. Thus, knowledge alone is not the only *stuff* of wisdom. Perhaps specific knowledge is not even necessary for wisdom to function. "The understanding of what has worth, of what is good, is at the same time the basis of wisdom."[4]

6. **They have *uncommon* common sense.** The ability to judge or discern what's best often hinges on common sense. Common sense involves a

freedom from eccentricities, an ability to discern facts or conditions that are not obvious and knowing those things that can be accomplished or are ascertainable. It involves knowing and doubting at the same time. It is also being able to know when to fight and when to walk away. The wise solutions to problems, such as that faced by Solomon with the two women claiming to be the mother of the surviving baby, require almost superhuman common sense, discernment, and judgment.

7. **They are reflective and introspective.** The wise ones had a strong sense of purpose in their lives. Not only was I impressed with the character and morality of those whom I interviewed, but also, I found that they were secure in knowing who they were. Their self-knowledge and self-efficacy strengthened the believability of what they said. They were authentic men and women. Critical personal reflection was inherent in their reactions to their experiences. That they carefully considered all aspects of problems presented in their lives became evident. They appeared to use reflection when needed in their lives—primarily when a genuine problem appeared.

8. **They exemplify self-sufficiency.** The nineteen wise ones took ownership of their own problems (to use Bethwell's terminology [see chapter 11]). They were self-reliant and preferred to be self-sufficient. They also generously helped others, focusing their attention on positive ways to help those around them and the environment in which they lived. They exhibited a strong work ethic.

9. **They seek balance in all things.** The wise individuals integrated their personal, intrapersonal, and environmental situations through the mechanism of balancing toward the "common good." They seem able to rise above their cultural and learned ways of thinking and knowing. Recognizing their own cultural, intellectual, and emotional viewpoints and feelings, wise people also respectfully recognize the beliefs and opinions of others. They can hold both views simultaneously in balance.

10. **They are altruistic and seek the common good.** The wise ones focused not only on what was *right* for them personally but on what was *good* for others and for their communities. Even when discouraged, they continued to work for the common good. Their concern and reverence were directed at conditions for healthy growth for all creatures living on the earth—especially human beings. They did not equate the *common*

good with material wealth or fame for themselves. They did associate the *common good* with decent living standards for everyone—with enough nutritious food to eat, good water to drink, and opportunities of employment. They chose to help other people through leading the way by example and by speaking of and reflecting healthy values. Their altruistic actions produced change—cultural, political, and personal—for the betterment of society and the earth's environment.

11. **They are humble.** The concept of humility has long been associated with wisdom.[5] All nineteen wise ones were all humble people. Even though each was accomplished, not one of them showed any arrogance or conceit. They walked their own paths and focused on serving others in true humility. Other people mattered more to the wise than the wise person mattered to himself or herself. Such caring, such respect, and such kindness are a rare thing, especially when it is shown to strangers. All of them denied being wise. True humility can't be faked.

Becoming Wise

How does a person become wise? The commonalities reflected by wise individuals seem to indicate that wisdom, as a human attribute, is undoubtedly acquired by a similar process. Culture, although influential, probably does not matter. It appears that certain elements inherited or encountered in their developmental process steered these wise ones toward the acquisition of wisdom.

The acquisition of wisdom undoubtedly begins in youth. There one begins to learn the important lessons of life and to experience the outcomes associated with the choices. The time-honored stories and rituals of one's culture provide vicarious and experiential insights into the values of the home, society, environment, and cultural heritage. Through the normal developmental and learning process, one gains an understanding of life without having to experience every possible situation.

Education alone, however, cannot make one wise. Education can provide knowledge about things, but wisdom entails more than mere knowledge—it requires the judgment for whether certain information is important. It also involves a deep understanding of one's self.

Some have suggested that educators begin teaching wisdom to children in middle school. I see at least three problems with this approach. First, where will we find wise teachers to teach wisdom? Second, wisdom demands mature reasoning and judgment—traits normally not well developed in middle school-age children. The third problem inherent in trying to teach wisdom in typical government-run schools arises with wisdom's values.

Values are an important part of a wise person's makeup. In America, public schools often do a poor job of teaching moral values. Teaching such would be an alleged breach of the separation of church and state—or so some claim. Most schools leave teaching and, more importantly, modeling moral values to parents, the extended family, or religious leaders—those in the best position to explain the values and time-honored stories and rituals of their religion and culture.

Many of the wise ones interviewed pointed out the role of storytelling as a significant element in their understanding of the important lessons in life. Stories and proverbs provided the basis for many of their most lasting moral lessons. Unfortunately, storytelling, as the wise ones pointed out, is a family custom that is dying throughout the world.

Stories relate the events of our lives to the lives of others. We learn them through oral traditions or the written word, fiction or nonfiction. These stories often concern other beings (human or animal) and their trials. Through self-reflection, the stories teach us not only about ourselves but also about morality and virtue and what helps (the good) and what hurts (the evil) all peoples and societies. Stories often present the moral contradictions and inconsistencies in our personal lives. Through them, we learn the hard lessons of life, experiencing them vicariously. Otherwise, we learn the hard lessons of life by painful personal experience.

Television and other technologies have supplanted stories told by parents around the hearth of the home each night. Although there is much still available to be learned in viewing appropriate television broadcasts, the moral values so essential to the acquisition of wisdom are absent in many television programs. Seeing several hundred murders depicted in television shows each year does not create a desire for wisdom. News broadcasts emphasize the sensational, present biased viewpoints, and tend to ignore or underreport stories and experiences that might give meaning to wise actions in life. Individuals are free to select what they watch or listen to, and in this area, the wise appear to make different choices than the foolish.

Becoming wise does not involve the process of joyful pleasure and entertainment. For the individuals I interviewed, it required determination and effort to remain true to what they knew would strengthen their characters and help them reach their goals in life. The numerous adversities they experienced were like a "refiner's fire" rather than a debilitating tragedy.

The understandable desire that people hold—to avoid any suffering, loss, or adversity—appears to work against the acquisition of wisdom. We rush to rescue those in trouble—people who could help themselves—but, in so doing, deprive them of the growth and development that comes with the struggle.

The wise focus outside themselves much of the time. Most religious traditions teach that one should think of their neighbor before one's self and give to those who are less fortunate. In Eastern religions, the path to wisdom, *nirvana,* is sought through meditation, quieting the mind to eliminate all thoughts of self. Other religious traditions ask their followers to try to eliminate selfishness through prayer and reflection. Selfish motives and the desire for instant gratification, so prevalent in Western societies, also work against the acquisition of wisdom.

If wisdom represents the pinnacle of human development, there should be more and more individuals becoming wise since people are living longer. Knowing what prevents us from becoming wise may help us realize what we can do to increase wisdom.

An awareness and an appreciation of time-honored traditions from all cultures could help. Exposure to many and varied cultures and traditions is also supportive of wisdom. Just as we can gain knowledge by going through a well-defined process of school or specialized training, we can seek to become wiser by using our minds, virtues, hearts, feelings, intuitions, and talents. We can learn what wisdom looks like from the wise—whether living among us or through their memes,[6] which can be found in literature, traditions, or stories.

Is seeking wisdom worth the effort? From the wisdom literatures of all religions, we learn that it is. For example, in the Old Testament, Proverbs 8:11 states, "For wisdom is better than rubies. All the things that may be desired can't be compared to it." Certainly, the turmoil and problems found throughout the world today beg for wise people to lend assistance. In all probability, there are thousands of human beings who could be called wise presently living in every culture. They work, mainly anonymously, to stabilize and strengthen people and encourage all to pursue, in the words of the United States Declaration of Independence, "life, liberty, and the pursuit of happiness." They have much to teach all of us. We can learn from them if we are willing.

What we can ill afford to do is to ignore the wise ones living among us today. By actively seeking wisdom, by being willing to "put our feet to the fire" and learning to think of others as well as ourselves, we will glean wisdom from whomever and wherever it can be found. We will take the first steps on a journey toward ensuring humanity's ultimate survival, thereby offering our own positive, unselfish contribution to the universe. Whether or not we become wise in the process, the journey will be worth it.

Endnotes

[1]   Quoted by Johan Wolfgang von Goethe, *Art and Antiquity*, 5, 1, Individual Points (1824).

[2]   John Simpson and E. S. C. Weiner, *The Oxford English Dictionary* (New York: Clarendon, 1989), p. 3794.

[3]   Keith Lehrer, B. Jennie Lum, Beverly A. Slichta, and Nicholas D. Smith, *Knowledge, Teaching and Wisdom* (Dordrecht, Netherlands: Kluwer Academic Publishers, 1996).

[4]   Ibid., 5.

[5]   Gabriel Marcel, *The Decline of Wisdom* (London: Harvill Press, 1955); Daniel N. Robinson, "Wisdom Through the Ages," in *Wisdom: Its Nature, Origins, and Development*, edited by R. J. Sternberg (New York: Cambridge University Press, 1990).

[6]   As discussed in Chapter XV, a *meme*, a term coined by Richard Dawkins, is a replicating idea or concept passed from generation to generation. Examples include music, poems, literature, technological inventions, scientific methods, etc.

Bibliography

Abrokwaa, Clemente K. "Indigenous Music Education in Africa." In Ladislaus M. Semali and Joe L. Kincheloe, eds. *What is Indigenous Knowledge? Voices from the Academy.* New York: Farmer Press, 1999.

Arlin, P. K. "Cognitive Development in Adulthood: A Fifth Stage?" *Developmental Psychology 11* (1975): 602-606.

Arlin, P. K. "Wisdom: The Art of Problem Finding." In Robert J. Sternberg, ed., *Wisdom: Its Nature, Origins, and Development.* Cambridge, England: Cambridge University Press, 1990.

Asimov, Isaac. *Atom: Journey across the subatomic cosmos.* New York: Truman Talley Books/Plume, 1992.

Assmann, Aleida. "Wholesome Knowledge: Concepts of Wisdom in a Historical and Cross-cultural Perspective. In D. L. Featherman, R. M. Lerner, and M. Perlmutter, eds., *Life-span Development and Behavior, 12.* Hillsdale, NJ: Lawrence Erlbaum Associates, Inc., 1994.

Austin, James. *Zen and the Brain: Toward an Understanding of Meditation and Consciousness.* Cambridge, MA: MIT Press, 1999.

Baird, David. *A Thousand Paths to Wisdom.* Naperville, IL: Sourcebooks, Inc., 2000.

Baltes, Paul B. and Smith, Jacqui. "Toward a Psychology of Wisdom and Its Ontogenesis." In Robert J. Sternberg, ed., *Wisdom: Its Nature, Origins, and Development.* Cambridge, England: Cambridge University Press, 1990.

Baltes, Paul B., Staudinger, U. M., Maercker, A., and Smith, J. "People Nominated as Wise: A Comparative Study of Wisdom-related knowledge. *Psychology and Aging, 10, 2,* (1995):155-167.

Banks, T. H. *Three Theban Plays: Antigone, Oedipus the King, Oedipus at Colonus.* New York: Oxford University, 1956.

Barnhart, Robert K., ed. *The Barnhart Concise Dictionary of Etymology: The Origins of American English Words.* New York: Harper Collins, 1995.

Basso, Keith. *Wisdom Sits in Places: Landscape and Language Among the Western Apache.* Albuquerque, NM: University of New Mexico Press, 1996.

Bellah, Robert N., Madsen, Richard, Sullivan, William M., Swidler, Ann, and Tipton, Steven, M. *Habits of the Heart: Individualism and Commitment in American Life.* Berkeley, CA: University of California Press, 1985/1996.

Bleyl, Merriam F. *The Wise Ones: A Multi-cultural Perspective.* Unpublished Ph.D. Dissertation, University of New Mexico, Albuquerque, NM, 2000.

Bleyl, Merriam F., with Boverie, Patricia. "Transformative Rungs on Wisdom's Ladder." In Edmund O'Sullivan and Jane Taylor, eds., *Learning Toward an Ecological Consciousness: Selected Transformative Practices.* New York: Palgrave/McMillan, 2004.

Birren, J. E., and Fisher, L. M. "The Elements of Wisdom: Overview and Integration." In Robert J. Sternberg, ed., *Wisdom: Its Nature, Origins, and Development.* Cambridge, England: Cambridge University Press, 1990.

Bowden, Mark. "Blackhawk Down: How a Relief Mission Ended in a Firefight." *The Inquirer,* Dec. 14, 1997.

Brookfield, Steven D. *The Skillful Teacher.* San Francisco: Jossey Bass, 1990.
_____ *Becoming a Critically Reflective Teacher.* San Francisco: Jossey Bass, 1995.

Cahill, Thomas. *How the Irish Saved Civilization: The Untold Story of Ireland's Heroic Role from the Fall of Rome to the Rise of Medieval Europe.* New York: Doubleday, 1995.

Cajete, Gregory. *Native Science: Natural Laws of Interdependence.* Santa Fe, NM: Clear Light, 2000.

Campbell, Joseph. *The Hero With a Thousand Faces.* Princeton, NJ: Princeton University, 1968.

Capra, Fritjof. *The Tao of Physics.* New York: Bantam Books, 1977.

Cherny, S. S., Fulker, D. W., and Hewitt, J. K. "Cognitive Development from Infancy to Middle Childhood." In Robert J. Sternberg and E. Girgorenko, eds. *Intelligence, Heredity, and Environment.* New York: The Cambridge Press, 1997.

Christian, Jacq. *The Wisdom of Ptah-Hotep: Spiritual Treasures From the Age of the Pyramids.* London: Constable and Robinson Ltd., 2004.

Christopher, Robert C. *The Japanese Mind.* New York: Fawcett Columbine, 1983.

Clayton, Vivian P. and Birren, James E. "The Development of Wisdom Across the Life-span: A Reexamination of an Ancient Topic." In Baltes, P. B., and Brim, O. G. Jr., eds., *Life-span Development and Behavior, 3.* New York: Academic Press, 1980: 103-135.

Coles, Robert. *Erik H. Erikson: The Growth of His Work.* Boston: Little, Brown, 1970.

Csikszentmihalyi, Mihalyi. *The Evolving Self.* New York: Harper Collins, 1993.

_____ *The Evolving Self: A Psychology for the Third Millennium.* New York: Harper Perennial, 1994.

_____ "Toward an Evolutionary Hermeneutics: The Case of Wisdom." In R. F. Goodman and W. R. Fisher, eds., *Rethinking Knowledge: Reflections Across the Disciplines.* Albany, NY: State University of New York Press, 1995.

Csikszentmihalyi, Mihalyi, and Rathunde, Kevin. "The Psychology of Wisdom: An Evolutionary Interpretation." In Robert J. Sternberg, ed.,

Wisdom: Its Nature, Origins, and Development. Cambridge, England: Cambridge University Press, 1990.

Cuomo, Kerry Kennedy, and Adams, Eddie. *Speak Truth to Power: Human Rights Defenders Who are Changing Our World.* New York: Crown, 1999.

Dalai Lama XIV, His Holiness, The. *My Land and People: The Original Autobiography of His Holiness the Dalai Lama of Tibet.* New York: Warner Books, 1962/1977.

_____ *Ethics for the New Millennium.* New York: Riverhead Books, 1999.

Damon, William. "Setting the Stage for the Development of Wisdom." In Warren S. Brown, ed., *Understanding Wisdom: Sources, Science and Society.* Philadelphia, PA: Templeton Foundation, 2000.

Davis, Garold N., and Davis, Norma S. *Behind the Iron Curtain: Recollections of Latter-day Saints in East Germany* (1945-1989), 1996.

Dawkins, Richard. *The Selfish Gene.* New York: Oxford University Press, 1976/1989.

_____ *The Extended Phenotype: The Gene as a Unit of Selection.* Oxford, England: W. H. Freeman, 1982.

Dawkins, R. *River Out of Eden: A Darwinian View of Life.* New York: Basic Books, 1995.

Dennett, D. C. *Kinds of Minds: Toward an Understanding of Consciousness.* New York: Basic Books, 1996.

Eliot, T. S. *Collected poems 1909-1962.* New York: Harcourt Brace, 1963.

Erikson, Erik H. *Childhood and Society.* New York: W. W. Norton and Company, 1963. Originally published in 1950.

Fisher, Walter R. "Narration, Knowledge, and the Possibility of Wisdom." In R. F. Goodman & W. R. Fisher, eds. *Rethinking Knowledge: Reflections*

Across the Disciplines. Albany, NY: State University of New York Press, 1995.

Frank, Anne. 1952. *The Diary of a Young Girl.* New York: Doubleday, 1952.

Franklin, Jon. *Molecules of the Mind: The Brave New Science of Molecular Psychology.* New York: Dell, 1987.

Fowler, George. *Dance of a Fallen Monk.* New York: Addison-Wesley, 1995.

Fuller, William C. *Russia: A History.* London: Oxford University Press, 1997.

Galef, David. *Even Monkeys Fall from Trees and Other Japanese Proverbs.* N. Clarendon, VT: Charles and Tuttle, 1987.

Gaski, Harald (ed). "Sami History and the Frontier Myth: A Perspective on Northern Sami Spatial and Rights History." *Sami Culture in a New Era: The Norwegian Sami Experience.* Karasjok, Norway: Davii Girji OS, 1997.

Goethe, Johan Wolfgang von. *Art and Antiquity, 5, 1* (1824), Individual Points.

Gorden, E. W., and Lemons, M. P. "An Interactionist Perspective on the Genesis of Intelligence." In Robert J. Sternberg and E. Grigorenko, eds., *Intelligence, Heredity, and Environment.* New York: Cambridge University Press, 1997.

Gracian, Baltasar. *The Art of Worldly Wisdom.* Martin Fischer, trans. New York: Barnes and Noble, 1993.

Grenville, J. A. S. *A History of the World in the Twentieth Century.* Cambridge, MA: The Belknap Press of Harvard University Press, 1994.

Griessman, Gene. *The Words Lincoln Lived By: 52 Timeless Principles to Light Your Path.* New York: Simon and Schuster, 1998.

Griffin-Pierce, Trudy. *Earth is My Mother, Sky is My Father: Space, Time, and Astronomy in Navajo Sandpainting.* Albuquerque, NM: University of New Mexico Press, 1992.

Gross, Eric K. "Evaluation/assessment of Navajo Peacemaking." NCJRS Document 187675. *U.S. Department of Justice Research Report*, April 5, 2001.

Gruber, H. E. "Cognitive Psychology, Scientific Creativity, and the Case Study Method." In M. D. Gemek, R. S. Cohen, and G. Cimino, eds. *On Scientific Discovery*. Dordrecht: Reidel, 1980.

Hætta, Odd Mathis. *The Ancient Religions and Folk Beliefs of the Sámi.* (Alta Museum Pamphlets, #1). Alta, Norway: Fagtrkk Alta as, 1994a.

_____ *Samene: Historie, Kulture, Samfun.* Oslo, Norway: Grøndahl, Dreyer, 1994b.

_____ *Die Sámit: Ureinwohner der Arktic.* Vaasa, Finland: Ykkös Offset, 1995.

Harden-Burrola, Elizabeth. "Public Forum Examines Casinos Pros, Cons." *The Gallup Independent*, Nov. 6, 2008. Gallup, NM.

Hayakawa, S. I. *Use the Right Word: A Modern Guide to Synonyms and Related Words.* New York: Funk and Wagnalls, 1968.

Heisenberg, Werner. *Physics and Philosophy.* New York: Harper Torchbooks, 1958.

Helskog, Knut. *The Rock Carvings in Hjemmeluft/Jiepmaluokta.* Alta, Norway: Bjørkmanns, 1996.

Herbert, Nick. *Elemental Mind: Human Consciousness and the New Physics.* New York: Penguin Books, 1993.

Hesser, James I. "Navajo Migration and Accumulation in the Southwest." *Museum of New Mexico Papers in Archaeology,* 6 (1962). Santa Fe, NM: Museum of New Mexico.

Hinckley, Gordon B. *Standing for Something: Ten Neglected Virtues That Will Heal Our Hearts and Homes.* New York: Times Books/Random House, 2000.

Hinman, Lawrence W. "Seeing Wisely: Learning to Become Wise." In Warren S. Brown, ed., *Understanding Wisdom: Sources, Science and Society*. Philadelphia, PA: Templeton Foundation, 2000.

Hock, Dee. *Birth of the Chaordic Age*. San Francisco: Berrett-Koehler Publishers, 1999.

Holliday, Stephen G. and Chandler, Michael J. "Wisdom: Explorations in Adult Competence." In J. A. Meacham, ed., *Contributions to Human Development, 17*. New York: Karger, 1986.

Hunt, E. Nature vs nurture: The Feeling of *Viya de*. In Robert J. Sternberg and E. Grigorenko, eds., *Intelligence, Heredity, and Environment*. New York: Cambridge University Press, 1997.

Iverson, Peter. *Diné: A History of the Navajos*. Albuquerque, NM: University of New Mexico Press, 2002.

Jensen, A. R. "The Puzzle of Nongenetic Variance." In Robert J. Sternberg and E. Grigorenko, eds., *Intelligence, Heredity, and Environment*. New York: Cambridge University Press, 1997.

Kaufmann, Walter K. "The Literature of Possibility: A Study of Humanistic Existentialism." In Hazel E. Barnes, ed., *Ethics, 70:4* (1960).

Kegan, Robert. *The Evolving Self: Problem and Process in Human Development*. Cambridge, MA: Harvard University Press, 1982.

_____ *In Over Our Heads: The Mental Demands of Modern Life*. Cambridge, MA.: Harvard University Press, 1994.

Kekes, John. *The Examined Life*. University Park, PA: The Penn State University Press, 1992.

_____ *Moral Wisdom and Good Lives*. New York: Cornell University Press, 1995.

_____ *The Art of Life*. Ithaca, NY: Cornell University Press, 2002.

Keller, Werner. *The Bible as History.* New York: William Morrow and Co., 1956.

Kitchener, K. S., and Brenner, Helene G. "Wisdom and Reflective Judgment: Knowing in the Face of Uncertainty." In R. J. Sternberg, ed., *Wisdom: Its Nature, Origins, and Development.* Cambridge, England: Cambridge University Press, 1990.

Knudsen, Anne Merete. *Refugees in Their Own Country.* Alta Museum Pamphlet #2. Alta, Norway: Alta Museum, 1995.

Kramer, D. A. "Conceptualizing Wisdom: The Primary of Affect-cognition Relations." In Robert J. Sternberg, ed., *Wisdom: Its Nature, Origins, and Development.* Cambridge, England: Cambridge University Press, 1990.

Kuoljok, Sunna, and Utsi, John E. *The Saami: People of the Sun and Wind.* *Jokkmokk,* Sweden: Ájtte, Swedish Mountain and Saami Museum, 1993.

Labouvie-Vief, G. "Modes of Knowledge and the Organization of Development." In M. L. Commons, J. D. Sinnett, F. A. Richards, and C. Armon, eds., *Beyond Formal Operations: Comparisons and Applications of Adolescent and Adult Development* Models, 2. New York: Praeger, 1989.

Lahey, L., Souvaine, E., Kegan, R. G., and Felix, S. 1986. *A Guide to the Subject Object Research Group: Its Administration and Analysis.* Cambridge, MA: Subject-Object Research Group, 1986.

Langer, Ellen J. *Mindfulness.* Reading, MA: Addison-Wesley, 1987.

Lappé, Frances Moore and Lappé, Anna. *Hope's Edge: The Next Diet for a Small Planet.* New York: Putnam, 2002.

Lehrer, Keith, Lum, B. Jennie, Slichta, Beverly A., and Smith, Nicholas D. 1996. *Knowledge, Teaching and Wisdom.* Dordrecht, Netherlands: Kluwer Academic Publishers, 1996.

Lichtheim, Miriam. *Ancient Egyptian Literature: The Old and Middle Kingdoms,* 1. Los Angeles, CA: University of California Press, 1973.

Link, M. A. *Navajo: A Century of Progress (1868-1968)*. Window Rock, AZ: Arizona: Navajo Tribe, 1968.

Locke, John. Peter H. Nidditch, ed., *An Essay Concerning Human Understanding*. New York: Oxford University Press, 1690/1975.

Maathai, Wangari M. "Opinion Interview." *New Scientist Magazine* (July 22, 2000).

_____ *Unbowed: A Memoir*. New York: Alfred Knopf, 2006.

_____ *The Challenge for Africa*. New York: Random House, 2009.

Magga, Ole Henrik. "Cultural Rights and Indigenous Peoples: The Saami Experience." In United Nations Educational, Scientific and Cultural Organization. *World Culture Report: Culture, Creativity, and Markets*. Paris, France: Darantière, 1998: 76-84.

Manker, Ernst. *People of Eight Seasons*. London: C. A. Watts, 1965.

Marcel, G. *The Decline of Wisdom*. London: Harvill Press, 1955.

MacDonald, Copthorne. *Toward Wisdom: Finding Our Way to Inner Peace, Love, and Happiness*. Willowdale, Ontario: Hounslow Press, 1996.

McCullough, David. *The Path Between the Seas: The Creation of the Panama Canal, 1870-1914*. New York: Simon and Schuster, 1977.

Meacham, John A. "The Loss of Wisdom." In Robert J. Sternberg, ed., *Wisdom: Its Nature, Origins, and Development*. Cambridge, England: Cambridge University Press, 1990.

_____ "Wisdom and the Context of Knowledge: Knowing That One Doesn't Know. In D. Kuhn and J. A. Meacham, eds., *On the Development of Developmental Psychology*. Basel, Switzerland: Karger, 1983: 111-134.

Mezirow, J. D. and Associates. *Fostering Critical Reflection in Adulthood: A Guide to Transformative and Emancipatory Learning.* San Francisco, CA: Jossey-Bass, 1990.

Minakata Museum. *Information Pamphlet.* Tanabe, Japan, 1999.

Monson, Thomas S. *Faith Rewarded: The Personal Account of Prophetic Promises to the East German Saints.* Salt Lake City, UT: Deseret Book, 1996.

Morison, Samuel Eliot. "The Rising Sun in the Pacific." *History of United States Naval Operations in World War II, 3.* Boston, MA: Little, Brown and Co., 2001.

Mosha, R. Sambuli. "The Inseparable Link between Intellectual and Spiritual Formation in Indigenous Knowledge and Education: A Case Study in Tanzania." In Ladislaus M. Semali and Joe L. Kincheloe, eds., *What is Indigenous Knowledge? Voices from the Academy.* New York: Farmer Press, 1999.

Natsoulas, Theodore. "The Kenyan Government and the Kikuyu Independent Schools; From Attempted Control to Suppression, 1920-1952. *Historian* (Winter, 1998).

New Scientist Magazine. Opinion: Interview with Wangari Maathai. (July 22, 2000).

Nozick, Robert. *The Examined Life: Philosophical Meditations.* New York: Simon and Schuster, 1989.

Paine, R. *Dam a River, Damn a people: Saami (Lapp) Livelihood and the Alta/Kautokeino Hydroelectric Project and the Norwegian Parliament.* WGIA Document 45. International Work Group for Indigenous Affairs. Copenhagen, Denmark, 1982.

Pagels, Heinz. *The Dreams of Reason: The Computer and the Rise of the Age of Complexity.* New York: Simon and Schuster, 1988.

Pakenham, Thomas. *The Scramble for Africa: White Man's Conquest of the Dark Continent.* New York: Random House, 1991.

Parson, Tim. "Wakamba Warriors are Soldiers of the Queen: The Evolution of the Kamba as a Martial Race, 1890-1970. *The American Society for Ethnohistory, 46* (1999).

Pepper, Karl R., and Eccles, John C. *The Self and Its Brain.* New York: Cambridge University Press, 1985.

Perry, T. A. *Wisdom Literature and the Structure of Proverbs.* University Park, PA: The Pennsylvania State University Press, 1993.

Pinker, S. *How the Mind Works.* New York: W. W. Norton and Co. 1997.

Pratt, David. "David Bohm and the Implicate Order." *Sunrise Magazine.* Theosophical University (Fall/March 1993).

Rawl, John. *A Theory of Justice.* Oxford: Clarendon Press, 1972.

Reader, John. *Africa: A Biography of the Continent.* New York: Alfred A. Knopf., 1998.

Riegel, K. F. "Dialectical Operations: The Final Period of Cognitive Development. *Human Development, 16,* 1973: 346-370.

_____ "The Dialectics of Human Development. *American Psychologist,* 1976: 689-699.

Robinson, Daniel N. Wisdom Through the Ages. In R. J. Sternberg, ed., *Wisdom: Its Nature, Origins, and Development.* New York: Cambridge University Press, 1990.

Rose, Steven. *The Making of Memory: From Molecules to Mind.* New York: Anchor Books, 1992.

Routledge, W. Scoresby and Routledge, Katherine. *With a Prehistoric People.* London: E. Arnold Publishers, 1905.

Ryle, Gilbert. *The Concept of Mind.* Chicago: Univ. of Chicago Press, 1949.

Salmon, Katy. "Forest Profile: Wangari Maathai Mobilizing the Mothers." *People and the Planet 8*, 2000.

Samali, Ladislaus M., and Kincheloe, Joe L., eds. *What is Indigenous Knowledge? Voices from the Academy*. New York: Farmer Press, 1999.

Samuelsen, Robert J. "We Face a Choice." *Newsweek Magazine* (1992).

Schloss, Jeffrey P. "Wisdom Traditions as Mechanisms for Organismal Integration: Evolutionary Perspectives on Homeostatic 'laws of life.'" In Warren S. Brown, ed., *Understanding Wisdom: Sources, Science and Society*. Philadelphia, PA: Templeton Foundation, 2000.

Sears, Priscilla. "Wangari Maathai: 'You Strike the Woman . . .'" *In Context: A Quarterly of Humane Sustainable Culture* (Spring 1991).

Sinnott, J. D. "Postformal Reasoning: The Relativistic Stage." In M. L. Commons, F. A. Richards, and C. Armon, eds., *Beyond Formal Operations: Late Adolescent and Adult Cognitive Development*. New York: Praeger, 1984.

Simpson, John, and Weiner, E.S.C. *The Oxford English Dictionary*. New York: Clarendon Press, 1989.

Smoley, Richard and Kinney, Jay. *Hidden Wisdom: A Guide to the Western Inner Traditions*. New York: Penguin/Arkana, 1999.

Srivista, Suresh, and Cooperider, David L., eds. *Organizational Wisdom and Executive Courage*. San Franciso: The Lexington Press, 1998.

St. Augustine. "Summa Theologica: Humility." (Secunde Secundae Partis, Q. 161). *De Virginit Xxxxi*.

Staudinger, U. M., Smith, J., and Baltes, P. B. "Wisdom-Related Knowledge in a Life Review Task: Age Differences and the Role of Professional Specialization." *Psychology and Aging*, 7, 2, (1992): 11271-11281.

Sternberg, Robert J. "Implicit Theories of Intelligence, Creativity and Wisdom." *Journal of Personality and Social Psychology*, 49, 3, (1985): 607-627.

_____ "Understanding Wisdom." In Robert J. Sternberg, ed., *Wisdom: Its Nature, Origins, and Development.* Cambridge, England: Cambridge University Press, 1990a.

_____ "Wisdom and Its Relations to Intelligence and Creativity." In Robert J. Sternberg, ed., *Wisdom: Its Nature, Origins, and Development.* Cambridge, England: Cambridge University Press, 1990b.
_____ *Wisdom: Its Nature, Origins, and Development.* Cambridge, England: Cambridge University Press, 1990c.

_____ "Sternberg: A Wayward Path to Wisdom." *Psychology Today 31* (1998): 3, 88.

_____ "Intelligence and Wisdom." In Robert J. Sternberg, ed., *Handbook of Intelligence.* New York: Cambridge University Press, 2000a: 631-649.

_____ *Handbook of Intelligence.* New York: Cambridge University Press, 2000b.

_____ "Intelligence and Wisdom." In Robert J. Sternberg (ed.), *Handbook of Intelligence.* New York: Cambridge University Press, 2000B: 631-649.

_____ What is Wisdom and How Can We Develop It?" *The Annals of the American Academy* (January 2004), 164-174.

Sternberg, Robert J. and Grigorenko, E., eds. *Intelligence, Heredity, and Environment.* New York: Cambridge University Press 1997.

Suzuki, David, and Knudtson, Peter. *Wisdom of the Elders: Honoring Sacred Native Visions of Nature.* New York: Bantam Books, 1992.

Taylor, Sally T. 2004. "The Fellowship of Christ's Sufferings as Reflected in Lear and Life" *Brigham Young Studies*, 43, 2 (2004).

Tennant, M., and Pogson, P. *Learning and Change in the Adult Years: A Developmental Perspective.* San Francisco: Jossey-Bass Publishers, 1995.

Valkeapää, Nils Aslak. Ralph Salisbury, Lars Nordstrom, Harald Gaski, trans. *The Sun, My Father*. Guovdageaidnu, Norway: DAT O.S., 1988.

Velasquez, Manuel, Andre, Clair, and Others. "The Common Good." *Issues in Ethics 5:2* (Spring, 1992).

Vygotsky, L. S. A. Kozulin, ed. *Thought and Language*. Cambridge, MA: Harvard University Press, 1986. Originally published in 1962.

Waters, Frank. *Masked Gods: Navaho and Pueblo Ceremonialism*. Athens, OH: Swallow, Ohio University Press, 1950.

Webster's New Collegiate Dictionary. 1984.

Wetmore, Alexander. *Song and Garden Birds of North America*. Washington, D.C.: National Geographic Society, 1964.

Willis, Clint. *A Lifetime of Wisdom: Essential Writings By and About the Dalai Lama*. New York: Marlowe and Company, 2002.

Witherspoon, Gary. *Language and Art in the Navajo Universe*. Ann Arbor, Michigan: The University of Michigan Press, 1997/1995.

Zion, James W. "The Dynamics of Navajo Peacemaking." *Journal of Contemporary Criminal Justice, 14, 1* (February 1998): 58-74.

Index

About The Author

Merriam Fields Bleyl, PhD, is fascinated by the phenomenon of human wisdom. She spent the last fifteen years investigating wisdom and interviewing wise individuals in Western and non-Western cultures. In 2000 she earned a PhD degree from The University of New Mexico in Organizational Learning and Instructional Technology. Her real interest is in the adult learner and in how humans acquire wisdom. She has an appreciation for the "wise ones" in all cultures.

After receiving her undergraduate degree from the University of Utah in 1962, she embarked on a long hiatus from formal education, during which she married, mothered four children, taught piano and creativity workshops, and served as a community volunteer. With thirty years of life experiences and a passion for learning more about how adults function in the world, in 2001 she started her own educational research company, *Wisdom in Life and Learning*. Contact Dr. Bleyl at mbleyl@mac.com.

She is occasionally an adjunct professor at the University of New Mexico in Albuquerque, where she teaches a course on wisdom.

She presented two papers and an experiential session at the 2004 and 2007 Transformational Learning Conferences, one of which, "Transformative Rungs on Wisdom's Ladder," was subsequently included as a chapter in Edmund O'Sullivan and Marilyn Taylor's *Learning Toward an Ecological Consciousness: Selected Transformational Practices*, published in 2004 by Palgrave-Macmillan. She also served as a panelist for the Conference on World Affairs at The University of Colorado at Boulder in 2004.

Dr. Bleyl lives with her husband in the small mountain town of Star Valley, Arizona—amidst magnificent Ponderosa Pines, marauding javelinas, and occasional herds of visiting elk. The grandmother of 12, she is also a musician, playing the piano, directing choirs, and musical plays. However, the topic of wisdom remains her passion.

LaVergne, TN USA
28 December 2009

168225LV00002B/8/P